NEW PROCLAMATION

New Proclamation
Year B 2012

Easter through Christ the King
April 7, 2012—November 25, 2012

L. P. Jones

Ira Brent Driggers

Susan E. Hylen

Tracy Hartman

David B. Lott, Editor

Fortress Press

Minneapolis

NEW PROCLAMATION
Year B 2012
Easter through Christ the King
April 7, 2012—November 25, 2012

Unless otherwise noted, scripture quotations are the author's own translation or from the New Revised Standard Version Bible, copyright © 1989 by the Division of Christian Education of the National Council of Churches of Christ in the USA, and are used with permission.

Scripture marked RSV is from the Revised Standard Version of the Bible, copyright © 1952 [2nd edition, 1971] by the Division of Christian Education of the National Council of the Churches of Christ in the United States of America. Used by permission. All rights reserved.

Scripture texts marked NAB are taken from the *New American Bible*, copyright © 1970 by the Confraternity of Christian Doctrine, Washington, DC, and are used by permission of the copyright owner. All rights reserved.

Illustrations: Joel Nickel, Peggy Adams Parker, Robyn Sand Anderson, Meg Bussey, and Paula Wiggins, © 2010 Augsburg Fortress.
Cover design: Laurie Ingram
Book design: Sharon Martin

Library of Congress Cataloging-in-Publication Data
The Library of Congress has catalogued this series as follows.
New Proclamation: Year B 2012 Easter through Christ the King
      p. cm.
    Includes bibliographical references.
    ISBN 978-0-8066-9631-7
       1. Church year. I. Moloney, Francis J.
    BV30 .N48 2001
    2511.6dc21 2001023746

Library of Congress Cataloging-in-Publication Data
ISBN 978-0-8006-9772-3

The paper used in this publication meets the minimum requirements of American National Standard for Information Sciences—Permanence of Paper for Printed Library Materials, ANSI Z329.48-1984.

Manufactured in the U.S.A.
15   14   13   12   1   2   3   4   5   6   7   8

Contents

Time after Pentecost / Ordinary Time
Trinity Sunday through Lectionary 16 / Proper 11
Ira Brent Driggers

Time after Pentecost / Ordinary Time
Lectionary 17 / Proper 12 through Lectionary 26 / Proper 21
Susan E. Hylen

Time after Pentecost / Ordinary Time
Lectionary 27 / Proper 22 through Christ the King / Reign of Christ
Tracy Hartman

Preface

For nearly four decades Fortress Press has offered an ecumenical preaching resource built around the three-year lectionary cycle, a tradition that this latest edition of *New Proclamation* continues. *New Proclamation* is grounded in the belief that a deeper understanding of the biblical pericopes in both their historical and liturgical contexts is the best means to inform and inspire preachers to deliver engaging and effective sermons. For this reason, the most capable North American biblical scholars and homileticians are invited to contribute to *New Proclamation*.

New Proclamation has always distinguished itself from most other lectionary resources by offering brand-new editions each year, each dated according to the church year in which it will first be used, and featuring a fresh set of authors. Yet each edition is planned as a timeless resource that preachers will want to keep on their bookshelves for future reference for years to come. In addition, *New Proclamation*, true to its ecumenical scope, has traditionally offered commentary on all of the major lectionary traditions. Now, reflecting changes in practices among the mainline Protestant denominations, those number just two: the *Revised Common Lectionary* (RCL) and the Roman Catholic *Lectionary for Mass* (LFM).

New Proclamation is published in two volumes per year. The first volume, published earlier this year, covered all the Sunday lections and major festivals from Advent through Easter Vigil. This second volume begins with new commentary on the Easter Vigil and covers the remaining Sunday lections and major festivals through Christ the King Sunday as well as Thanksgiving Day. For those churches that celebrate minor feast days and solemnities, including saints' days and the Feast of the Transfiguration (August 6), denominational days such as Body and Blood of Christ (Corpus Christi) (June 10) or Reformation (October 31), and national days and topical celebrations, a separate volume covering the texts for those days is available: *New Proclamation Commentary on Feasts, Holy Days, and Other Celebrations* (ed. David B. Lott; Fortress Press, 2007).

Longtime users of *New Proclamation* will note that this latest edition adopts a fresh look, which ties the series in visually with Augsburg Fortress's popular worship resource *Sundays and Seasons*. We hope that this change not only makes the text more readable and accessible, but also encourages readers to use these fine resources in tandem with each other. We also invite you to visit this volume's companion Web site, www.NewProclamation.com, which offers access not only to this book's contents, but also to commentary from earlier editions, up-to-the-minute thoughts on the connection between texts and current events, user forums, and other resources to help you develop your sermons and enhance your preaching.

What has not changed with this edition is the high quality of the content that *New Proclamation* provides to preachers and those interested in studying the lectionary texts. Each writer offers an introduction to her or his commentary that provides insights into the background and spiritual significance of that season (or portion thereof), as well as ideas for planning one's preaching during that time. In addition, the application of biblical texts to contemporary situations is an important concern of each contributor. Exegetical work is concise, and thoughts on how the texts address today's world, congregational issues, and personal situations have a prominent role.

The writers in this volume reflect the sort of variety that has always marked the *New Proclamation* series. In his commentary on the Easter texts, L. P. Jones not only demonstrates his distinguished background as a New Testament scholar, specializing on John, but writes from the perspective of his current work as a Presbyterian congregational minister. Ira Brent Driggers and Susan Hylen bring their work as New Testament professors and their commitment to the church in writing about the pericopes for the first months of Ordinary Time, bridging exegesis and application expertly. And homiletics professor Tracy Hartman wraps up the volume by bringing special attention to women in the texts for the final weeks of the church year. All four breathe new life into the lectionary texts and will help preachers do the same as they proclaim the gospel within the congregations they serve. We are grateful to each of these contributors for their insights and their commitment to effective Christian preaching, and are confident that you will find in this volume ideas, stimulation, and encouragement for your ministry of proclamation.

David B. Lott

Easter

L. P. Jones

Easter is a season. It takes much more than a single day to celebrate the resurrection, God's victory over death in Jesus, and the new life, renewal, and transformation God extends to us in Jesus Christ. Our liturgical calendar recognizes and celebrates that. Easter begins in the dim quiet of the Great Vigil and continues through the mighty wind and tongues of fire of Pentecost. Tradition gives us the Great Fifty Days during which to give thanks for Jesus' triumph over sin and death and the hope the Easter proclamation offers all who come to God through him. Most of us have little trouble using the forty days of Lent to consider the cost of discipleship and to follow Jesus up the road to Jerusalem. Surely the proclamation that the tomb could not hold him, that God liberated him from death's strong bonds, and that he appeared to reassure, commission, and send the Spirit to his disciples also deserves a season of praise and thanksgiving. Sports seasons extend indefinitely and fund-raising seasons follow each other so closely we struggle to discern when one ends and the next begins. Celebrating the season of Easter allows us to declare the appearance of the risen Lord too profound and life changing to limit our responses to a single day or week. We need a week of weeks for news this good and hope this profound!

Many Christians have grown accustomed to singing their Alleluias, picking up their Easter flowers, hunting eggs with their children, enjoying a meal with family or friends, and then setting all that aside until the next year. Fifty days of proclamations and acts of liturgy, service, and fellowship can help them not only to embrace but also to be shaped by the message of Easter. Seven weeks of celebration will not diminish the joy of Easter Day. Instead, as we build on the pageantry and themes of that great day for consecutive weeks, we allow its message and meaning to shine more fully on souls and spirits that need its light.

In most sanctuaries the blare of trumpets helps to proclaim that Jesus is risen. Why limit the brass to Easter Day? The good news deserves to be heard, and horn players, rarely timid folk, have a rich repertoire from which to draw tunes to help our spirits soar. Most hymnals include more Easter hymns than a congregation can sing on a single day. "Christ the Lord Is Risen Today!" rings as true on the Sixth Sunday of

Easter as on Easter Day. We sing "Silent Night" more than once each Christmas. Why limit our favorite Easter hymn to once each year? If we prefer not to repeat an entire hymn, during the season of Easter the first verse of a congregational favorite could serve as an opening act of praise, a response to the Declaration of Forgiveness, or a closing celebration of the season.

Easter celebrates the new life we receive through the death and resurrection of Jesus. During the season of Easter we could lead the prayer of confession from the font and, prior to declaring forgiveness, pour water into the font and declare, "In the waters of baptism we are buried with Christ in his death, and from them we are raised to share his resurrection." The congregation could respond, "Alleluia! Christ is risen indeed!" or sing an Easter chorus or refrain. Since Holy Communion provides strength for the living of our baptisms, congregations unaccustomed to weekly Eucharist could gather at the table throughout the season, keeping the feast to declare the good news.

As Easter people we can extend our celebration of the Great Fifty Days beyond the sanctuary. What better way to celebrate new life than playing with a child? We can challenge our congregants to take a child or a group of children to the park to feed the ducks. That would give tired parents a few extra moments of their own and keep our vow to nurture those we baptize in word, deed, love, and prayer. If time with a child doesn't help us to give thanks for life, we need help! Those who prefer to stay indoors can bake cookies with those children, eat a few while they're warm, save some for the parents, and deliver the rest to someone who could use a smile. Those concerned about nutrition can skip the cookies and bake some bread. What we do matters less than doing something to express our joy and gratitude. Since the blessings of Easter come to us as community and shape us as a community, we truly receive them as we do something to celebrate community.

Easter celebrates what God alone can do. Yet for most of us God uses very human agents to claim and bless our lives. We can celebrate and proclaim that during the season of Easter by naming some of the saints who have guided us during our journey in faith and each week visiting, calling, or writing a note to express our gratitude. Or we could simply challenge each congregant to pick seven individuals, couples, or families they'd like to know better and invite one per week to coffee, ice cream, or cupcakes. As we rejoice in the connections that strengthen the community of faith, we give glory to God, whose gifts make that possible.

Easter celebrates God's breaking forth with light and life in places least expected. We can celebrate by making a sack of sandwiches and handing them out on the street, meeting with friends to prepare a meal to be delivered to a local spousal-abuse shelter, joining with a neighbor to plant flowers on a neglected spot of land, or attempting in some other way to bless the community around us. If someone asks why and our saints are too timid to declare, "Because Jesus is risen and I want to celebrate!" invite them to shrug and say, "Because my crazy pastor asked me to." We celebrate resurrection and new life as we help others to feel glad they are alive. The faithful with whom we serve probably have more and better ideas than we do. Ask them for their ideas and invite them to be creative. In bringing light from darkness, hope from despair, and life from death, God certainly is creative. That's why we need fifty days to celebrate. The tomb is empty! Jesus is risen! Alleluia! Amen!

April 7–8, 2012
Resurrection of Our Lord / Easter Vigil

Revised Common Lectionary (RCL)
/ *Evangelical Lutheran Worship (ELW)*

Genesis 1:1—2:4a*
Psalm 136:1-9, 23-36

Genesis 7:1-5, 11-18; 8:6-18; 9:8-13
Psalm 46
Genesis 22:1-18
Psalm 16
Exodus. 14:10-31; 15:20-21*
Exodus 15:1b-13, 17-18
Isaiah 55:1-11*

Isaiah 12:2-6
Proverbs 8:1-8, 19-21; 9:4b-6 or Baruch
   3:9-15, 32—4:4
Psalm 19
Ezekiel 36:24-28
Psalm 42 and Psalm 43

Ezekiel 37:1-14
Psalm 143
Zephaniah 3:14-20
Psalm 98
The following four texts and responses are
in the ELW *only*:
Jonah 1:1—2:1
Jonah 2:2-3 (4-6) 7-9
Isaiah 61:1-4, 9-11
Deuteronomy 32:1-4, 7, 36a, 43a
Daniel 3:1-29*
Song of the Three 35–65
Romans 6:3-11
Psalm 114 (not *ELW*)
John 20:1-18 (*ELW*) or Mark 16:1-8

Lectionary for Mass (LFM)

Genesis 1:1—2:2 or 1:1, 26-31a
Psalm 104:1-2, 5-6, 10 + 12, 13-14, 24
   +35 or Psalm 33:4-5, 6-7, 12-13, 20-22
Genesis 22:1-18 or 22:1-2, 9a, 10-13,
   15-18

Psalm 16:5 +8, 9-10, 11
Exodus 14:15—15:1
Exodus 15:1-2, 3-4, 5-6, 17-18
Isaiah 54:5-14
Psalm 30:2 + 4, 5-6, 11-12a + 13b
Isaiah 55:1-11
Isaiah 12:2-3, 4bcd, 5-6
Baruch 3:9-15; 32—4:4

Psalm 19:8, 9, 10, 11
Ezekiel 36:16-17a, 18-28
Psalm 42:3, 5; 43:3, 4 or Psalm 51:12-13,
   14-15, 18-19

Romans 6:3-11
Psalm 118:1-2, 16-17, 22-23
Mark 16:1-7

The beginning of the Great Fifty Days occurs at dusk on Holy Saturday or before dawn on Easter Sunday. The Great Vigil of Easter, perhaps the oldest worship service of the church, combines the sacraments of baptism and eucharist in a celebration of the triumph of light over darkness, God's beginnings over human endings, and Jesus' life, ministry, death, and resurrection over sin and death. Even when we note that Easter Day attendance eclipses that of Christmas Day, we can still lament the fact that so many Christians throng to worship on Christmas Eve, yet comparatively few gather on the eve or predawn morning of Easter Day. Surely the light and life God brought forth from Jesus' dark and death-filled tomb deserve additional celebration. In a culture that tailgates before kickoffs and holds midnight madness before the first official practice of the college basketball season, crowds of Christians assembling in darkness would bear witness to our conviction that God's triumph in Jesus Christ makes all things new.

Even so, a lengthy Easter Vigil can prove too demanding. One observer has noted, "The Vigil is not for the faint of heart!"[1] Faithful pastoral care and proclamation call for a service that includes not only a procession behind the paschal candle but also dramatic readings and other participatory acts. The Gospel narratives for Easter feature movement. A liturgy with varied sounds and voices, words sung and spoken, and movement of eyes and bodies can allow the faithful to hear and experience the Word.

Traditionally the Vigil includes four segments: the Service of Light; the Service of the Word; the Service of Baptism or Reaffirmation of the Baptismal Covenant; and the Service of the Eucharist. The symbolism of the Service of the Light speaks most clearly when worshipers gather outside the church building, witness the lighting of the new fire and the paschal candle, and process into the church. The meaning presses deeper as the faithful light their candles and sing to the risen Jesus in their light.

The Service of the Word need not include all the suggested readings to place the resurrection in the context of God's steadfast love. Intentionally selected voices could enhance the service. A young person reading the story of the interrupted sacrifice of Isaac could make those gathered shudder at that demanding text. A reader with African heritage could lend meaning to the reading of the passage through the sea. A saint who has come to affirm the light of Easter despite the pain of recently having a loved one pass through the valley of the shadow could make Ezekiel's valley of dry bones and Zephaniah's song of joy even more compelling. A woman's voice could give Mark's story of the first Easter and the frightened women fleeing the empty tomb the feel of a firsthand account. Some of those voices might highlight the pain behind these texts. That seems appropriate. We gather in the darkness to seek and celebrate Easter light because we often find darkness all too real.

*When a selection from the twelve Old Testament readings given here is what is used in a particular Vigil, the *ELW* indicates that these four are always among those chosen. The passage from Romans and the Gospel are also always used.

In the ancient church, the Vigil was the primary time for baptism. Even without candidates for baptism, tradition, the readings, and the new life Easter proclaims call for reaffirmation of what God does and we accept in baptism. Luke and John include scenes of the risen Jesus breaking bread with his followers. The Vigil climaxes as the candles on the altar are lighted and the Service of the Eucharist begins, inviting the gathered body of Christ to feed on the Bread of Heaven and Cup of Salvation and begin the Great Fifty Days of celebration.

The service of the Easter Vigil could provide the basis for proclamation. The preacher can affirm both those present and the message and ministry of the church by reflecting on why we gather at such an unusual hour for such an involved service. Following the risen Christ is not always convenient and often requires effort; yet it makes us a distinct people with a distinct message and ministry to share. If that fails to stir homiletic juices, the many and varied readings for this service offer a rich variety of images and messages.

Readings from Hebrew Scripture

The readings from Hebrew Scripture cover the breadth of salvation history. Since it is not necessary to read them all, selecting those that clearly refer to baptism, Eucharist, light's conquest of darkness, or another theme can unify the service. Amidst a culture that often stresses self-sufficiency to our detriment, those planning the service could select lections that stress the acts of God that shape our lives by providing for the faithful what we cannot secure for ourselves. Many characters appear in the account of the crossing of the sea (Exod. 14:10-31; 15:20-21), but all the action in the story belongs to God. Similarly, when Isaiah describes a covenant of peace made with an abandoned wife (Isa. 54:5-14), only God truly acts and, apart from the last two verses, God is the subject of every sentence. Isaiah's declaration of deliverance (Isa. 61:1-4, 9-11) calls a prophet to an impressive array of tasks, but the text focuses on God, who anoints the prophet and covers him with righteousness and salvation. The final verse of the invitation to an everlasting covenant (Isa. 54:5-14) proclaims that what God does for the people will manifest God's name perpetually,[2] and in Ezekiel's vision of renewal (Ezek. 36:24-28), God restores the exiled community in order to sanctify the divine name. These narratives remind us that we assemble in the darkness not to recognize our potential but to celebrate our conviction that God alone knows the fullness to which God will call us. Easter celebrates surpassing, not reaching, human limits. The Great Vigil could challenge the faithful to name and ponder where and how the gifts and presence of God shape the most formative moments of our lives.

The most troubling of these texts is the interrupted sacrifice of Isaac (Gen. 22:1-18). When God orders Abraham to sacrifice Isaac and blesses him for obeying, unanswered questions arise that the provision of a ram in the thicket does not lay to rest. The moral dilemma central to this story haunts us. Yet the faithful have not gathered in the darkness because they lack queries or distress. Despite the burdens brought to the darkness, we gather to express trust and confidence in God. Although it offers no answers, it may help to recall that during committal services pastors declare that the faithful gather in the sure and certain hope of the resurrection to eternal life, through our Lord Jesus Christ. We gather in hope, aware that our hearts ache and uncertainties linger, yet dependent on and hopeful for the presence and grace of God. The Great Vigil does not eliminate or ignore our unresolved issues. It invites us to find resurrection light shining in the darkness.

Epistle Reading
Romans 6:3-11 (RCL, LFM)

This lection repeatedly stresses the union of believers with Christ, proclaiming that we have been baptized into Christ, baptized into Christ's death, buried with Christ, united with him in death, crucified with him, and have died with him, so that we will be united with him in resurrection and live with him. What begins with baptism passes through death and crucifixion and ends with death to sin and newness of life with Christ. This is no gentle journey. It is a battle with all that keeps us from life. Yet Paul strikes a triumphant tone because the crucified Christ with whom we are united will not die again and forever lives with God. Paul claims not that the baptized no longer sin and will not die, but that our story extends beyond the reach of sin and death. The final verse, which begins with an imperative, underscores this. Paul charges us to accept a new identity: dead to sin and alive to God in Christ. That brings the promised future of the preceding verses into the present. Our task is not to wait for new life to begin, but to live now in gratitude for and celebration of what God has done.

Psalmody
Psalm 114 (RCL)
Psalm 118:1-2, 16-17, 22-23 (LFM)

Psalm 114 recounts some of the acts by which God led Israel from bondage in Egypt to the land of promise. The declaration that Judah became "God's sanctuary" (114:2) affirms that God dwelt in the people even before they dwelt in the land. The selected verses from Psalm 118 give thanks for God's mercy, power, and wonder, and call us to imitate the psalmist by declaring God's works. Both lections invite the faithful to ponder the acts of God and give voice to our praise.

Gospel
Mark 16:1-8 (RCL)
Mark 16:1-7 (LFM)

Two aspects of Mark's resurrection narrative surprise and may disturb us. First, although a messenger announces that Jesus has been raised, the risen Jesus never appears. Second, the women who hear the messenger's announcement flee the tomb in amazement and say nothing to anyone. That does not seem to provide a fitting ending to "the good news of Jesus Christ, the Son of God" (Mark 1:1).

The narrative begins on a positive note. Three women, followers of Jesus who had witnessed his crucifixion and death from a distance (15:40), come to the tomb to anoint him. The male disciples have fled, but these women remain. The spices they carry make the purpose of their visit ambiguous. Do they come to anoint a dead body, or do they bring spices to the tomb because they believed Jesus' predictions that he would rise and thus come to anoint their risen King? Their question along the way about how to deal with the stone suggests that they may not anticipate a miracle. Yet they express no surprise at the stone's removal and enter the tomb without hesitation. Perhaps they have come to hear good news.

Inside the tomb the women find a young man dressed in a white robe. His apparel and location on the right side imply that he may be more than merely a young man. Whether or not they recognized him as an angel, the women have cause for alarm. Encountering an angel lies outside ordinary experience. If this young man does not have a divine connection, he could be linked with those who crucified Jesus and thus could mean them harm. Yet the women do not flee. Whether they have stumbled into the presence of God or of a dangerous stranger, they hold their ground. In a relatively long and deliberate speech, the young man affirms that the women came looking for the crucified Jesus, declares that Jesus has been raised from the dead, and instructs the women to inform the other disciples that Jesus has gone ahead of them to Galilee and that they will see him there. Then the women flee in trembling bewilderment.

What can we do with these fleeing, bewildered, and silent women? Since we have read or heard this narrative, we have reason to assume that the women eventually said something to someone. They certainly had a story to tell: no dead body in the tomb where they had seen it placed; an announcement of resurrection from no ordinary messenger; and a declaration that Jesus awaited his followers in Galilee. Surely God or the young man in the tomb could have found other messengers to send to the other disciples. Yet that would make it no less tragic for the women to keep to themselves what they found and experienced at the tomb.

Why would the women, who remained nearby when the other disciples fled and had the courage to enter and remain in the tomb, flee in silent bewilderment? If they did not consider the message of resurrection true, they had no reason for fear. They would feel sad, even heartbroken, but not bewildered. On the other hand, if the women believed the message, they had cause to tremble, just as a terrified Peter found himself uncertain what to say after witnessing Jesus' transfiguration (Mark 9:6). The women needed time to slow down their heart rates and feet, to allow their tongues to catch up, and to find words for what they experienced.

Any disappointment the women may have felt at not seeing the risen Jesus would not diminish the significance of what has happened. As they and other disciples travel to Galilee, where they first met Jesus, they may encounter the risen Jesus anywhere. Why tarry in the tomb? The place to see Jesus is where he's always been: with the hungry and sick; in the midst of storms and controversies; teaching disciples and calling them to fullness of life.

What does this story invite us to proclaim? A faithful response to that question can embrace the two surprising and disturbing aspects of the narrative.

Let's begin with the bewildered and silent women. Many of us know their silence well. We have heard the good news from unexpected sources and experienced the risen Jesus in acts of service and devotion. The news we have to share may not seem as profound as that of the women, but some people will hear that news from us like they will hear it from no other. Jesus can become manifest without us, but that makes it no less disappointing for us to keep the good news we have experienced to ourselves. Mark's silent ending to the story of resurrection challenges us to find our voices. Yes, sometimes what we experience defies reason and we may tremble to believe it is true. Yet when God enters and transforms our lives, surely we must tell someone. Our witness to the face of Christ we saw at a soup kitchen, an after-school ministry, or a food pantry could bring him into view for a neighbor or friend. Our report of hearing good news during moments of brokenness could assure someone we know that darkness yields to light. Giving voice to our experiences of resurrection, even when we lack complete understanding, deepens our gratitude and adds a song of joy to a world in need of good news. I've yet to complain when more than one songbird blesses my morning walk with my bride. There's always room for another voice in the choirs that forever proclaim God's glory.

What about the absence of the risen Jesus in this narrative? When the women arrived that morning, they could have found the tomb filled with death. Instead, they found it occupied by a living being with a message of life. Surely they longed to see Jesus, but discovering that he was alive was no small consolation. The women did not see the risen Jesus there because he had gone ahead of them to Galilee. We, too, see and encounter Jesus in places where he always conducts his ministry. We encounter him as we face adversity that challenges us to depend more completely on God. We find him in our midst as we open our arms to receive those whom others reject and as we serve the least of these in his name. We see him as celebrations of the goodness and grace of God and of life in the faith community stir our souls. We find him present as we worship in his name, gather at the font to receive baptism, and come to his table to receive the gifts of God for the people of God.

We have seen and experienced the risen Jesus. That is why we gather to worship in the dark of night. Believing in the risen Jesus does not answer every unanswered question or erase all our disappointments. The new life we receive in baptism does not eliminate the struggle of living into God's promises and keeping our baptismal vows. Even the most profound experiences that assure us that Jesus is alive do not take the cost out of discipleship. The resurrection does not deny the painful reality of the crucifixion. Yet from the very tomb where Joseph laid Jesus' lifeless body comes the message that God has raised him and that he goes ahead of us. Life, not death, has the final word. Jesus lives, and because he is alive we may meet him anywhere, especially his typical places of ministry and possibly in the middle of the night with others who come in darkness to encounter the light. Alleluia!

John 20:1-8 (*ELW*)

For discussion of this text, please see the Gospel lection for Easter Day, below.

Notes

1. Laurence Hull Stookey, *Calendar: Christ's Time for the Church* (Nashville: Abingdon, 1996), 101.
2. The Hebrew word translated "memorial" in Isa. 55:13 is *shem*.

April 8, 2012
Resurrection of Our Lord / Easter Day

Revised Common Lectionary (RCL)
Acts 10:34-43 or Isaiah 25:6-9
Psalm 118:1-2, 14-24
1 Corinthians 15:1-11 or Acts 10:34-43
Mark 16:1-8 or John 20:1-18

Lectionary for Mass (LFM)
Acts 10:34a, 37-43
Psalm 118:1-2, 16-17, 22-23
Colossians 3:1-4 or 1 Corinthians 5:6b-8
John 20:1-9

Only Christmas Eve rivals Easter Day. Worshipers fill every available space, familiar faces present week after week and others we seldom see and hardly recognize. They include folks not familiar with the liturgy, family members present more out of obligation to a loved one than spiritual longing, children on a sugar high from raiding baskets that appeared earlier this morning, and a few baptized long ago who remember that this day is special but perhaps little else. The liturgy also swells. Brass players squeeze between the flowers and choristers, extra music comes from added choirs, and leaders in word and song stretch to rise to the occasion. With such a full sanctuary and liturgy, there seems little room for proclamation. This is Easter Sunday. Some deem it a trial to endure. How can a mere preacher speak credibly to a congregation with such diverse needs and expectations? Others find it an impossible task. When everyone knows the story, how can even the most skilled and faithful proclaim a fresh word?

Yet the reality this day celebrates and the message it proclaims give us our identity. Today we express our conviction that good triumphs over evil, love defeats hatred, light prevails over darkness, life overcomes death, and God's acts in and through Jesus Christ permanently shape the world. As Archbishop Desmond Tutu eloquently declared, "Easter says to us that despite everything to the contrary, [God's] will for us will prevail, love will prevail over hate, justice over injustice and oppression, peace over exploitation and bitterness."[1] Yes, many worshipers may come for lesser reasons and the pomp and fanfare may seem to overwhelm the spoken word. Nevertheless, all these people have gathered and God sends the news the preacher has to share to them all.

Easter Day is not a trial, but it calls for witness. Today preachers have an opportunity to proclaim not only the story passed down for generations but also how they and the communities they serve have experienced that story. Not only in ancient texts but also in our lives we have seen light shine in the darkness, beginnings spring from endings, and life break forth where death appeared to reign. Those gathered know the story's beginning and end, but may not have seen and certainly need to hear how it continues to shape our lives. Preachers have the opportunity, privilege, and call not to prove that resurrection light shines but to point to it: to name a place where ministry in Jesus' name has sprung forth with new life; to recall a situation in which timid steps taken in hope led to a bold beginning; to tell the story of a light that darkness could not extinguish; to declare where the risen Jesus has appeared. The long-faithful deserve affirmation of the path they walk. The curious and even the bored may unexpectedly have their eyes opened. Easter Sunday calls the preacher to join Mary Magdalene in announcing, "I have seen the Lord!" (John 20:18).

First Reading
Acts 10:34-43 (RCL)
Acts 10:34a, 37-43 (LFM)

Peter's speech contrasts his understanding that "God shows no partiality" (Acts 10:34) with God's selection of specific individuals to witness Jesus' ministry and resurrection. Just as Jesus offered the healing and power of his ministry to all, God extends open arms not to an exclusive community but to all the respectful and upright. God complements that general invitation by selecting a specific group of individuals to witness Jesus' resurrection. These witnesses, who have seen and shared bread and cup with the risen Jesus, have the responsibility to make what they have experienced known to all. God has chosen them not to elevate them above others but to use them to encourage everyone to accept the divine embrace.

As we move from the text to our lives, we hear a call to humility and service. We have the privilege of gathering at the Lord's table and participating in ministry in Jesus' name only because God has blessed us with that privilege. God calls us to respond by pointing those around us, especially the oppressed, to God's call and embrace.

Isaiah 25:6-9 (RCL alt.)

Isaiah envisions an extraordinary banquet prepared by God in Jerusalem. Only the finest food and wine fill the tables, but the rich fare pales in comparison with the invitation list. God prepares the meal for "all people" and assures their attendance by destroying the shroud over "all people" and the sheet over "all nations" and wiping away the tears from "all faces." This feast brings together the breadth of God's creation. Isaiah also describes the table conversation during the banquet. The guests will recognize their host as their God for whom they have waited and rejoice in the salvation God has provided.

If these words bring to mind the Eucharist, please recognize that the invitation in this lection extends to all. God calls those who regularly taste the Bread of Heaven and Cup of Salvation to live in expectation of a table set for everyone. As we move from Holy Communion to other tables, God calls those who eat well to live in expectation of a day when all will feast not on meager fare but on the fullness God offers. Waiting on salvation surely means not only praying for that day but also preparing for it.

Psalmody
Psalm 118:1-2, 14-24 (RCL)
Psalm 118:1-2, 16-17, 22-23 (LFM)

For discussion of Psalm 118, please see the psalmody for the Easter Vigil, above.

Second Reading
1 Corinthians 15:1-11 (RCL)

Everything Paul declares about the resurrection of Jesus describes it as the good news of salvation that believers receive as a gift. Twice Paul affirms that he has proclaimed only what he first received. He underscores his conviction that both Christ's death for our sins and his burial and resurrection on the third day happened in accord with Scripture. His chronology of Jesus' resurrection appearances first to Cephas, then the Twelve, then to more than five hundred sisters and brothers, then to James, then to all the apostles (clearly not the same as the Twelve for Paul), and finally to him further illustrates how believers depend on the tradition passed on to them. The risen Jesus appeared not to all but to those selected by God to bear witness. Paul's humble description of himself as "one untimely born" and "the least of the apostles" completes the picture of dependence on God and the gifts of God. Even when he boasts that he has labored harder than the others, he quickly corrects himself and states that it was not him but the grace of God in him.

This emphasis on salvation as a gift makes it curious for Paul to question whether the Corinthians have come to believe in vain (v. 2) and to assert that God's grace toward him has not been in vain (v. 10). Yet ultimately Paul confesses that it does not matter who does the proclaiming as long as the hearers believe. Even if Paul works harder than anyone else, first importance lies in bearing faithful witness to the gift of God he has received. We avoid believing in vain not by attempting to earn anything but by accepting and living in the good news of salvation we have received.

Acts 10:34-43 (RCL alt.)

For discussion of this passage, please see the first reading, above.

Colossians 3:1-4 (LFM)
1 Corinthians 5:6b-8 (LFM alt.)

For discussion of these texts, please see the second reading for Easter Evening, below.

Gospel
John 20:1-18 (RCL, *ELW* alt.)
John 20:1-9 (LFM)

John's resurrection narrative unfolds with deliberate drama. Everything begins with Mary Magdalene traveling alone to the tomb. All four canonical Gospels place Mary at the tomb on Easter morning, but only John has her travel alone. In the Fourth Gospel something significant always transpires when only Jesus and another character share the stage, but only later will that happen in this narrative. When Mary discovers that the stone no longer seals the tomb and concludes that someone has moved Jesus' body, she runs to inform Peter and the Beloved Disciple. That pair runs together to the tomb. When they arrive, the Beloved Disciple only stoops to look into the tomb, but Peter brashly charges inside and discovers additional evidence that something has happened to Jesus' body. Then the Beloved Disciple enters the tomb, sees, and believes that Jesus has conquered death. We expect trumpets to blare, but instead receive the news that they did not yet understand the Scripture and that the two disciples returned to their homes.

Mary remains at the tomb weeping. Only the Fourth Gospel depicts Mary weeping at the tomb. The significance of that also will appear later. When Mary looks into the tomb, she sees two angels, who ask her to explain her tears. She repeats to the angels the fear she shared with the disciples. Then she turns and sees Jesus. Once again we anticipate trumpets, but instead we learn that she does not recognize him.

In the conversation that follows, Jesus first asks Mary why she weeps and then poses to her the question he asked when the first would-be disciples approached him (John 1:38). For the third time Mary gives voice to her fear, this time promising to honor Jesus' body if this gardener will tell her where it is. Jesus responds by calling her by name, and she recognizes him. Mary has fulfilled Jesus' promises that his disciples will endure weeping and mourning before they can rejoice (John 16:20-22) and that when the Good Shepherd calls his sheep by name they will recognize his voice (John 10:3-4). Yet before the trumpets can blare, Jesus tells Mary not to hold on to him.

Jesus has conquered death and continues his ministry beyond the cross and tomb. That is good news, but not the entire good news. Jesus, who came from God, now will return to God. His glorification becomes complete not in his resurrection but in his ascent to God. After explaining this to her, Jesus commissions Mary, at this point the sole witness to resurrection and recipient of the news of ascension, to make all this known to the other disciples. This time Mary does not run, but she obeys. She leaves the tomb, goes to the disciples, and preaches the first Easter sermon, "I have seen the Lord." Now it's time for the trumpets!

John's resurrection features a great deal of movement, but the story unfolds at its own pace. It takes time to see everything in the tomb, time for Jesus to appear, time for Mary to recognize her Lord, and time for the completion of Jesus' glorification. Even faith unfolds deliberately. First the Beloved Disciple believes that Jesus has conquered death. Then the risen Jesus appears to Mary and calls her by name and she can believe that he has risen and continues to love his own. Finally, Jesus declares that he will return to the Father, inviting his followers to believe that through him they are born of God (John 1:13) and belong to God. The deliberate unfolding of the narrative calls for humility and patience. Sometimes fear and sorrow take us on a path to wonder. Sometimes we see more than we recognize and only a familiar voice discloses the fullness before us. Sometimes a moment that seems only for us most truly belongs to the community. Grace and truth come in God's time, but they find their way to us. Not every time is right for trumpets, but the time for trumpets always comes. Alleluia!

Mark 16:1-8 (*ELW*, RCL alt.)

For discussion of Mark 16:1-8, please see the Gospel for the Easter Vigil, above.

Preaching the Gospel

Why do people fill the pews on Easter Sunday? As noted above, some come to honor family and tradition more than to sate spiritual longing; yet they keep coming. It often surprises me that I believe they come because they want to believe it's true. They long to believe, some in spite of themselves, that the tomb could not hold Jesus and that resurrection to new life by the grace of God is real. They know that struggle and suffering come to all, that evil abounds, and that darkness often spills into landscapes, communities, and souls. The faithful come to hear a word of affirmation, and those on the edges come to discover whether they have seen but not recognized something in front of them. They know the story. They come to have it address this time and place and intersect with their lives. Peter's sermon in the first reading declares that even some of those who participated in Jesus' preresurrection ministry never saw their risen Lord. In the Gospel lection Peter leaves the tomb with secondhand faith, if that, and Mary has to linger and have her tears repeatedly questioned before resurrection light dawns on her. The first generation of believers depended on the witness of those to whom Jesus appeared. Our generation turns not only to them but also to the preacher, wondering whether there is news to share and witness to bear.

The preacher's call and privilege are to point to what gives us the audacity to stand there, to name where we and our community have seen and experienced the risen Jesus, where resurrection light and life have dispelled our darkness. The stories and experiences we share do not belong to us alone, but we have the task and honor of inviting all to hear them, of naming the risen Jesus where we have seen him. As we name those places and experiences, we give the gathered saints permission and assistance to name the places and experiences known to them. We proclaim where we have seen him not to deny painful realities, but to proclaim that another reality draws and defines us.

I once had a colleague in ministry who was the son of an abusive alcoholic. At the age that our youth participate in confirmation classes, he witnessed his father murder his mother. He and his sister escaped only because he found a new hiding place. Such stories typically lead to more tragedy, but through the love and influence of foster parents and a supportive congregation, the risen Jesus called and claimed as his own the child who became my colleague.

Several years ago a declining congregation in a rapidly changing community contemplated closing its doors. Then the members opened their seldom-used building to offer a safe place and tutoring to local children. Despite the shoestring budget and significant cultural differences, the risen Jesus appeared and inspired a new beginning.

One Advent a group in a congregation knitted mittens for a class of elementary students. One boy, who lived in a shelter, proudly wore his mittens all day. At the end of the day, he asked his teacher to rewrap them. When she noted that he couldn't wear them home if she wrapped them, he explained that he wanted to give them to his little sister for Christmas. I don't know whether that boy saw the risen Jesus, but in him his teacher did. So did I.

Objectively, these stories prove nothing. We cannot prove the risen Jesus any more than Mary Magdalene could verify what she saw and heard outside the tomb. We share our stories and experiences not to prove a point but to give voice to our conviction that light shines in the darkness, hope overcomes despair, and life outlasts death. As we keep looking for the risen Jesus, especially while participating in ministry in his name, he appears and brings new life with him. We have seen the Lord. Alleluia! Let the trumpets sound!

Note

1. Desmond Tutu, *The Words of Desmond Tutu*, selected by Naomi Tutu (New York: New Market, 1989), 91.

April 8, 2012
Resurrection of Lord / Easter Evening

Revised Common Lectionary (RCL)

Isaiah 25:6-9
Psalm 114
1 Corinthians 5:6b-8
Luke 24:13-49

Lectionary for Mass (LFM)

Acts 10:34a, 37-43
Psalm 118:1-2, 16-17, 22-23
Colossians 3:1-4 or 1 Corinthians 5:6b-8
Luke 24:13-35

First Reading
Isaiah 25:6-9 (RCL)
Acts 10:34a, 37-43 (LFM)

For discussion of these readings, please see the first reading for Easter Day, above.

Psalmody
Psalm 114 (RCL)
Psalm 118:1-2, 16-17, 22-23 (LFM)

For discussion of these responses, please see the psalmody for the Easter Vigil, above.

Second Reading
1 Corinthians 5:6b-8 (RCL, LFM alt.)

Malice and wickedness appear even in a community formed by the goodness and grace of God. Paul recognizes and laments that when he notes the presence of an utterly unacceptable immorality among the believers in Corinth (1 Cor. 5:1). He fears that this influence will corrupt the entire community. To illustrate his point Paul reminds them that Jewish tradition forbids the use of yeast during Passover and that even a little yeast readily becomes evident in a batch of dough. Malice and wickedness do not disappear when ignored. Despite his concern, Paul considers the community truly "unleavened" because Christ, their paschal lamb, has been sacrificed. Celebrating the festival, the gift of God in Jesus, requires the confrontation of the offending party in sincerity and truth. If necessary, Paul advises expelling the immoral from the community (5:13). Here he stresses maintaining what God has accomplished in Christ.

Church discipline makes the headlines primarily when we fail to practice it. No one benefits when one believer too readily labels another as leaven; but the entire church suffers when believers choose to keep silent while wickedness rises in the community of faith.

Colossians 3:1-4 (LFM)

Temporal and eternal realities merge in this description of the life of the baptized. Having established that the Colossians have been buried and raised with Christ in baptism (Col. 2:12), Paul returns to that topic to encourage them to let baptism shape their lives. New life for the baptized begins here and now, not as a result of ascetic practices (2:20-23) but as a gift from God bestowed when believers are raised with Christ. Paul commands the baptized to seek and think about what is above, not to deny earthly life, but to allow eternal realities to direct and sustain them. Just as wisdom and knowledge are hidden in God (2:3), so are the lives of the baptized. The baptized live very much in this world, but Christ is their life, and when Christ appears in glory, they will appear with him, or as the Johannine Jesus promises, "I . . . will take you to myself, so that where I am, there you may be also" (John 14:4).

Paul's words elevate rather than diminish earthly life. Because our life is with Christ in God, at any moment "what is above" may become manifest along the path we walk. In both times of confusion and moments of clarity, our eyes may be opened to see Christ with us. That promise and possibility call us not to attempt to escape the dust and heat of daily life, but to discover goodness and grace within it. When we encounter suffering and need, our life with Christ in God calls us to respond with compassion, acts of justice, and longing for the fullness to which God draws us. In the verses that follow this lection, Paul challenges the Colossians to cast aside immorality, impurity, anger, fury, and slander and to put on heartfelt compassion, humility, and patience (3:5, 8, 12 NAB). The baptized, who live with Christ in God, have the privilege, opportunity, and call to bless "what is on earth" with "what is above."

Gospel
Luke 24:13-49 (RCL)
Luke 24:13-35 (LFM)

The phrase "that same day" (24:13) links this narrative with the women's trip to Jesus' tomb, the announcement to the women that Jesus has risen, the women's report of their experience to the other disciples, the disciples' conclusion that the women's report is an "idle tale," and Peter's visit to the empty tomb (vv. 1-12). Although it is Easter, several followers of Jesus have found the tomb empty, and messengers from God have declared that Jesus has risen, as yet no follower has seen the risen Jesus or believed the women's testimony. Luke covers the initial characters who appear in this lection with a cloud of ambiguity by identifying them merely as "two of them" (v. 13). Grammatically, the nearest antecedent is the apostles (v. 10); yet later these two will rejoin "the eleven and their companions" (v. 33). Perhaps Luke simply depicts them as followers of Jesus capable of recognizing him. For most of this narrative that capacity remains unfulfilled.

While the two travelers discuss what has transpired in Jerusalem, the risen Jesus makes his first appearance in this Gospel; but "their eyes were kept from recognizing him" (v. 16). Even when the risen Jesus appears in plain view, it takes more than mere sight to recognize him. The unrecognized Jesus initiates conversation by asking what they have discussed as they walked. Then Luke reports that they looked sad. Their sadness underscores their failure to believe the women's testimony that Jesus, who ironically now travels with them, has risen. For these disciples the report of the empty tomb and the resurrection proves insufficient to awaken belief that Jesus has risen on the third day as he promised (Luke 9:22; 18:33).

As the two disciples summarize their experiences, they praise Jesus and attest to his crucifixion but go no further than calling him "a prophet mighty in deed and word" (v. 19). They confess that they "were hoping" (v. 21 NAB) he would redeem Israel. By using the imperfect tense to describe their hope, Luke makes it uncertain whether they still hold on to that hope or left it behind in Jerusalem. They report the testimony the women offered after visiting the tomb, but stress the fact that no one has seen Jesus, the very Jesus with whom they speak. That prompts the unrecognized Jesus to call them foolish and "slow of heart" (v. 25). Ironically, Jesus suggests that Scripture alone should have convinced them to believe even as he stands unrecognized before them. Clearly, quickening their hearts will require something beyond the merely human.

After an impromptu Bible study session, the two disciples reach their destination. The still-unrecognized Jesus keeps walking. Custom dictated that a guest only accept an invitation after a host insisted, but more than courtesy seems at work here. The risen Jesus will not force himself on his disciples. The disciples may not have the ability to recognize Jesus without divine assistance, but they must take some initiative. The unrecognized Jesus gives in to their urging, stays with them, and apparently hosts the meal they share. The verbs for taking, blessing, breaking, and distributing the bread (v. 30) are the same Luke uses in the narratives of the feeding of the five thousand (9:16) and the Last Supper (22:19). This is no ordinary meal, if any meal deserves to be called ordinary. That soon becomes clear to the disciples. In a single, relatively short sentence Luke reports that during the table fellowship the disciples' eyes were opened and they recognized Jesus, who then vanished (literally, "became invisible"). The two disciples have traveled seven miles or more with Jesus without recognizing him; yet when God opens their eyes he immediately disappears. Recognizing the risen Jesus is a God-given blessing, but it is something to report and not a place to stay. The two disciples waste no time traveling back to Jerusalem to rejoin "the eleven and their companions" (v. 33). Before they can bear witness to their experiences, they learn that Jesus has appeared to Simon. Evidently the risen Jesus remains itinerant.

In the Revised Common Lectionary the story continues as Jesus appears among the disciples while they share their experiences. Again the disciples fail to recognize him. This time they consider him not a stranger but a spirit.[1] Jesus speaks more gently to his undiscerning disciples than he did earlier, but still chides for them for being frightened and questioning. His invitation for his frightened disciples to touch and verify the wounds of his crucifixion leads to joy, but also disbelief and amazement. Jesus then eats in their presence, further assuring them that he has a body and is not a spirit. Then he conducts another Bible study session and "open[s] their minds to understand the scriptures" (v. 46). This does not lead to an unqualified statement of recognition of the risen Jesus, but it does conclude with a commissioning of the disciples. They, who have witnessed his resurrection, however inadequate their perception, will in turn proclaim repentance and forgiveness in his name. First, however, they must receive a gift promised by God and be "clothed with power from on high" (v. 49). Jesus commissions these disciples even without an unqualified statement of recognition of him. Luke never goes beyond declaring that they had joy but "were disbelieving and still wondering" (v. 41). That evidently suffices for God. Witnesses to the risen Jesus are privileged, but they remain dependent on God. They cannot recognize the risen Jesus without the aid of God and Scripture, and they cannot bear witness to what they have seen and heard without power from God.

Preaching the Gospel

Those who preach on this text often focus on the opening of the disciples' eyes during table fellowship with Jesus and their report, after the fact, that their hearts burned within them while the Jesus they had not recognized interpreted Scripture with them. Luke's evocative metaphors for what the disciples experienced when they finally recognized Jesus certainly invite reflection. Many of us have discerned the significance of an experience only after someone or something graciously placed it in a different perspective. Nevertheless, a preacher faithful to Luke's narrative must note that opened eyes and burning hearts, wondrous as they are, do not bring this narrative to its climax. In the LFM lection the scene reaches its peak as the two Emmaus-road travelers rejoin other followers of Jesus and share their experiences of resurrection. If the two had remained in Emmaus, only they would have benefited from their experience. Returning to Jerusalem allowed them to pool their discoveries with other believers and extend the blessings to the entire body. In the RCL lection the scene reaches its fullest height as the risen Jesus appears again and commissions the disciples to proclaim repentance and forgiveness in his name. In both lections, the blessings received through Scripture and at table strengthen the disciples for mission.

Word and table are fueling stations, not stopping points. That does not diminish the joy we experience at table or our excitement when Scripture illumines our lives. Rather, it challenges us to do something in Jesus' name with our joy and excitement. God intends not for the good news to stop with us, but for it to flow through us so others can hear and experience it.

Shifting to another aspect of this rich text, we can observe that although the risen Jesus is present in all but two verses of the narrative, he is clearly recognized only in one of them, the one in which he immediately vanishes (Luke 24:31). Luke depicts moments of certainty as relatively uncommon and fleeting. That may not sound like very good news for Easter, but doesn't it honestly describe our experience? Like the two disciples on the Emmaus road, we often think we know exactly what happened. Then conversation, reflection on Scripture, and table fellowship (especially conversation, reflection, and table fellowship with someone different) change our perspective and point to how Jesus is at work in our midst. Sometimes we conclude that we have walked as far as we can, only to have the blessing and breaking of bread deepen our recognition of our table partners and provide fuller understanding of the path both behind and ahead of us. We cannot control when Jesus will become recognizable, but we know how to make room to receive that gift when it comes. On the Emmaus road we move from certainty through humility into community.

This evocative narrative also invites reflection on the reality that there are no perfect disciples, only empowered disciples. In the scene along the road and in Emmaus, disciples walk with the risen Jesus without recognizing him and are chided for failing to believe the women's testimony and the witness of the prophets. Yet Jesus still breaks bread with them and opens their eyes. In the scene in Jerusalem the disciples wonder and disbelieve even amidst the joy of having the risen Jesus with them. Yet Jesus promises them that God will empower them to participate in ministry in his name. Discipleship requires humility and perseverance. Sadness, confusion, fading hope, wrong conclusions, and inadequate perceptions do not disqualify us as long as we stay on the road, open the Scriptures, and come to table with Jesus. That's good news.

Note
1. The Greek word rendered "ghost" is *pneuma*.

April 15, 2012
Second Sunday of Easter

Many faithful church members associate the Second Sunday of Easter with two things: a vacation for the senior pastor, especially in multistaff congregations, and "doubting Thomas." Pastors who have the option understandably entrust their flock to a valued associate on the Sunday that follows the many services and demands of Holy Week and Easter Day. Few fault them; but the church celebrates Easter as a season. The faithful may more readily recognize that and extend the celebration if the brass and the person they most often see in the pulpit do not disappear so quickly after the Alleluias return to the service.

What about Thomas? Exegetes regularly note that the word *doubt* does not appear in the Greek text of John 20:27. Jesus challenges Thomas to become "believing," not "unbelieving."[1] The narrative makes little distinction between Thomas and the other disciples. The disciples do not believe Mary's proclamation that she has seen Jesus, and Thomas does not believe theirs. At first they all are unbelieving and only the appearance of the risen Jesus convinces them. Nevertheless, some of us will follow tradition and label Thomas a doubter. So why not say a good word for him and the considerable company he keeps in our communities? One famous doubter named Thomas reminds us, "We too often forget that Christian faith is a principle of questioning and struggle before it becomes a principle of certitude and of peace. One has to doubt and reject everything else in order to believe firmly in Christ, and after one has begun to believe, one's faith itself must be tested and purified."[2] In the Gospel reading for this day, Jesus provides what Thomas needs to believe. When doubters stay with the community and the community embraces them, Jesus finds a way to claim them as his own. Nearly all the lections for this Sunday extol the blessings of unity. A little gentleness with doubters makes room for Jesus to make us one.

First Reading
Acts 4:32-35 (RCL, LFM)

Luke describes the faith community as a body of believers with one heart and soul. They share not only belief in their risen Lord but also mutual concern and affection as they generously use their abundance to support the common good. As a result, they all have what they need. Those who have more than enough do not distribute their surplus in ways that make those who lack indebted to them. Instead, as Barnabas illustrates, when they sell their property they lay the proceeds at the feet of the apostles, who make the distributions for and from the community. Although the sharing of possessions receives most of the attention in this narrative, one verse does not appear to relate directly to it. Between the description of what the believers have in common and the illustrations of how they distribute resources, Luke notes that the apostles bore witness to Jesus' resurrection with "great power" and that "great grace was upon them all" (4:33). This apostles' testimony fulfills the promise and commission of the risen Jesus (Luke 24:47-48; Acts 1:8). It also points to the heart of what the believers share. Earlier in Acts 4 the religious authorities threaten the apostles because of their witness to Jesus. Yet the apostles continue to speak with "great power." That fidelity in the face of opposition helps to explain the "great grace" they receive. The witness given by the apostles reminds the community of the power and presence that make them who they are. Their shared belief in the risen Jesus flows into unity of heart and soul and generous distribution of their possessions.

Especially during the season of Easter, those called to proclaim the gospel have the opportunity to bear witness to the resurrection and the new life God offers us in and through it. More than a century ago, Phillips Brooks advised: "Beware of the tendency to preach about Christianity, and try to preach Christ. . . . It is good to be a Herschel who describes the sun; but it is better to be a Prometheus who brings the sun's fire to the earth."[3] As we name and share understandings and experiences of our risen Lord and new life in him, we proclaim the good news that makes us who we are and we encourage our community to celebrate what binds us together. We often allow varied and incompatible beliefs to divide us. Our conviction that we have new life in the risen Jesus does not eliminate our differences, but it outshines them. As that conviction shapes and guides us, we open ourselves to the "great grace" of unity of heart and soul.

The story of Barnabas illustrates this. His actions provide a striking contrast with the deceit practiced by Ananias and Sapphira (Acts 5:1-11) and give him credibility when he introduces Paul to the apostles (Acts 9:26-27). In addition, Barnabas exemplifies the grace that flows when a community manifests its belief in the risen Lord by sharing one heart and soul. Luke describes Barnabas as a Levite and a Cypriot. As a Levite, Barnabas belonged to a priestly family; yet he contributes his abundance not to temple but to the community. As a Cypriot, a diaspora Jew, Barnabas not only finds acceptance among the believers in Jerusalem but even receives a new name. God alone knows the doors that open as we invite our risen Lord to guide and shape us.

Psalmody
Psalm 133 (RCL)

This psalm uses two evocative illustrations to affirm the goodness and pleasure known in a community that lives in unity. First, living in unity resembles the anointing of a priest. The precious oil flows from the head, down the beard, and reaches the robes, saturating priest and vestments with its fullness. Second, living in unity resembles the dew that falls on Mount Hermon, which comes so abundantly that it extends more than one hundred miles to the south to Jerusalem. Nothing in the psalm indicates what prompts this reflection, but both illustrations point to Jerusalem, where God ordains the blessing of perpetual life. The lack of unity so often on display in and around Jerusalem may make the message seem unrealistic. We read it, however, during the season of Easter, which reminds us to place our deepest hopes in what God ordains.

Psalm 118:2-4, 13-15, 22-24 (LFM)

For discussion of this text, please see the psalmody for the Easter Vigil, above.

Second Reading
1 John 1:1—2:2 (RCL)

The opening verses of 1 John create two distinct groups: "we," the author and those with him, and "you," the recipients of the letter. "We" have witness to provide regarding what has existed from the beginning of the community, what "we" have heard, seen, and touched. This witness points to the "word of life," described as revealed life and eternal life (1:1-2). "We" desire that "you" enter this life by having fellowship (*koinōnia*) with us, which means fellowship with God and Jesus Christ. The name of Jesus does not appear until the end of verse 3. This implicitly declares that "you" encounter Jesus through the witness "we" offer, making it possible for joy to become complete.

After the author summarizes his message as "God is light" (v. 5), the "you" disappears for five verses and the "we" refers to the author and recipients of the letter (vv. 6-10). A series of conditional statements declare that we have fellowship with God and each other only as we walk in light, confess that we sin, and accept the forgiveness and cleansing God extends in Jesus. If we fail to do that, we sin and separate ourselves from eternal life. Neither providing witness nor accepting that witness suffices in and of itself. Only walking in the light and accepting what God alone provides keeps us in the light.

In the only use of the first-person singular pronoun in this passage, the author indicates that he has written this letter so that his little children not sin. The use of "I" adds tenderness to the appeal, but then the pronoun becomes plural with the reminder that when anyone sins we can depend on Jesus, our advocate and atoning sacrifice. That applies not only to us, but to "the whole world" (2:2). We all sin and, thanks be to God, we all have the opportunity for fellowship with God and each other.

This passage stresses the importance of one generation of Christians offering testimony about Jesus to the next and emphasizes the forgiveness and word of life that God provides in Jesus. Believers do not come together solely to share pews and ministerial tasks. We gather to share what we know about and experience in Jesus. Forgiveness stands at the heart of this. We all sin and sin separates us from life itself; but God faithfully forgives and cleanses. That underscores how blessed we are to have God and each other.

I John 5:1-6 (LFM)

For discussion of this text, please see the second reading for the Sixth Sunday of Easter, below.

Gospel

John 20:19-31 (RCL, LFM)

John's story of the first Easter evening opens with Jesus' disciples hiding behind locked doors. Fear of the authorities rather than jubilation over Mary's proclamation that she has seen the Lord (20:18) shapes their lives. Evidently they do not believe her. Before we can contemplate that, Jesus appears in their midst, greets them with peace (fulfilling John 14:27), and displays the wounds he suffered during the crucifixion. When they recognize him and respond joyfully, Jesus sends them forth as God first sent him (fulfilling John 17:18) by breathing on them, telling them to receive the Holy Spirit, and empowering them to forgive and retain sins. He entrusts his ministry to them. The disciples remain silent in the narrative. Indeed, no male follower of Jesus has spoken since the narrator indicated that the first day of the week had come (John 20:1).

Then the scene abruptly shifts and we learn that Thomas was not with the others when Jesus appeared to them. The disciples break their silence and echo Mary, declaring, "We have seen the Lord" (v. 25). Thomas, like the disciples following Mary's report, does not believe them and states what it will take for him to believe. Before anyone comments on those demands, the narrative jumps ahead a week to describe another appearance of Jesus, this time to Thomas as well. Jesus extends his peace to all and invites Thomas to examine the proof he has requested. Thomas immediately makes the most complete confession of faith in John's Gospel, "My Lord and my God!" (v. 28). Now that Thomas has what he wanted and the others have what they needed, Jesus extends his blessing to those who will come after them and believe without seeing. His words include all non-first-century believers in the community of faith and assure the disciples that the witness they bear will prove effective. The narrator underscores this by addressing readers directly to affirm that he has told this story to prompt belief in Jesus and acceptance of life in his name (fulfilling John 1:12-13).

Although the disciples do not believe Mary and Thomas does not believe them, the narrative comes to a series of climaxes when people do believe. When the fearful disciples assemble behind closed doors, Jesus ignores that barrier and their lack of faith and appears to them. When they recognize him, he commissions them for ministry. When Thomas refuses to believe without firsthand evidence, Jesus again ignores the barriers and provides the proof Thomas demands. Without taking time to verify by touch what his eyes see, Thomas proclaims Jesus his Lord and God. Jesus then includes all subsequent disciples in the joy of that moment by extending his blessing to all who believe without seeing. Instead of chastising or rejecting unbelieving disciples, Jesus does what he must to draw them into life. Just as his resurrection declares the triumph of life over death, his appearance and declarations in this narrative indicate that unbelief will not stop him from calling and tending his own. That's good news!

Preaching the Gospel

The good news that Jesus emerged victorious from the tomb, that life triumphs over death, and that darkness does not overcome light can prove hard to believe. Even when someone we trust delivers that message, we sometimes remain incredulous. The unbelieving live within as well as beyond the community of faith. How should we respond? This Gospel story invites us to make room. The disciples to whom Jesus first appeared did not believe Mary, but they remained together. Jesus appears to them not with threats but with peace. When they recognize him, he commissions them. Thomas does not believe those disciples, yet he remains with them a week later. Jesus appears again, not to scold but to bless. Then the author of John looks gently toward the readers and assures us that Jesus has a blessing for us as well, an opportunity for those who stay with the community (and read this book) to believe and have life in his name.

Our faith journey includes passages and seasons of unbelieving. The faith community has the privilege and call to make room for those who abide in it even while they do not believe all that it proclaims. Grief and tragedy can make the world frightening. When our foundations tremble and shake our certainty, we need the community more than ever. Various and competing claims about passages of Scripture can fill the faithful with more questions than answers. Those who keep listening for God even when the word seems silent need conversation, not condemnation. The church exists not solely for those who have what they want but also for those who long to believe there is more and for those who may not believe there is more but remain in its life and ministries all the same.

Unbelief need not be tragic. The hungry served at soup kitchens need compassion in Jesus' name more than unwavering convictions. A bass with unorthodox theology still adds notes to an anthem that glorifies God and inspires the congregation. We all experience times when prayer seems spoken into a vacuum, Scripture seems mute, or the loaf and cup seem merely that and nothing more. Yet as we continue to pray, read, partake, and wait, Jesus finds us. When we stay in community even while unbelieving, we do not reject Jesus. We simply cannot say all the words with conviction. As the certain and uncertain stand together and serve in Jesus' name, we manifest our common conviction that a community of faith depends foremost not on what we can get our hearts and heads around but on the God who gives us those hearts and hands and works in and through them, often in ways beyond our limits. Easter proclaims not how far we can reach but how God draws us to new life.

Notes

1. The Greek text contrasts two adjectives, *apistos* and *pistos*. These words do not appear together elsewhere in John, but grammatically one is the antithesis of the other. The risen Jesus appears to help Thomas move from *apistos* to *pistos*.
2. Thomas Merton, *Conjectures of a Guilty Bystander* (New York: Image Books, 1968), 70.
3. Phillips Brooks, *Lectures on Preaching* (New York: E. P. Dutton, 1877), 21.

April 22, 2012
Third Sunday of Easter

Revised Common Lectionary (RCL)	**Lectionary for Mass (LFM)**
Acts 3:12-19	Acts 3:13-15, 17-19
Psalm 4	Psalm 4:2, 4, 7-8, 9
1 John 3:1-7	1 John 2:1-5a
Luke 24:36b-48	Luke 24:35-48

Two weeks have passed since Easter Day. The crowds may have waned and the flowers probably have lost their blossoms, but it remains the season of Easter and in today's Gospel reading it is still Easter Day. So let the brass sound, raise the banners, fill the air with Alleluias, and invite those gathered to celebrate. What God has done and continues to do in Jesus deserves joyful recognition. In today's Gospel, even fear and incredulousness do not disqualify Jesus' disciples from receiving his commission. We have ample time to ponder how to respond to God's call in Jesus. It's Easter! Let's rejoice in gifts from God that come to us not because of who we are and what we have done but because of whose we are and the wonders God works.

First Reading
Acts 3:12-19 (RCL)
Acts 3:13-15, 17-19 (LFM)

Peter's speech in this narrative follows the healing of a lame man at the Beautiful Gate of the temple, the first healing story in Acts. Peter implies that he merely wants to make certain that the crowd does not attribute that healing to John's and his personal piety and power. To do that, however, he addresses a larger and more controversial issue.

Peter initially connects himself with his hearers by addressing them as "men, Israelites" (3:12),[1] descriptions that apply to John and him as well. They all worship the same God. After Peter informs the crowd that the God they all worship has glorified Jesus (but not revealing how), the connections fade as he accuses them of rejecting Jesus, choosing a murderer over "the Holy and Righteous One," and "killing the Author of life" (vv. 14, 15). The wickedness of their actions intensifies with those successive descriptions of Jesus. Then Peter proclaims that God raised Jesus from the dead (thus glorifying him) and that he and John bear witness to that. The speech then returns to the healing of the lame man, identifying the name of Jesus and faith in that name as the power that restored the lame man's health. Peter softens his tone, referring to the crowd as "brothers" (v. 17 NAB), attributing their heinous acts not to malice but to ignorance, and proclaiming that those acts fulfilled prophetic descriptions of what God's Messiah would suffer. Finally, he offers to close all the distance between himself and his hearers. When they repent and turn to God to have their sins erased, they truly will worship the same God.

Peter's speech contrasts personal piety with the power of God. Peter and John lack the resources to heal. Yet as witnesses of the resurrection and believers in what God offers in Jesus, they have received the gift of forgiveness and can share God's gift with others. Peter wants no credit for the healing, but he wants the crowd to accept his witness to Jesus' resurrection. God's power to wipe away the sins of the repentant is the true miracle.

Psalmody
Psalm 4 (RCL)
Psalm 4:2, 4, 7-8, 9 (LFM)

Although it opens with a plea for help, this prayer exudes confidence. Unnamed adversaries attack the psalmist's honor and he has grown angry, but he has more than sufficient strength on which to draw. Some strength comes from others. The psalmist affirms that he has company as he looks for good. Some strength comes from within. He has learned to trust God and continue offering sacrifices even when disturbed. The greatest strength comes from God. God has previously provided room in a confining situation (4:2) and now elates the psalmist's heart as in a year of abundant harvest. Despite the difficulties, the psalmist can sleep peacefully, a gift from the God who broadens every narrow path.

Second Reading
1 John 2:1-5a (LFM)

In the first words of this lection, the author of 1 John refers to the readers as "my children." Far from being condescending, that appellation reveals affection and tenderness. Having noted earlier that we all sin (1:8), the author wants us to avoid sin, but even more writes to assure us that when we sin God provides not only expiation but also the risen Jesus to serve as our advocate. First John identifies our advocate (*paraklétos*) as Jesus and not the Holy Spirit (John 14:16). These words come long before Trinity became a doctrine. The author speaks as a pastor more than a theologian. He assures the faithful that Jesus actively defends us when we sin. He does not leave us or the world (2:2) to our own devices. To receive assistance from "the righteous one," we need only keep the commandments. The author does not identify those commandments, but proclaims that obedience to them unites us with God. He focuses on what we do as believers more than on what we believe.

The author knows that we sin and challenges us to believe that Jesus can and will compensate for our sins. Contemporary Christians may wrestle with the first conviction more than the last. We often insist that we make mistakes, but reject being called sinners. Yet few honestly consider the baptized innocent of greed, adultery, envy, slander, and other decidedly sinful behaviors. This text offers three challenges. First, we can acknowledge that we sin. We do not merely make mistakes; we add to the brokenness in and of the world. Second, we can believe in forgiveness. In Jesus Christ, God's capacity to provide new beginnings overcomes our failures and limitations. Third, we can do something in Jesus' name. First John does not provide the details for what it means to keep Jesus' word, but it insists that living in union with God requires not merely a verbal confession of faith but also acts that express our faith.

I John 3:1-7 (RCL)

Many years ago a professor told a classroom of doctoral students that they already had an "A" in his class. Then he challenged them to keep it. This lection may make us feel like those students. The opening verses refer to the faithful as children destined to become as pure as God. Then the author declares all sinners guilty and insists that everyone who sins neither sees nor knows God. Since we all sin (1 John 1:8), can any of us keep our "A"?

We avoid that question by focusing on God, not ourselves. Yes, we sin and our sins render us guilty. We reflect the righteousness of God only as we do what is right (3:7). Yet instead of suggesting that we have the capacity to avoid sin, the author challenges us to have confidence that when we sin and turn to God, we have an advocate, Jesus Christ, who atones for the sins of the world (2:2). That does not imply that our sins do no harm. Rather, it proclaims that despite our sins, in Christ God claims us as God's own, children of God born "not of blood or of the will of the flesh or of the will of man, but of God" (John 1:13). Any purity we have comes not from our lack of sins but from our hope in God and our confidence that as the ways and will of God become manifest, God will be revealed not only for us but in us. Becoming children of God is a gift, not an achievement.

Gospel
Luke 24:36b-48 (RCL)
Luke 24:35-48 (LFM)

As Luke tells the story, the risen Jesus and his disciples kept late hours on Easter Day. In the passage that precedes this lection, two disciples who have yet to recognize Jesus invite him to stay with them because "it is almost evening and the day is now nearly over" (24:29). Table fellowship with Jesus opens their eyes, and when he vanishes they return to Jerusalem. There they learn that Jesus has appeared to Simon also and then they share their story with "the eleven and their companions" (v. 33).

This same group remains together that evening as this lection begins. While they discuss their experiences, Jesus mysteriously stands among them and greets them with peace. Although Jesus has appeared to Simon and been recognized by the two with whom he broke bread in Emmaus, his appearance still terrifies these disciples. Luke implies that they recognize him, but weakens that by noting that they consider him a ghost (*pneuma*). Jesus questions their fear and their doubting hearts, and then invites them to touch him and shows them his hands and feet. When that does not erase their doubts, he eats a piece of fish in their presence. Although he can vanish and appear inexplicably, he has a body and is not a spirit.

Luke does not describe how the disciples responded to Jesus' proof of his corporeal existence. Instead, Jesus immediately turns to the primary purpose of this appearance. He has come to affirm what he has previously taught them: that he had to fulfill everything written about him in Scripture (Luke 9:21-22, 44; 17:25; 18:31-33). As he repeats that lesson, he elevates the significance of the role his disciples will play. He opens their minds to understand that Scripture anticipates not only his suffering, death, and resurrection, but also their preaching of repentance and forgiveness of sins in his name. The witness he and Scripture commission them to provide will begin the proclamation of the gospel to all nations.

After Jesus appears, the disciples do not speak. The narrator describes them first as startled and terrified, and then as joyful but incredulous. Jesus adds doubting to that depiction. Yet they say nothing. Nor, apart from handing Jesus a piece of fish, do they take any significant action. They do not touch Jesus when he invites them to verify that he has a body. They do not worship, ask questions, or make exclamations. That does not, however, diminish their position. They receive a commission from Scripture and Jesus to bear witness to Jesus' suffering, death, and resurrection. For now it suffices that they recognize him and accept what he has come to reveal.

Preaching the Gospel

No contemporary Christian knows for certain how she or he would have responded if present in the events described in Scripture. We have inherited centuries of proclamation about and witness to Jesus. Most of us heard him called our risen Lord long before we could understand or interpret that title. It helps to remember that when we read stories about Jesus' disciples. We do not know how the evangelists shaped their stories to fit the messages they intended to proclaim; nor can we imagine the challenge of responding to Jesus before his story became woven into the human narrative.

Luke's story about Jesus' appearance to his disciples late on the first Easter evening depicts them as silent and relatively inactive. That comment is descriptive, not judgmental. Luke does not portray the disciples as unwilling participants. Rather, he describes them accepting in very human fashion the wonder and mystery of the moments unfolding before them. God's gift and what God alone can do lie at the heart of the Easter story, not our understanding of or participation in it. When we hear the Easter story and accept it as formative, we have the call, privilege, and opportunity to bear witness to how it shapes our lives. We do that in many ways: feeding the hungry, visiting the imprisoned, comforting those who ail or mourn, befriending the rejected, and more, all in Jesus' name. All that activity should not, however, blind us to the blessing of simply enjoying time with Jesus, savoring moments when we receive far more than we contribute.

We worship not only because it glorifies God and strengthens us for service but also for the pleasure of it. Believing and longing to believe that life triumphs over death and that forgiveness can open securely closed doors deserves spirit-filled singing and awe-filled silence. Similarly, we turn to Scripture not only to encounter the Word and have light shed on our path, but also for the joy of it. Friendships form and deepen as we share the comfort of hearing again a familiar story and the excitement of discovering a new favorite. Jesus' disciples did not fail to speak or act that Easter evening; they savored that time with Jesus. A caring pastor could follow that scene into proclamation of those times we spend together not to achieve a goal but to receive the gift of the risen Lord.

A second homiletic possibility lies in the captivating description of the disciples as joyfully incredulous (Luke 24:41). Even if we dealt with doubting believers on the Second Sunday of Easter, this image invites additional reflection. Sometimes doubts plague us and make us question our place in the community of faith. That deepens when what others find compelling leaves us unconvinced. In Luke's story the risen Jesus appears in Jerusalem as mysteriously as he vanished in Emmaus and invites his disciples to verify by sight and touch that it is he. The joy they feel in his presence leaves room for disbelief. The very notion that it appeared to be or might be him sufficed! This does not imply that we should never ponder doctrines that trouble us or that what we believe and do not believe does not matter. Rather, it gives us permission to ask our questions joyfully.

One of the most gifted teachers in a congregation questioned every statement in the Apostles' Creed. Yet his students clamored for him to teach another class, and when the congregation stood to recite the creed during baptism, no one gazed on the child with truer pleasure. Some of those who hold out their hands for the Bread of Heaven and no small number of those who train to participate in Holy Communion have doubts about our catechetical statements about the sacrament, yet they delight in its celebration and truly commune. Luke depicts Jesus appearing and staying with his disciples on the first Easter evening even though they were incredulous. Surely Jesus continues to accept and commission followers who do not allow what they do not believe to get in the way of the joy of belonging to him and finding life in his name.

God's gift and what God alone can do lie at the heart of the Easter story, not our understanding of it. Happy Easter! Thanks be to God.

Note

1.   The NRSV and NAB read "You Israelites," but the Greek word translated "you" is *andres*.

April 29, 2012
Fourth Sunday of Easter

F ew of the faithful who gather on Good Shepherd Sunday have significant awareness of or experience with sheep and shepherds. Yet Christian hymnody and art have provided many comforting images of Jesus calling, claiming, and protecting us. We find comfort in our relationship with God. Thanks be to God for that. Faithful acceptance of that comfort leads not to complacency but to grateful recognition of how the presence, power, and love of God have reached us. We celebrate the good news of resurrection and new life in part by recalling the people and events through which we have experienced the care of the Good Shepherd and found ourselves blessed by the gifts of God.

First Reading
Acts 4:5-12 (RCL)
Acts 4:8-12 (LFM)

The first reading continues a story that began in Acts 3. While going to the temple to pray, Peter and John encounter a lame man begging for alms. Instead of dropping coins into his hand, they invite him in Jesus' name to stand and walk. When the man jumps to his feet and begins to praise God, Peter identifies the power behind the healing as faith in the name of Jesus, "the Holy and Righteous One" (Acts 3:14) rejected by the astonished onlookers. Peter calls the crowd to repent, but the authorities arrest John and him and hold them in custody. Our lection begins here.

Contrasts of power appear throughout this narrative. The authorities have the power to arrest Peter and John and compel them to give an account of their actions.

They do not, however, know the power or name that enabled a man lame from birth to walk. Peter acknowledges the power of the authorities by identifying them as rulers. Yet the Holy Spirit has filled Peter and he knows the name behind the miracle. When Peter refers to the healing of the lame man as a good deed, some might attribute the miracle to the apostles. Peter points the authorities and all the people of Israel to the true power, the name of Jesus. He then quotes Scripture to draw a contrast between the rejection of Jesus by the authorities and his assertion that no other name offers salvation. Power belongs not to those in positions of privilege but to those who recognize the name of the crucified one whom God raised from the dead. Those who fail to recognize or accept that power place themselves outside salvation. Luke heightens this contrast by using the verb *sōzō* to describe both the healing of the lame man (v. 9) and the declaration that only the name of Jesus saves humanity (v. 12). The authorities do not comprehend the source of the miracle because they do not understand how humanity receives salvation. They fail to recognize true power.

The authorities have the power to place in custody those who did a good deed to a lame man, but they do not have access to the power that healed the man. Peter and John lack the power to secure their own freedom, but they have access to the power that made a lame man walk and brings salvation to humanity. We typically assume that those in positions of privilege and authority have power. This passage and the life of faith identify power not as something to possess but as something that acts through us and for us. Jesus' followers lacked the power to stop his crucifixion. Yet power finds room to bring life in the witness they bear to his resurrection. As followers of Jesus, instead of seeking to exercise power, we pray for power to act for, in, and through us to allow the lame to walk, to enable the powerless to speak a truth authorities do not want to hear, and to equip humanity to accept salvation. In the Gospel reading for this Sunday, Jesus proclaims that he knows his sheep and his sheep know him. In this reading, the fullness of life flows to those who know Jesus' name.

Psalmody
Psalm 23 (RCL)

The most familiar psalm opens with a claim of tranquility: "The Lord is my shepherd, I shall not want" (23:1). More literally translated, the psalmist declares, "I shall lack nothing." As the phrases that follow indicate, times of lack and difficulty precede those words. The presence of other powers prompts the psalmist to claim, "The Lord is my shepherd," and familiarity with their absence deepens the longing for and appreciation of green pastures, still waters, right paths, and restoration of the soul. The journey leads through the darkest valley and God prepares a table in the presence of enemies. The psalmist has faced challenges, but those trials have only strengthened the conviction that God provides care sufficient for every need and lasting for all of life. Most of the action in this psalm belongs to God. The psalmist claims not to lack, walks through the valley, and anticipates dwelling in the house of the Lord; but God guides, restores, comforts, prepares, and anoints. Goodness and mercy, attributes of God, pursue (*rādap*) the psalmist. So the psalmist calmly but defiantly declares to any would-be sovereign, "I have a shepherd in whom I have no lack, who makes my rest, my journey, and my home secure."

Psalm 118:1 + 8-9, 21-23, 26 + 21 + 29 (LFM)

For discussion of this text, please see the psalmody for the Easter Vigil, above.

Second Reading
1 John 3:16-24 (RCL)

The verses that lead into this lection set up a contrast of Cain, "who was from the evil one and murdered his brother" (3:12), with Jesus, who manifested love by laying down his life for us. Those who hate each other follow Cain (v. 15), but eternal life dwells in those who follow Jesus. This contrast does not invite martyrdom. Instead, it points to a process through which believers become increasingly bound to Jesus and each other. When we see and help another believer, we follow Jesus' example. Those actions assure us that we have a healthy relationship with God, which gives us the confidence for even bolder action and makes room for additional gifts of God to dwell in us. When we obey Jesus' commandment, when we accept his laying down of his life for us as an act of love and exhibit similar love for each other, by the power and presence of the Spirit, we live in Jesus and he lives in us.

The gospel often calls the faithful to love and serve others in Jesus' name. First John calls members of the body of Christ to love and serve each other. When we limit our love to one another, we become sectarian. When we consider this love foundational to all to which God calls us, we prepare for broader ministries in Jesus' name. As we stand beside each other in times of confusion, walk with each other through valleys of grief, rejoice with each other in moments of triumph, and allow those experiences to draw us more fully into each other, our acts of love manifest our identity as Jesus' disciples (John 13:35) and deepen our capacity to care for others. What we practice shapes us. When fear of embarrassment causes us to avert our eyes from friends in need, when we say nothing to a family dealing with job loss because we don't know what to say, or when we allow a wound to fester rather than seek or offer forgiveness, we miss opportunities to strengthen the ties that bind and also make it easier to repeat those actions. Similarly, when we sit quietly with a friend even though we have no words to offer, when we risk the discomfort of acknowledging that we gave offense to or were hurt by someone with whom we serve, or when we take the time to become better acquainted with those with whom we worship, we experience being bound in Jesus and strengthen those bonds for the future. Following Jesus does not require extreme actions. Offering kindness and gladdening each other's hearts manifests who and whose we are. The practice of love draws us into more perfect love.

I John 3:1-2 (LFM)

For discussion of this text, please see the RCL second reading for the Third Sunday of Easter, above.

Gospel

John 10:11-18 (RCL, LFM)

The Gospel reading describes complementary relationships that lead to the formation of a new community. The primary relationship, that between Jesus and the Father, provides the foundation for everything the narrative describes and envisions. Jesus and the Father know each other, and Jesus accepts and obeys what the Father commands. Jesus explicitly states that he has the power to lay down his life and take it up again and that he does this willingly. His act of obedience deepens the Father's love of him. John emphasizes not the cost Jesus pays but the love he expresses and generates.

The bond between Jesus and the Father flows into the relationship between the Good Shepherd and the sheep. In contrast to the hired hand, who neither owns nor cares for the sheep, Jesus knows and is known by the sheep, just as Jesus and the Father know and are known by each other. Four times in eight verses Jesus declares that he lays down his life for the sheep (10:11, 15, 17, 18). John later declares this an ultimate manifestation of love (15:13). Here, Jesus' willing obedience to the Father and care for the sheep allow the love of God to embrace the sheep through him.

No one takes Jesus' life from him. He lays down his life in obedience to God and as a gift to his sheep. Jesus offers this gift not only to the sheep initially addressed but also to other sheep outside that fold, who also listen to Jesus' voice. Anything that makes the sheep distinct fades as Jesus establishes a new community for all who listen to his voice, resulting in one flock and one Shepherd. The unity of the sheep, like Jesus' laying down of his life, is a gift he conveys. Knowing the Good Shepherd means accepting the other sheep. The sheep know God because they know Jesus, and they belong to each other because they all listen to Jesus' voice.

Preaching the Gospel

In the first reading, Peter proclaims that only the name of Jesus extends salvation to humanity. Psalm 23 assures the faithful that with the Lord as our shepherd, goodness and mercy pursue us, we lack nothing, and we have a place to dwell our whole life long. The Gospel lection provides the comforting image of Jesus as the Good Shepherd who knows his own and lays down his life for them. Pondering those images can give us an inflated sense of worth. We must have value to receive such extensive care. The faithful preacher will point us in a different direction not only because this is Easter, a season to celebrate what God alone can do, but also because we miss the point when we allow today's readings to make us feel smug.

Today's readings describe a relationship with God that comes as a gift. The power that heals a lame man in Acts 4, a power not recognized by the authorities, did not belong to Peter and John; it worked through them. The Lord is our shepherd not because we did something to claim a place in the flock but because God claims, calls, and cares for the sheep. The Good Shepherd lays down his life of his own volition and draws his sheep into his relationship with the Father. Faithful discipleship requires us to accept and respond to those gifts; but we only have those opportunities because God first extends those blessings to us.

Typically, God uses other people to offer the gifts of faith and community to us. If we have received baptism, someone who had a relationship with Jesus carried or led us to the font. If we know the stories of Jesus, someone taught them to us or helped us to hear them. If we believe in a good and gracious God, whose care of humanity resembles that of a good shepherd, someone did something to help us to draw that conclusion. Even mystics who have profoundly personal experiences of God depend on others to provide a foundation and context for their distinct encounters. We belong to God and each other because in some way and through someone God claimed us. Jesus' life, ministry, death, and resurrection reached us because others allowed his power, story, and love to become manifest in and through them. Everyone in the community that bears Jesus' name belongs to and depends on each other.

Perhaps the greatest challenge in these readings arises when Jesus mentions his "other sheep" (10:16). The Gospel reading begins with Jesus contrasting his actions as the good shepherd with the hired hand. It ends with a description of Jesus' willing obedience to God's command. Between those glimpses into Jesus' identity, immediately after he declares that he knows his sheep and his sheep know him, Jesus mentions the "other sheep." These sheep do not have secondary or inferior status. They also listen to Jesus' voice and become part of the one flock under the care of one shepherd. Regardless of who we think those "other sheep" are, they belong to Jesus as much as we do, and we belong to them as much as we belong to Jesus. What a compelling and challenging picture of Christian unity!

Acknowledging the existence of one flock and one Shepherd will not make it easier to live in community; whether we have in mind a single congregation or the diverse communions that comprise the body of Christ. Yet taking that image seriously challenges us to become humbler and more accepting of each other. All sheep have gifts to offer, but none of the sheep can lay exclusive claim to the Good Shepherd. Instead, the Good Shepherd lays down his life to claim us and unite us with each other. John's inclusion of the "other sheep" challenges all believers to look first not at what makes us distinct but at what binds us to each other. That sounds impossible. Given the energy we invest in separating ourselves into homogeneous enclaves, it may not even be practical. Yet it is Easter. Surely God, who assures that darkness never overcomes light and makes it possible for life and love to prevail over death and hatred, can provide glimpses of shared identity and mission. Even the most timid of those glimpses calls us to believe, to listen, to follow, and to find in each other's embrace the presence and love of God.

May 6, 2012
Fifth Sunday of Easter

Easter focuses on what God alone can do. Only God can assure that darkness does not overcome light and can bring life from tomb. Even when we acknowledge our complete dependence on God, however, we want to know what God expects of us. How can we manifest our acceptance of and gratitude for God's gifts? Today's Gospel lection repeatedly calls us to bear fruit, and the other lections illustrate ways to respond to that call. In the readings from Acts, the interactions between the Ethiopian eunuch and Philip, and between Barnabas and Saul, illustrate the encouragement believers can provide for each other. The selected verses from Psalm 22 depict a vast array of people using different means to give praise and glory to God. The lections from 1 John point to the blessings that flow as believers support each other with acts of love. These texts challenge us to ponder who in the community of faith finds it easier to believe because of our discipleship and who in the community around us finds God more credible because of what we do in Jesus' name. It is Easter and the focus remains on what God alone can do. Through the fruit we bear, our active lives of faith join our voices in singing, "Alleluia!"

First Reading
Acts 8:26-40 (RCL)

Luke provides a relatively detailed description of the Ethiopian eunuch Philip encounters on the road from Jerusalem to Gaza. The eunuch has significant power and privilege, and his queen trusts him sufficiently to allow him to travel the considerable distance from Ethiopia to Jerusalem. He traveled to Jerusalem to worship, which implies that he sought something other than his standing, wealth, and privilege. That pilgrimage may not have ended as he desired. Purity laws prohibited eunuchs from entering the temple. Yet he continues to seek God through Scripture, specifically reading Isaiah, who in a passage other than the one cited here makes room for eunuchs in the temple (Isa. 56:4-5).

Philip encounters this eunuch because he obeys first when an angel tells him to travel that road and then when the Spirit directs him to join the man in the chariot. His obedience yields an opportunity to share the good news about Jesus with someone outside his community. When the eunuch requests baptism as well, Philip enters the water with him. Purity laws may keep the eunuch out of the temple and lack of a guide may hinder his understanding of Scripture, but nothing prevents his baptism. This gives him a joy that even Philip's mysterious disappearance does not diminish.

"What is to prevent me from being baptized?" (8:36). When others ask that question for themselves or those dear to them, we have God-given opportunities to pave a way to the font. As we focus not on the differences we see but on how God may have placed us in a position to open a door to faith and community, we travel in faith together to places beyond our reach alone.

Acts 9:26-31 (LFM)

This reading follows the story of Saul's conversion. According to Luke, after Saul received baptism he remained for some time with the disciples in Damascus and proclaimed Jesus as the Son of God in the synagogues. Only after a conspiracy against his life does he travel to Jerusalem. The disciples in Jerusalem evidently know nothing about Saul's conversion and preaching. When they last saw him, he intended to destroy the church (Acts 8:3). Barnabas, known to the believers in Jerusalem as a "son of encouragement" (Acts 4:36), steps forward to assure the apostles that Paul has seen the Lord and joined the community. Supported by that recommendation, Saul has the opportunity to speak about Jesus in Jerusalem as well, building up the community he once sought to destroy.

Today's Gospel lection calls believers to bear fruit. In this passage Saul bears witness to Jesus in Jerusalem only after Barnabas bears fruit by assuring the apostles that Saul has become a follower of Jesus. The encouragement we provide for each other helps not only the newly converted but also the long-faithful to step into more active roles in community. Supportive words about what we have seen and experienced in each other open doors for new ministries. We proclaim the good news not only by sharing the story of Jesus with those who have not heard it but also by helping each other find places in our ministries to use the gifts and experiences God has given us.

Psalmody
Psalm 22:25-31 (RCL)
Psalm 22:26-27, 28 + 30, 31-32 (LFM)

The selected verses of Psalm 22 bring to a close a personal prayer for deliverance. After appealing for help and receiving assurance that God has heard and offered rescue, the psalmist promises to praise God in the congregation and invites others to join the song (22:22-23). The psalmist extends this invitation to an amazingly broad array of people, calling the poor, the families of the nations, the dead, and generations yet unborn to worship God and witness as vows are paid. The diverse list of those called to worship and their varied responses to God describe worship not only as praise offered to God in the congregation but also as feeding the hungry, living our gratitude daily, opening our hearts to those outside our faith community, and telling children stories about what God has done. Individual suffering prompts this prayer, but the closing words call for trust in a God worthy of praise by all who live, have lived, and shall live.

Second Reading
1 John 4:7-21 (RCL)

As this section of the letter begins, the author once again addresses the readers as "Beloved."[1] Although certainly a term of endearment that reflects the warm bond between the leader and the people, "beloved" also and more significantly describes the God-given identity of the members of the faith community. The love so frequently mentioned in these verses refers not to a human emotion or virtue, but to the nature and gift of God. God, who is love, reveals this divine attribute to humanity in order to draw human beings into the fullness of life with God and each other. First John never declares humanity lovable, but often describes us as loved and called into love by God. We enter this love as we confess Jesus as the Son of God, and believers manifest this love through their acts of love for each other.

We can easily trivialize this message. During a discussion of ethics and the covenant of marriage, a New Testament professor remarked, "Falling in love is easy. It takes effort and commitment to grow in love and stay in love." First John points to the effort love requires by stating that when we love each other, "God lives in us, and his love is perfected in us" (4:12). The verb translated "lives" is *menō*, a verb that appears frequently in the Johannine literature, which can mean abide, stay, dwell, last, and endure. First John calls for persistent care for other believers that draws us more fully into the presence and nature of God. We cannot initiate love; we love because we are beloved. Yet we can decide again and again to make ourselves available to love by loving others.

Preachers can guide the faithful to the depth of the author's meaning in two significant ways. First, we can note that 1 John calls us to love all our brothers and sisters in faith. In even the best of communities, some of us are harder to love. Yet remember that this passage does not declare us lovable but describes us as beloved. The love to which 1 John calls us manifests itself not in words alone, but in "truth and action" (v. 18). That requires effort and commitment, but the entire body becomes stronger and more suited for Jesus' ministries as even those whom we find it hard to love know that we value them. Second, although it lies somewhat outside the theme of this letter, we can allow our practice of loving each other to prepare us for ministries beyond the walls of the church. Strengthened by our mutual bonds, we can reach out in Jesus' name not only in obedience to divine commands but also because we truly long for the least of these to have a better life. Loving like that means we will often have our hearts broken, because love makes us vulnerable to disappointment and to the deepest experiences of betrayal. Yet loving like that helps a world too often tarnished by the worst we can do to shine in the light of the best that God makes manifest in and through us.

I John 3:18-24 (LFM)

For discussion of this text, please see the second reading for the Fourth Sunday of Easter, above.

Gospel
John 15:1-8 (RCL, LFM)

The final "I am" sayings in the Fourth Gospel, which describe Jesus as the vine and his disciples as the branches, focus on relationships. Jesus has a unique relationship with God, which flows into an intimate relationship with believers and binds all three firmly together. By calling himself the true vine and the Father the vine grower, Jesus declares absolute dependence on God. He extends this dependence to the disciples by calling them his branches. A gardener can graft branches from one vine onto another, but no branch can grow without a vine. Jesus' followers cannot exist without him, and because he is the true vine they can exist only in him. The frequent use of the verb *menō* strengthens this image.[2] God, an active vine grower, intends these relationships to endure. God also expects the branches to bear fruit, much fruit. Those who do not bear fruit find themselves removed from the vine, and those who bear fruit are pruned to make them more productive.

Although we may find it comforting to hear ourselves called branches of the true vine, a significant call and challenge come with the comfort. The natural cycle of the growing season illustrates the theological truth and the challenge John conveys. When a farmer plants a vine and branches begin to grow from it, the farmer works to assure that the branches yield fruit. That includes pruning healthy branches and removing unhealthy ones. When the branches yield their fruit, the farmer proudly displays them to the neighbors or in the market. God blessed the world with Jesus, expecting him to call disciples. God's word in and through Jesus removes disciples (e.g., John 6:60-66) and prunes those who remain (e.g., John 13:10-11). God expects those disciples to bear fruit, to believe that they belong to the vine and to support each other. The fruit the disciples bear makes the goodness and glory of God even more widely known. This image includes judgment, but it focuses on the possibility of believers completing what God begins in Jesus.

Preaching the Gospel

Even those without green thumbs and with little interest in gardening can find homiletic possibilities in John's image of the vine and branches. In the ivy that adorns many of our lawns, no one branch stands out from the other. The branches weave themselves close together to cover the ground and hold in the moisture. Similarly, the community of faith thrives as members seek to support and complement rather than stand out from one another. Some of us go out of our way and pay extra for vine-ripened tomatoes. We also know that lasting relationships between believers, leaders, and God yield the best fruit of the ministry we enter through baptism. Some vines tenaciously take control of entire hillsides. The honeysuckle vines on our hillside not only attract hummingbirds and butterflies but also hold the soil on the steep slope in place. In the same way faith communities with a deep commitment to ministry in Jesus' name and strong bonds of mutual affection offer blessings to any neighborhood in which they grow. Let those listening for a sermon idea put down the books for a moment and take a walk. Somewhere nearby a prolific vine invites theological reflection that can yield homiletic fruit.

The repeated call in John 15 for believers to bear fruit also invites reflection and proclamation. When many of us receive baptism or affirm our baptism, we not only profess Jesus as Lord but also promise to obey his word and show his love, that is, to bear fruit. That promise and John 15 challenge us to ask ourselves, "Who has benefited from my baptism?" No community or disciple can do everything to which God calls us equally well, but every Christian community and individual has the ability to bear fruit that blesses someone. When we have the ability to make money or amass resources, Jesus calls us to find ways for others to benefit from that fruit. When we have more than we need to eat, Jesus calls us to make certain that others benefit from our surplus. When we receive the gift of 168 hours each week, Jesus calls us to use some of them in ways that benefit others. The purpose of grapevines is to bear grapes; the purpose of Jesus' followers is to bear fruit. We bear fruit not to earn our identity but to express it by helping others to have more to eat, more hope, more purpose and direction, and more reason to believe in goodness, grace, and God.

The final verse of this lection, which declares that God is glorified when we bear fruit, inspires another possibility. The first question in the Westminster Catechism asks what the chief purpose of humanity is and declares in response that our chief end is to glorify God and enjoy God forever. In a world in which heinous acts of violence by faithful fanatics have too often not only shattered the common good but also marred the image of God, surely we can help our communities accept ministries in

Jesus' name that give God glory. Many of us bemoan the loss of influence the church and the gospel have experienced in our society. Rather than point fingers, we can ask ourselves what fruit that we bear does something to change that. God wants not simply fruit, but "much fruit" (John 15:8). God nurtures in each congregation the capacity for a bold ministry that will point to the presence, goodness, and love of God. If maintaining our present ministries leaves little or no resources for a bold ministry, perhaps we need to seek the pruning that will allow us to bear much fruit and glorify God.

Notes

1. The author addresses the reader with this term in 1 John 2:7; 3:2, 21; 4:1, 7, 11.
2. *Menō* is the verb translated as "abide" in John 15:4, 5, 6, 7. As noted in the discussion of the second reading, it can also mean "stay," "dwell," "last," and "endure."

May 13, 2012
Sixth Sunday of Easter

Revised Common Lectionary (RCL)	**Lectionary for Mass (LFM)**
Acts 10:44-48	Acts 10:25-26, 34-35, 44-48
Psalm 98	Psalm 98:1, 2-3a, 3b-4
1 John 5:1-6	1 John 4:7-10
John 15:9-17	John 15:9-17

Do we enjoy life in and with the community of faith? Do we enjoy participating in the ministries of Jesus? If not, we may have forgotten how it all began, what drew us to the font and faith, and the grace and goodness that have freely flowed our way. The readings for this Sunday illustrate in various ways the love of God and each other that fills communities of faith with joy. Each one also includes a call for the faithful to respond, to use our lives to make a difference. God expects us to use, not hide or hoard, the gifts and blessings we receive. Yet each time goodness and grace become manifest around and in us, God makes our world new. That's something God alone can do. It's Easter! Alleluia!

First Reading
Acts 10:44-48 (RCL)
Acts 10:25-26, 34-35, 44-48 (LFM)

When the gifts of the Holy Spirit interrupt his preaching, Peter echoes the Ethiopian eunuch's expectant "What is to prevent me from being baptized?" (Acts 8:36) with his own astonished "Can anyone withhold the water for baptizing these people who have received the Holy Spirit just as we have?" (10:47). Several divine acts precede Peter's question. First, an angel appears in a vision and instructs Cornelius, a Roman centurion, to send for Simon Peter. Then Peter falls into a trance while praying and has three consecutive visions instructing him to kill and eat unclean creatures. When Peter objects, a voice commands him not to deem profane anything God has cleansed. Peter restates that message when he opens his sermon to Cornelius and his household, declaring that God's acceptance and salvation extend beyond the boundaries of Judaism. Then the Holy Spirit falls on Peter's Gentile hearers, dramatically illustrating Peter's sermon. The Gentiles in Caesarea receive the same gift the Spirit bestowed on the Jews in Jerusalem, the ability to speak in tongues (2:4; 10:46).[1] Barriers once considered firm have become permeable. Samaritans (8:12), an Ethiopian eunuch (8:38), a former persecutor of the church (9:18), and now Gentiles have received baptism and belong to one faith community.

We all have people we consider outside our group. Sometimes we prefer or drive them there. Sometimes they choose to be there. Peter's experience warns members of the faith community not to use indelible ink with any dividing lines we draw. The Holy Spirit moves at will, falling on whomever the Spirit chooses. When the gifts of the Spirit appear, the faithful look for ways to affirm and participate, even if that challenges our carefully drawn and sometimes cherished boundaries. Easter focuses on what God alone can do. God alone decides who receives the gifts of the Spirit. God calls and challenges us to recognize and give thanks for those gifts no matter where or on whom they appear.

Psalmody
Psalm 98 (RCL)
Psalm 98:1, 2-3a, 3b-4 (LFM)

We all have favorite songs of faith. When we sing those songs, memories of past events that formed us in faith join the praises we offer in the present. Not everyone, however, shares our experiences and favored melodies. That does not mean we should not continue to sing a beloved hymn or song; but it justifies adding new words and melodies to our repertoire that praise God for present acts that form people in faith.

Psalm 98 praises God for steadfast love and faithfulness shown to the people of Israel. Yet the psalmist proclaims God as sovereign and judge of all the world and its people and invites not only humanity but also the waters, the earth, and all within them to respond joyfully to the wonders God works. The opening verse calls for a new song. A new song does not deny past blessings, but recognizes and celebrates what God does and provides now. We all have our favorite songs of faith, but each act of God adds something new to receive with gratitude and to celebrate with joy.

Second Reading
1 John 5:1-6 (RCL)

As 1 John draws to a close, the author weaves its major themes together. We love God primarily by loving fellow believers. Such love keeps the commandments, which we accept not as burdens but as a way of joining God's triumph over the world. Jesus stands at the center of this. Those who believe that Jesus is the Christ and Son of God have been born of God and conquer the world. Even love of fellow believers stands secondary to recognizing and accepting God's revelation in Jesus. We sometimes call this Christianity's scandal of particularity. We unequivocally place Jesus at the heart of everything we understand and believe about God, faith, and life. That does not prohibit us from appreciating and interacting with people in other faith traditions. Rather, it provides the foundation on which we stand in all our relationships. We sometimes struggle to discern clearly where and to what Jesus calls us, but we always seek to respond to his call by following him, obeying his word, and showing his love.

The final verse of this lection continues that focus by declaring that Jesus came by water and blood. Commentators wax eloquently about the possible meanings of this. Those who stress the sacraments of baptism and holy communion in our ministries no doubt will consider the water and blood references to them regardless what the experts conclude. When we do, let's focus not solely on the blessings the sacraments offer to believers but also on the ministries they call us to offer others. God conquers the world by defeating evil, not by purging those who differ from us. The sacraments strengthen and equip us to participate in that struggle.

Those familiar with the Gospel of John will hear in the mention of water and blood echoes of John's crucifixion scene in which blood and water flow from Jesus' pierced side (John 19:34). That flow culminates in the references in John to the life Jesus makes available through his gifts of living water and blood (John 4:10, 12-14; 6:53-55; 7:37-38). The narrator not only attests that this fulfills Scripture but also interrupts the narrative to assure the reader that he witnesses this event and to affirm that it is true (John 19:35-37). Jesus lays down his life as an act of obedience to God and of love for his friends (John 15:13). As today's Gospel reading asserts, those who believe that Jesus is the Christ and the Son of God must respond to that by bearing fruit: loving the children of God and living lives that make the love of God known.

1 John 4:7-10 (LFM)

For discussion of this text, please see the second reading for the Fifth Sunday of Easter, above.

Gospel
John 15:9-17 (RCL, LFM)

The passage begins with Jesus reminding his disciples that just as he remains in God's love by laying down his life for them and thus keeping God's commandments (10:18), he expects them to remain in his love by believing in him and loving each other and thus keeping his commandments. He adds that he has offered them this opportunity to make it possible for his joy to enter them and their joy to become complete. Jesus knows the difficulties his followers will face (e.g., 16:2), but still considers discipleship not a burden to bear or a requirement to fulfill, but a joy. As we believe in what God reveals in Jesus and share love with other believers, we receive glimpses of God and goodness that give us reason to rejoice even in the face of hardship. Joy comes not in the absence of struggle, but in blessings worth the struggle.

After promising joy to his followers, Jesus returns to a primary Johannine theme, the love God offers the world and into which God calls us. At the beginning of the foot washing, the initial act in Jesus' final hours with his disciples, John declares that Jesus loved his disciples and "loved them to the end" (13:1). Those words describe the foot washing and the crucifixion it foreshadows as acts of love. This passage enhances that message by declaring the laying down of one's life for one's friends the greatest love. Jesus' crucifixion, his act of obedience through which God glorifies him, is an act of love. Love refers not to a human emotion but to a gift from God. Jesus' act of love draws us into God and affirms our worth. In the words of William Sloane Coffin: "It is not because we have value that we are loved, but because we are loved that we have value. Our value is a gift, not an achievement."[2]

The gift of God becomes even more intimate as Jesus refers to his followers as friends. Earlier he called them servants (13:14-16), but the completion of his act of love will make them his friends, his chosen friends. The disciples rarely understand Jesus' actions and struggle to grasp his identity. They belong to him only because he has chosen them. He has loved them and revealed his God-given ministry to them; and soon he will lay down his life for them. Jesus extends those gifts to all his followers. We belong to the community of faith only because in Jesus' name someone led us here, welcomed us here, and made a place for us here. We do not have faith alone. We have faith because Jesus has acted through someone or something to claim us as God's own.

Lest our status as the chosen make us smug or self-centered, Jesus closes this passage by commissioning us to bear fruit, fruit that will last. The verb translated "last" is *menō*, which played a prominent role in last Sunday's lections. This verb describes how Jesus abides in his followers and they abide in him (John 15:4). Jesus calls for acts of love with staying power: caring that costs us something; honest conversations that lay foundations for new beginnings; confession and forgiveness that overcome sin; commitment to the community that sets aside personal preference to seek the common good. Yes, it warms our hearts for Jesus to call us his friends; and yes, like us, Jesus has high expectations of his friends. As he used others to make us his friends, he intends to use us to extend that same friendship to those he chooses.

Preaching the Gospel

Most of us can recall a childhood memory of waiting to be chosen while sides were being decided for a game or event. Even if we had little fondness for the activity, we wanted someone to choose us quickly. In John 15 Jesus declares that he chooses us. This choosing typically takes place as Jesus acts through parents, friends, and complete strangers to draw us to church and the font, to make us welcome, and to include us in his ministries. Jesus chooses us, all of us. We respond to our selection most faithfully not through feelings of superiority but through gratitude for the blessings we have received. A sermon that invites the faithful to name those who helped draw them to faith, possibly supplemented by church members briefly sharing their own stories, could not only give an entire new meaning to "election" but also renew appreciation for life in a congregation. Since Jesus not only chooses us but also commissions us to bear fruit, he challenges us to do for others what family, friends, and strangers have done for us. It all begins with an invitation, an act of love that Jesus chooses us to issue.

The joy mentioned at the beginning of the Gospel lection points in another direction. Many professional athletes and musicians have reportedly declared, "If they didn't pay me to do this, I'd do it for free!" They say that in part because they enjoy the game or love the music. They understand its nuances and take pleasure in aspects of their craft that many never notice. They probably also have considerable natural ability, which helps them to play well. And even the best have practiced. They've spent hour after hour repeating the same actions until they become almost automatic. Everyone whom Jesus chooses for his ministry has gifts and abilities for that to which he calls us. God gives us those gifts not so we can hoard or hide them, but so we can bear fruit. What in the ministries of Jesus would we do "for free"? Joyful participation begins as we recognize what we do well. Some of us humbly question our abilities. What do our friends say we do well? Jesus may be using their voices to call us. Finally, how faithfully do we practice what we do well? Do we automatically welcome newcomers, invite new acquaintances, bring donations for the hunger fund, or volunteer when vacation Bible school time arrives? Jesus wants fruit that lasts. Our fruit lasts when it becomes such a part of us that we know in our hearts we'd "bear it for free"!

What can we say about Jesus calling believers his friends? Those words warm our hearts, but they also challenge us to be the kind of friends on whom Jesus can depend. After all, no one can gladden our heart like a friend, and no one can break our heart like a friend. The author of 1 John advises, "No one has ever seen God; if we love one another, God lives in us, and his love is perfected in us" (4:12). Surely being a friend of Jesus works the same way. What plan do we have for being a friend of the people with whom we worship, especially those whom we've had little time or opportunity to befriend? What plan do we have for being a friend of those who look to our faith community for assistance? We can't help them all, but Jesus probably can point us to one or two who would consider our acts of friendship a blessing. Our efforts can gladden or break Jesus' heart. Please remember that we do not do this to make the team. Jesus has already chosen us. We befriend in Jesus' name to express who we are and declare what we believe. We do it for the joy of it. Alleluia!

Notes

1. Luke uses the same Greek verb (*laleō*) and noun (*glōssa*) in both passages.
2. William Sloane Coffin, *Credo* (Louisville: Westminster John Knox, 2004), 6.

May 17, 2012 (or transferred to May 20)
Ascension of Our Lord

Revised Common Lectionary (RCL)
Acts 1:1-11
Psalm 47 or 93
Ephesians 1:15-23
Luke 24:44-53

Lectionary for Mass (LFM)
Acts 1:1-11
Psalm 47:2-3, 6-7, 8-9
Ephesians 4:1-13 or 4:1-7, 11-13
Mark 16:15-20

In recent decades human beings have hurled a variety of spacecraft into the heavens. We have viewed Earth as an oasis of blue in the dark expanse of space, deepened our knowledge of every planet in our solar system and many of the other heavenly bodies relatively near us, and hit a golf ball on the surface of the moon. The Hubble telescope has helped us to discover that the observable universe has a radius of fourteen billion light-years. Light travels a little less than six trillion miles in a year. That makes the observable universe more vast than we can comprehend. Yet in all this exploration and discovery we have encountered no divine throne room, no specific place to designate as the heavenly abode of God. Have our scientific achievements and scientific worldview rendered our confession that Jesus ascended into heaven and is seated at the right hand of God a quaint relic of our heritage now devoid of meaning? Not necessarily.

When we consider Jesus' ascension a fact to confirm rather than a facet of our faith, we miss the point. The Apostles' Creed marks Jesus' ascension as the completion of his earthly ministry and the theological climax of his resurrection. Unlike those whom Jesus raised from the dead, Jesus never faced death again. Nor did God raise Jesus so he could wander the earth (or the universe) and continue his peripatetic ministry eternally. Rather, we believe and affirm that Jesus returned to the God from whom he came, the God who sent him, the God in whom he lives and belongs forever. Because we believe and affirm that about Jesus, we believe that, by the grace of God, we also return to God when we complete our lives. Death marks not our end but our point of return to the Author of life.

Our scientific understanding provides support for this belief and affirmation. The first law of thermodynamics states that energy can be transformed but not created or destroyed. Once energy exists, it endures in some form. From a faith perspective, what God creates returns to God. Isaiah declares that more eloquently:

> For as the rain and snow come down from heaven,
>   and do not return there until they have watered the earth,
> making it bring forth and sprout,
>   giving seed to the sower and bread to the eater,
> so shall my word be that goes out from my mouth;
>   it shall not return to me empty,
> but it shall accomplish that which I purpose,
>   and succeed in the thing for which I sent it. (Isa. 55:10-11)

We may struggle to define heaven and wrestle with to where Jesus ascended. Yet when we declare that Jesus ascended into heaven and is seated at the right hand of God, we affirm our conviction that God accomplishes what God purposes. Only God can do that, and that's very good news! It's Easter! Alleluia!

First Reading
Acts 1:1-11 (RCL, LFM)

The opening verses of Acts affirm several convictions of Christian faith. First, Luke affirms that the ministry of Jesus stretches "from the beginning until the day when he was taken up to heaven" (1:1). The God who sends Jesus also receives him back. His return affirms the goodness of the one who sends him. God does not exhaust and then discard Jesus, but receives him back in triumphant reunion. Our belief in and longing for life eternal spring not from mere wishful thinking, but from our conviction that by the grace of God life returns to its source and thus continues. Second, the instructions given the disciples in this passage affirm waiting as a necessary and active aspect of the ministry to which Jesus calls us. The risen Jesus spends forty days with his disciples and commands them not to leave Jerusalem until they receive the gift of the Holy Spirit. Jesus feeds us not by quickly thrusting a bag of burgers and fries out a drive-through window, but with a full meal of study, prayer, and reflection that takes time to prepare and partake of.[1] Finally, Jesus' last earthly words to his disciples (1:7-8) affirm that some things lie outside what we can know. Faithful disciples can ponder them, but should not allow them to interfere with our call to bear witness to what we see and experience in Jesus. God calls us into the life, ministry, death, resurrection, and ascension of Jesus not to enjoy the show but to enter and continue those realities. As we receive baptism and share our experiences and the gifts God provides in ways that draw others to the font and the life of faith, we participate in and continue what God purposes. Thanks be to God for the Spirit who gives us the power to respond.

Psalmody
Psalm 47 or 93 (RCL)
Psalm 47:2-3, 6-7, 8-9 (LFM)

Psalm 47 proclaims that the God who chooses the people of faith rules over every nation. Although convinced that God ultimately subdues all nations under the people of the covenant, the psalmist avoids exclusive claim on God by stressing God's rule over all the earth. The opening verse calls for acts of joy and praise by "all you peoples," and the final verse envisions everyone gathering "as the people of the God of Abraham."

Psalm 93 celebrates God's rule over all by declaring that even the motion and roaring of primeval waters praise God, whose magnificence they cannot rival. The creation and its continued existence depend on God, who established it. Because God's rule has no end, what God decrees remains ever trustworthy. Both psalms offer appropriate messages to say and sing during Easter as we celebrate the triumph of God and on the feast of the Ascension of Our Lord as we affirm our conviction that what comes from God returns to God.

Second Reading
Ephesians 1:15-23 (RCL)

Knowing that we do not labor alone gives us hope. Paul or someone writing in his name offers thanks to God after hearing about other believers' faith in Jesus and love for the saints. Although Paul prays for those believers to receive even more complete awareness of the hope to which God calls them, what he has heard about them primarily inspires him to extol God, who offers a "glorious inheritance" (1:18) to all the saints. He describes God as the Father of glory and author of hope, whose power exceeds what the faithful can measure. Although the saints cannot fathom this power, we affirm it as we acknowledge Jesus' resurrection and ascension. The Lord Jesus in whom we believe draws us into his body, where we experience "the fullness of him who fills all in all" (v. 23). Through Jesus we enter the fullness of that which we cannot measure.

We belong to Jesus, but he does not belong to us. The life of faith is a life of response. Jesus calls and we follow where he leads. Jesus provides other saints to work alongside us, and we give thanks for them and pray for their ministries. God lifts Jesus from death to life in the fullness of divine embrace, and we trust Jesus to draw us there with him. God marks us "with the seal of the promised Holy Spirit" (v. 13) and we have hope.

Ephesians 4:1-13 or 4:1-7, 11-13 (LFM)

Paul or someone writing in his name challenges believers to accept their call from God with grateful and humble recognition that they walk[2] in faith alongside other believers. He issues this challenge because of his conviction that all believers share "one hope of your calling, one Lord, one faith, one baptism, one God and Father of all" (4:4-6). The faithful receive varied gifts from the risen and ascended Christ, but each one equips them to strengthen the one body of Christ.

Christians spend considerable time trying to distinguish ourselves from one another. Even within individual communions and congregations, we regularly debate who does and does not belong. We may not state it that bluntly, but when we declare any doctrine or practice mandatory for all, we exclude someone. Our baptism into Jesus Christ calls us to give account for what we believe and how we live. Yet we place our ultimate trust not in our responses to baptism but in the one into whom we are baptized. That does not mean that anything goes, but it calls for humble gratitude in all we are and do. As we celebrate the Ascension of Our Lord, we express our conviction that Jesus returned to God, who sent him, and our hope that we also will return to God, from whom we came. Our one call, one faith, one baptism, one Lord, and one God challenge us to embrace each other in ministry far more than we face off to determine who belongs.

Gospel
Mark 16:15-20 (LFM)

In an ending added to the Gospel of Mark long after its composition, Jesus ends his earthly ministry by commissioning his followers to proclaim the good news to everything created. Only then does God carry Jesus to his seat of power, where he helps his disciples in the ministries into which he calls them. The commissioning includes the promise that believers will use Jesus' name to cast out demons, speak in tongues, pick up snakes and drink poisons without harm, and heal the sick. The final verse of this lection explains that these signs come not from the believers themselves but from the risen and ascended Jesus. The signs do not verify a believer's discipleship and do not serve as a prerequisite to inclusion in the faith community. They represent the promise that as the baptized participate in Jesus' ministries, Jesus himself will supply the power and verification they need. Jesus does not commission the baptized to take his place; he calls us into ministries that represent and bear witness to him.

Some readers may find it troubling when Mark declares that baptized believers receive salvation whereas those who do not believe face condemnation. Although it extends a clear warning that failure to accept baptism comes at a cost, the text focuses on the commissioning and the signs of power and wonder that will support the ministry of the baptized. To refuse to accept baptism and commissioning not only deprives the person called to faith but also denies gifts of God to the entire creation. As we respond faithfully to baptism and Jesus' commission, we not only enter but also extend the rule and embrace of our risen and ascended Lord.

Luke 24:44-53 (RCL)

For discussion of this text, please see the Gospel for Easter Evening and the Third Sunday of Easter, above.

Preaching the Gospel

Twenty-first-century saints do not flock to churches to celebrate the Ascension of Our Lord. When we move the lections for the Ascension to the Seventh Sunday of Easter, many of the faithful may wonder why, or they may metaphorically pat us on the head and sigh, "That's what pastors do." Few of the faithful can explain why we include an affirmation that Jesus ascended into heaven in the Apostles' Creed. That includes those called to preach! We probably feel tempted to ignore the Ascension and hope no one notices. Instead, why not blow the dust off this declaration and ask God to breathe new life into it? After all, it is Easter, when we celebrate what God alone can do.

The Ascension of Our Lord expresses our confidence that the way things end affirms our conviction about how things begin, namely, our confession that Jesus returns to God affirms our conviction that he came from God. In the movie *The Bucket List*, an agnostic character portrayed by Jack Nicholson quips when asked about his belief in God, "We live, we die, and the wheels on the bus go round and round." For Nicholson's character, death ends the journey for us, and others continue to ride the bus. As we celebrate Jesus' ascension, we declare, "We live, we die, and we return to life." Not only the wheels of the bus, but all God creates continues to go round and round. Our struggle to grasp how that can be should surprise us no more than the fact that we cannot fathom an observable universe so broad that it takes light twenty-eight billion years to travel from one edge to the next. Some things lie beyond our understanding. That makes them no less true and no less formative. Affirming that we return to the God from whom we came inspires us to celebrate and serve God on the all-too-short journey in that grace-filled cycle.

Those uncomfortable tackling Jesus' ascension may want to take a different approach. I always try to take care of my tools, but when I borrow a tool from a friend, I make extra effort to return that tool in the same working order in which I received it. No one wants to return a tool broken or worse for wear. Today's Gospel lection declares that Jesus commissions the baptized to proclaim the good news to all God created. God entrusts creation into our care. How carefully and faithfully do we use what belongs to God? We could smugly note that we fare better in the text than those who do not believe, but that does not remove our call to participate in Jesus' ministry so his signs of power and presence can accompany us. We may feel ill equipped to perform exorcisms; but we can support spousal-abuse shelters and engage in ministries of justice and compassion so Jesus can cast out demons. We may have no desire to speak in tongues; but we can learn a contemporary song that encourages others to join the baptized in worshiping God. Jesus will tend to the rest. I personally have no desire to pick up a snake, venomous or not, and the day when someone could successfully dare me to drink something deadly lies behind me. Yet when one church member says something hurtful to another or someone makes it harder for a person on the margin to step toward the community, I feel compelled to respond. It ends better when we respond in love, but love takes even more courage than apathy and anger. As for laying hands on the sick, all of us have had the experience of visiting a hospitalized or ailing saint and leaving feeling that we encountered the living God. Thanks be to God for the promise that Jesus works with us in the ministries to which he calls us. For six weeks we have celebrated God's victory in and through him. Today let's ponder where we make room for that victory to embrace us and carry us up.

Notes

1. Note that the verb translated "staying with" in Acts 1:4 often means "to eat with."
2. The verb translated "to lead a life" (Eph. 4:1) often means "to walk."

May 20, 2012
Seventh Sunday of Easter
(if Ascension not observed here)

Even dedicated saints sometimes doubt their ability to respond to God's call and assume that others could do a better job. We have different talents and abilities, but all of us can make significant contributions to the ministries of the risen Jesus. That message echoes through today's lections. In the reading from Acts, God provides a way forward even in the face of failure. The selected psalms celebrate blessings that strengthen the faithful. The lections from 1 John promise that our love of each other helps us to find God in our midst. In the Gospel reading, Jesus himself prays for the faithful and describes them as prepared for ministry in his name. We cannot control Jesus' ministry, yet God not only invites us into it but also gives us all we need for faithful service. It's still Easter and wonders continue to flow. Alleluia!

First Reading
Acts 1:15-17, 21-26 (RCL)
Acts 1:15-17, 20a, 20c-26 (LFM)

After telling the story of Jesus' ascension into heaven (Acts 1:6-11), Luke describes what Jesus' followers did while waiting for the baptism of the Holy Spirit. The summary of their initial days in Jerusalem does not mention Judas, whom Luke mentioned last during the betrayal in Gethsemane (Luke 22:47-48). Nor does it imply that the group of believers lacked anything while "constantly devoting themselves to prayer" (Acts 1:14). Yet in his first speech in Acts, Peter declares it a scriptural and divine necessity for someone who has accompanied the disciples from the beginning of Jesus' ministry until his ascension to take the place of Judas and bear witness to the resurrection. Nothing in the narrative explicitly states what makes this an exigency. Instead, Luke presses on and reports that after prayer and the casting of lots, God selected Matthias. It seems only human to feel a twinge of sorrow for Justus, the other candidate. Actually, Luke tells us as much about him as Matthias because neither appears again in the narrative (or anywhere else in the New Testament). So why tell this story?

Perhaps Luke assures us that what God begins in Jesus will always continue. Nothing softens the pain of Judas's betrayal of Jesus. Yet even the failure of someone in the inner circle cannot keep what God does in and through Jesus from moving forward. Luke does not imply that individuals do not matter. After all, he names Judas and Matthias. Instead, he assures us that the ministry continues. If we see the glass as half empty, Luke warns believers that God can and will replace any of us. If we deem the glass half full, Luke promises that God will provide a way forward and encourages us to take our place among the faithful.

Psalmody
Psalm 1 (RCL)

During my early teens a friend and I often rode our bicycles to a nearby creek where we spent hours under, around, and in a row of huge sycamore trees. During spring and summer we found comfortable places in the massive branches from which we spied on those traveling the road or tossed rocks at limbs we launched into the creek. During the fall we trod noisily through leaves as large as our shoes. Supplied with a constant source of water, those trees flourished.

Psalm 1 compares such fortunate trees with those who do not simply reject poor advice and shun immoral ways but habitually take pleasure in seeking and accepting God's guidance. Whereas unfavorable winds readily blow the less devoted off course, these happy saints have stability in all seasons. The God whose instruction they seek guards the paths they travel.

Psalm 103:1-2, 11-12, 19-20 (LFM)

This reflection on the goodness of God begins with the psalmist inviting every part of himself in which life dwells to bow in recognition of the blessings that flow from the character and presence of God. The second couplet in this lection addresses the faithful and illustrates what makes such reverence appropriate. God's kindness toward the reverent exceeds measurement, and God's forgiveness places sins utterly beyond human reach. The last two verses invite the angels to add their blessings as well, blending human and heavenly praise of the sovereign of all. That implicitly connects worship in the forgiven and faithful human community with the adoration of those who dwell in the very presence of God.

Second Reading
1 John 5:9-13 (RCL)

As 1 John draws to a close, the author finds three ways to affirm the faith of those to whom he writes. First, he identifies them as believers and assures them that through faith they receive eternal life from God (vv. 11-13). Second, he declares that they have placed their trust in divine rather than human witnesses. The source of the human testimony goes unstated, but the verses immediately prior to this lection identify the divine witnesses as the Spirit, the water, and the blood (5:8). In the Gospel of John, blood and water flow from the side of the crucified Jesus (John 19:34). This flow may verify Jesus' bodily existence and probably symbolizes the life he provides through his gifts of living water and blood (John 4:10, 12-14; 6:53-55; 7:37-38). Those addressed by 1 John accept these witnesses. Third, the author contrasts the faithful with those who do not believe, who call God a liar and have no access to eternal life.

A comparison with the Gospel of John strengthens this affirmation. In the penultimate chapter of John, the narrator declares that he has written "so that you may come to believe that Jesus is the Messiah, the Son of God, and that through believing you may have life in his name" (John 20:31). The author of 1 John addresses "you who believe in the name of the Son of God, so that you may know that you have eternal life" (5:13). The Gospel calls readers to faith. The epistle assures the readers that they have faith and eternal life.

When did we last affirm the faith of others? What do we believe God offers people of faith and how often do we point to those gifts? We accomplish little good when we disparage those who do not believe, but a little affirmation of those with whom we worship and serve could provide strength for the journey. Sunday school teachers and youth leaders cannot definitively answer every question posed to them; but they help the next generation to discover the blessings of believing that we belong to God. Those who make hospital visits and prepare meals for the bereaved cannot answer the prayers they hear and utter; but their presence and comfort bring light to darkness and help to make God real. As fallible saints share life and ministry, they cannot erase all the harm done in the name of God; but as they show up to follow Jesus, they gladden each other's hearts and affect the lives of those they serve but never see. What we affirm may differ slightly or significantly from the assurances offered in 1 John; but because we are Easter people, what we believe matters, and faith breathes more deeply as we name and celebrate it.

1 John 4:11-16 (LFM)

For discussion of 1 John 4:11-16, please see the second reading for the Fifth Sunday of Easter, above.

Gospel
John 17:6-19 (RCL)
John 17:11b-19 (LFM)

The prayer Jesus offers in John 17 has a curious narrative context. Since Jesus prays to God, we can reasonably assume that he speaks privately, outside his disciples' hearing. Yet the transition into this scene includes no change of time, place, or characters (and little change in topic). The flow of the narrative invites us to consider the disciples very much present as Jesus converses with God. The Gospel of John seldom shies from ambiguity. The prayer scene, the final segment of Jesus' acts and words of farewell to his disciples, implies that Jesus has so completely grafted his disciples into him that they remain very much with him as he prays. The inclusion of this prayer in the Gospel invites readers into that same inner circle.

As Jesus prays he affirms his relationship with God. He came from God, was sent by God, and approaches his return to God. That repeats what the narrative has claimed repeatedly about him. Most of the prayer addresses Jesus' disciples. Although the disciples shine no more brightly in John than in the Synoptic Gospels, here Jesus affirms that they belong to God, that God gave them to him, that they have believed he came from and was sent by God, that he has protected them (losing only the one destined to be lost) and been glorified in them, that he now dedicates himself to his final acts on their behalf, and that he sends them forth as God sent him. No other passage in the Gospels speaks so highly of Jesus' followers.

In addition to providing his disciples this glowing reference, Jesus petitions God on their behalf. Each request relates to the ministry entrusted to them. Jesus asks God to protect them so that their unity will reflect his unity with God. This most likely refers to their ministry. Jesus wills to do what God commands and prays for his disciples to have similar devotion to God's purposes. Jesus also prays for his joy to become complete in them. He has mentioned this joy earlier in his words of farewell (15:11; 16:20-24). As he willingly embraces that for which God has sent him, he prays for his followers to accept the challenges they will face with confidence that God will act in and through them. Jesus also asks not that God remove them from the world, but that God protect them from evil. This repeats his plea that they not lose the God-given unity of their mission. Then Jesus prays for God to set the disciples apart to share with the world the truth that he came from and was sent by God.

Nothing in the prayer suggests that Jesus doubts that his disciples will fulfill their mission. He has often declared himself completely aligned with the command and will of God, and here he depicts his disciples as fully prepared and consecrated for what he sends them into the world to do. That challenges and invites followers of Jesus who read this prayer to believe he has similar confidence in and dedication to them.

Preaching the Gospel

During the prayer that brings his words and acts of farewell to an end, Jesus declares his disciples fully prepared for the ministries he sends them into the world to complete. Do we dare to believe that about ourselves? Only God's gifts can prepare us, so we have ample room for humility. Yet we might attempt more bold ministries in Jesus' name if we had a portion of the confidence the Gospel of John reports that Jesus has in us.

Jesus declares that his disciples belong to God, who gave them to him. Have we ever considered ourselves gifts to Jesus? That sounds presumptuous, but John's Jesus says that without blushing. A helpful Easter sermon could identify talents, abilities, and resources we receive from God that make us "gifts to Jesus" as we use them in his ministries. Preachers often implore the faithful to step up and do more. Why not celebrate Easter by telling them how and why we admire them and using Jesus' prayer to invite the saints to recognize that we fallible followers have precisely what Jesus needs to become visible in the world? Such a sermon would appropriately include a call to action. John's depiction of believers as belonging to God, entrusted to Jesus, consecrated to service, and equipped with sufficient gifts for ministry in Jesus' name challenges us to respond. God gives us to Jesus. What presents has Jesus received in us lately? What gifts would we like him to receive this summer?

As a young teenager I had the privilege of playing pitcher on our Pony League baseball team. I could throw reasonably hard and accurately, but often lacked confidence. When I arrived at the park near the beginning of one season, our coach, Coach Crump, handed me a ball and told me I was pitching against last year's championship team. I evidently did not respond enthusiastically, because Coach Crump looked at me and asked, "What's wrong with you?" What followed was not my proudest moment. I whined, "We lost to them three times last year. I'm not sure I'm good enough." Coach Crump placed his hand on my shoulder, looked me in the eye, and said: "You let me worry about them. You're on my team and I want you to pitch." Then he told me again to warm up and walked away.

Playing for Coach Crump was not a small thing. At the end of the previous year, as we took infield practice before a game, our third baseman made a throw to me at first base that I missed. The ball slammed into Coach Crump's head and he crumpled to the ground. He was hospitalized for several days. Yet when the new season began, Coach Crump returned to the team. I never wanted to pitch well as much as that evening when he told me I was his and handed me the ball. Forget about self-confidence. I was pitching for Coach Crump.

Unless we consider baptism, the selection of church officers and leaders, and other calls to ministry solely human acts, they confirm that we belong to God and that Jesus commissions us for ministry. Those blessings and our God-given talents and abilities equip us for ministry. We cannot do everything, but we can respond to God's call. Those called to serve on administrative boards do not have a direct conduit to God, but they have the capacity to work together to discern the movements of the Spirit and help the congregation follow faithfully. The saints who agree to greet those who come to worship have many weaknesses, but as they make guests feel welcome and receive familiar faces warmly, the presence and embrace of Jesus flow through them. Nursery and child-care volunteers may need their bulletin when the time comes to recite the Apostles' Creed, but they help us all to respond faithfully to our promise to support the baptized in their life in Christ. Not all of us readily understand accrual-basis accounting. Not all of us have the courage to face the limits of our faith with a group of middle-school youth. Yet all of us have the capacity for faithful service when our friends in the body of Christ invite us to accept leadership roles. We belong to God in baptism and Jesus promises to remain with us always. We will not win every game, but we can take the ball and pitch. Grace, forgiveness, and God take care of the rest.

May 27, 2012
Day of Pentecost

In the reading most people associate with Pentecost, the Holy Spirit fills Jesus' disciples, driving them from the places where they have assembled privately into the streets of Jerusalem where they publicly proclaim what God did in and through Jesus. According to Luke, pilgrims from a variety of nations heard this proclamation in their own languages. We need not interpret the story literally and conclude that the Spirit transformed Jesus' Galilean followers into polyglots. The proclamation in varied languages symbolizes the ways that the disciples spoke about Jesus to people where and as they were. Something wondrous happened. In a relatively short time the followers of Jesus went from being a small band of Jews in an isolated segment of the Roman Empire to an empire-wide phenomenon. Jews and Greeks, city dwellers and country folk, women and men, slave and free, educated and illiterate joined together. They did not all agree. Some of their disagreements fill the pages of the New Testament. Yet their devotion to Jesus and their service to others in his name united them.

Disagreements among Jesus' followers remain rampant. Some seem trivial; others reflect deeply held convictions. Yet most of the homeless, hungry, and hurting couldn't care less about our doctrine and dogma. Pentecost invites us to look beyond the labels we use to divide ourselves from one another and to glimpse our God-given unity in Jesus and his ministry. As we truly recognize that unity, we become more able to work together and more willing to be transformed by the life and ministry we share.

First Reading
Acts 2:1-21 (RCL, LFM)

On Pentecost we bring out our red paraments, vestments, and clothing to celebrate the tongues like fire that appeared among Jesus' disciples and signified the end of their time of waiting to receive power for ministry. The story begins with the sound of a rushing wind and the sight of tongues like fire, but that seems primarily for our benefit. The narrative focuses on proclamation. First, the Spirit-filled disciples proclaim their stories of God's power in a variety of languages to an astonished crowd. When the hearers struggle to understand what this means, Peter stands with the others and delivers his initial sermon, beginning with a quotation from Joel that promises an outpouring of the Spirit on all flesh that will inspire prophecy, visions, and dreams. The Spirit drives the disciples out of their private preparations into public view where they tell their story.

What can we expect to receive from the Spirit? According to Luke we can expect to feel a sense of urgency to act, to hear or see signs of God's presence that drive us from preparation into action. We can expect to have opportunities to share our stories. Most of us will not speak in foreign languages, but we all can participate in acts of ministry that speak to people where and as they are. When those to whom God has sent us want to know why we have come, we can expect the Spirit to equip one or all of us to explain that the ministry and message of Jesus belong not to a private group but to the world. Three thousand people probably will not join the faith community as a result of our message (cf. Acts 2:41), but that misses the point. We can expect the Spirit to equip and empower us to serve. Any success that follows belongs to God.

Ezekiel 37:1-14 (RCL alt.)

Ezekiel's vision of a valley filled with very dry bones addresses times when disappointment or devastation leaves a community with little or no hope. When God asks whether the bones can live, the prophet responds not with coyness or timidity but with conviction that God alone can restore life in a situation void of life. Faith calls us to "hope for what we do not see [and] wait for it with patience" (Rom. 8:25).

Restoration comes in two stages, both of which begin with God's initiative. First, the prophet obeys God and assures the bones that they will live. Then he follows God's command and calls for the breath/spirit to enter the enfleshed bones and bring them to life. The bones receive flesh as they respond to the prophet's words. They receive life with the gift of the breath/spirit. As the psalmist declares, "When you send forth your spirit, they are created; and you renew the face of the ground" (Ps. 104:30). Bones and humans have a responsibility to respond, but hope of renewal lies in what God provides. We do not make or create new life; we receive it.

This vision addresses a community. The bones lie in the valley together and receive flesh and breath/spirit together. When all seems lost, new life finds us as we remain together, respond to a common call, and accept the gifts of breath/life that God provides.

Psalmody
Psalm 104:24-34, 35b (RCL)
Psalm 104:1 + 24, 29-30, 31 + 34 (LFM)

We often feel closest to God in nature. Moonlit waves crashing against the shore can fill us with wonder at the breadth of all that is. Seeing the first hummingbird of the season return to the feeder and knowing that those tiny wings may have carried it nonstop across the Gulf of Mexico can inspire awe at the beauty and splendor of all creatures. Psalm 104 invites and encourages the celebration of creation. It calls God to rejoice as well (v. 31). All life depends on the one whose spirit creates and renews. That makes life too precious to take for granted and renders God always worthy of praise.

Second Reading
Romans 8:22-27 (RCL)

A tsunami strikes Japan, killing thousands, destroying infrastructure, and causing the release of radioactive material. We, along with creation, groan. A bomb explodes in a crowded marketplace, shattering innocent lives. We, along with creation, groan. As communities and individuals we confess with Paul, "I do not understand my own actions. For I do not do what I want, but I do the very thing I hate" (Rom. 7:15). We, along with creation, groan. Creation pulses with blessing and God claims us in Jesus, but we still fall short of life abundant and eternal. So we hope, and as we hope the presence and goodness of God find us.

Paul insists that as we patiently hope for what we cannot see, the Spirit prays for us. He challenges us to add to our prayers of supplication and intercession prayers in which we make room for the Spirit to speak to God for us and to speak for God to us. Such prayers acknowledge realities that make us groan without resigning ourselves to them. Hope increases as we believe that when we lack words and understanding the Spirit prays for us. We do not powerlessly accept whatever will become; we hope for the Spirit to draw us into the will of God.

Challenges and disappointments always accompany us as we journey in faith. How could they not? We long for nothing less than fullness of life for all creation. We hope not because only good things happen, but because goodness endures in the face of all that happens. Hope points us beyond our limitations to the God who creates and claims us, the Christ who saves and remains with us, and the Spirit who sustains and renews us.

Acts 2:1-21 (RCL alt.)

For discussion of this text, please see the first reading, above.

I Corinthians 12:3b-7, 12-13 (LFM)

Each believer receives a call to ministry and gifts sufficient for that ministry from the same Spirit, the same Lord, and the same God. The gifts of the Spirit and the ministries in which we use and manifest them do not set us over or beneath each other; they equip us for ministry side by side. All of the varied gifts we receive have the potential to strengthen the community into which we were baptized. That makes each gift a blessing and it challenges the faithful to ask regularly, "Who has benefited lately from the gifts I've received from God?"

We often fall into the temptation of ranking the gifts of the Spirit. Most of us admire those with the gifts for teaching, visiting the homebound and hurting, and inspiring the community to feed the hungry. Sometimes, however, we recognize the value of particular gifts of the Spirit only when no one receives or uses them. The gifts of hospitality expressed in greeting and ushering may not seem extraordinary. Yet our experiences of worship would diminish significantly if no one offered a word or sign of welcome. We sometimes belittle those who always consider the glass half full; not, however, during times when we need others to hope for us. Whether employees or volunteers, what would we do without those who pick up and tend to everything we leave behind when we gather to worship, pray, and play? Each gift, service, and work comes from the same Spirit, Lord, and God. When we disparage any gift, we disparage the giver. The faithful and grateful celebrate them all.

Galatians 5:16-25 (LFM alt.)

Paul defines life in the community of faith by encouraging believers to walk by the Spirit and not to finish what the flesh desires.[1] Rather than establishing a dualistic division between the spirit and the body in an individual, Paul's terminology challenges believers to live and act in ways that build up the community of faith. The phrase "the desire of the flesh" (v. 16) symbolizes anything that makes it harder for believers to live and work together.

Everything that pleases us does not strengthen the faith community or help others to believe in God. Yet temptations to choose what brings us pleasure abound. Most of us readily shun sorcery and orgies, but find refraining from jealousy, envy, and selfishness altogether another matter. Paul advocates not looking for a law to cover every possible act of discord, but rather measuring every thought and action by whether it strengthens community. The majority of the fifteen "works of the flesh" (v. 19) listed involve putting our own wants first or excessively seeking personal gratification. The nouns listed as "fruit of the Spirit" (v. 22) refer primarily to ways of treating and responding to others that foster shared life. Behind these lists stands the conviction that we inherit the realm of God together. In matters of faith, God takes us farther together than we travel alone.

No one always responds to others with gentleness and self-control and never feels envious or acts selfishly. We find it equally beyond our limits to love our neighbors as ourselves, forgive seventy times seven times, and rejoice always. As we long for the realm of God, we choose to reach for heights we cannot touch rather than settle for life as it is. Easter and the gifts of the Spirit point to new life. Responding faithfully means trusting God to transform us, not lamenting our need to change.

Gospel
John 15:26-27; 16:4b-15 (RCL)
John 15:26-27; 16:12-15 (LFM alt.)

In the Fourth Gospel Jesus has profound unity with God, from whom he comes and to whom he returns. That theme appears in this lection as Jesus notes that he will return to God and that what belongs to God also belongs to him (John 16:5, 15). Jesus' words of farewell extend his unity with God and his ministry to the Spirit/Advocate and the disciples.

Earlier Jesus consoled his troubled followers by reaffirming their faith (14:1-14). Now he reinforces his consolation by informing them that after he returns to God the Spirit/Advocate will come to them and reveal the complete truth of his message and ministry. The Spirit/Advocate comes directly from God and Jesus and has a unique mission to call people into accountability for their response to Jesus (16:8-11). Yet the Spirit/Advocate has the same basic ministry as the disciples. Both bear witness to Jesus (15:26-27). Their ministries differ in degree, not in kind. God-given unity makes this possible. All that belongs to God belongs to Jesus, and Jesus declares that the Spirit/Advocate will declare what belongs to him to the disciples (16:14). Earlier Jesus warned the disciples, "Apart from me you can do nothing" (15:5). The promise of the Spirit/Advocate assures them that as they accept what God provides they will not be apart from him.

With these words the Fourth Gospel addresses each subsequent generation of Christians. Jesus has a unique ministry and relationship with God. He calls us to respond by believing he came from God, accepting his revelation about God, and living in loving community with others. His words of farewell deepen the intimacy of our call. We do not simply respond to Jesus with the hope of receiving a reward one day. Rather, as we accept the guidance and gift of the Spirit, we participate in Jesus' ministry where and as we are, and we live in unity with Jesus, God, and the Spirit here and now. Just as Jesus came not only to reveal God but also to be the revelation of God, believers not only bear witness to him but also continue and extend his ministry. Jesus makes God known (1:18). Through and with the Spirit, his followers do the same.

John 20:19-23 (LFM)

For discussion of this text, please see the Gospel for the Second Sunday of Easter, above.

Preaching the Gospel

On Pentecost we end the season of Easter where we started: with absolute dependence on God. Only God can bring life from a death-filled tomb and only God can send the Spirit. Yet our dependence on God does not leave us with nothing to do. God sends the Spirit to equip us to continue Jesus' ministry, not only serving others and each other in his name but also discovering his presence in and around us as we do. On Pentecost we celebrate the wonder of the ways our often timid discipleship becomes, by the grace of God, the very work of God.

We often recognize and celebrate the ways we bear witness to Jesus and experience the presence of God when we gather at the font, come to the Lord's table, and participate in public acts of worship and service. We should never take such special moments for granted, and most of us could do a more faithful job of inviting others to come. Each such invitation bears witness to Jesus. We receive and live into the promise of the Spirit and of Pentecost not only in those visible ways but also in any act or word that helps others to hear the good news where and as they are, any act or word that makes it easier and more meaningful for others and each other to become or remain a part of the community of faith.

When a saint enters a convalescent care center and a member of the congregation comes to share time and stories of life and faith, the ministry of Jesus continues and he remains present. When a patient ear and caring smile offer acceptance to a young person who wonders whether the community has room for someone with so many unanswered questions, the ministry of Jesus continues not only in his name but with his presence. When a mission team shows up following a hurricane or flood, their presence and participation reveal the presence of God. When seemingly small acts of acceptance, friendship, and forgiveness make it easier for people with faith and people longing for faith to dream dreams of a more just and compassionate world, to envision a future with hope, and to live and serve together, we experience the ministry and presence of Jesus. During the passing of the peace, an elder in our congregation often takes my hand, looks me in the eye, and says, "God loves you, and so do I." Jesus becomes manifest in any Spirit-filled act of ministry that proclaims that message. Union with God does not come solely when the fever of life is over and the busy world is hushed. The presence and gifts of the Spirit draw us into the embrace of God in every deed or word that points to what we receive in Jesus.

Note

1. The Greek verb translated "live" in Col. 5:16 is *peripateō*, which usually means "walk," and the verb translated "gratify" is *teleō*, which means "finish" or "complete."

Time after Pentecost / Ordinary Time
Trinity Sunday through Lectionary 16 / Proper 11
Ira Brent Driggers

In the season after Pentecost the church celebrates the gift of the Holy Spirit. In the Jewish calendar, Pentecost marked the fiftieth day from Passover (*pentékosté*, "fiftieth"), commemorating the end of Israel's intervening seven-week harvest (Exod. 23:16; 34:22; Lev. 23:15-22; Num. 28:26-31). It was on this festival day that, according to Luke, the Holy Spirit descended upon the first community of believers gathered in Jerusalem (Acts 2:1-47) in fulfillment of the risen Jesus' promise to the apostles (Luke 24:49; Acts 1:5).

Luke describes the manifestation of the Holy Spirit in sensational language typical of a theophany (an appearance of God). It sounded "like the rush of a violent wind" and produced tongues "as of fire," so that believers spoke in various foreign languages (Acts 2:1-5). This spectacle amazed devout Jewish pilgrims who heard testimony to "God's deeds of power" (Acts 2:11) in their own native tongues—oddly, spoken by Galileans. When the pilgrims voiced their confusion over the meaning of this event, Peter offers an authoritative explanation: this is the fulfillment of God's promise to "pour out my Spirit upon all flesh" (Acts 2:17, quoting Joel 2:28), so that "everyone who calls on the name of the Lord shall be saved" (Acts 2:21, quoting Joel 2:32). Yet Peter is also quick to connect this charismatic moment to the historical life, death, and resurrection of Jesus of Nazareth, through whom God saves not only Israel but all of humanity, by the forgiveness of sins and the conquering of death (Acts 2:22-42). Peter insists, in other words, that Pentecost did not inaugurate some purely spiritual, subjective experience, much less create a "new" community vis-à-vis Israel. Rather, it extended the salvation that Israel's God accomplished through a singular person, the living Messiah and Lord: "Repent, and be baptized every one of you in the name of Jesus Christ so that your sins may be forgiven; and you will receive the gift of the Holy Spirit" (Acts 2:38; cf. 1 Cor. 6:11; Gal. 3:14; Titus 3:6). According to Luke, this Spirit-filled speech elicited the repentance of "some three thousand persons" who, upon their baptism, joined the Jerusalem church in apostolic instruction and fellowship: prayers, the breaking of bread, and the sharing of property (2:41-47).

We can get so caught up in the extraordinary spiritual gifts of Pentecost that we lose sight of the story's larger purpose, which is to demonstrate the continuing presence of God among believers. Pentecost assures us, in other words, that the ascension of Jesus does not leave the church "orphaned" (to borrow the language of John 14:18). The Holy Spirit is the name that Scripture gives to the continuing guidance and empowerment of God—indeed, of Christ himself (Acts 16:7; Rom. 8:9; Phil. 1:19; 1 Peter 1:11)—within the believing community. That John's Gospel depicts the giving of the Spirit rather less spectacularly than does Luke (John 20:19-23) hardly takes away from this fundamental meaning. It would be more accurate to say, then, that Pentecost marks the *birth* of the church since, without the guidance and empowerment of Christ, we would be left with just another voluntary association of (essentially like-minded) individuals, a mere collection of people rather than the very "body of Christ" (as Paul calls it) in the world. That is why Luke's account of Pentecost concludes with an emphasis on *fellowship* (Acts 2:37-47). The Holy Spirit draws people into a communion that only God can create, a communion of persons from various walks of life, now reconciled to God and to each other, who, based on that reconciliation, give to each other "as any had need" (Acts 2:45). Stated simply, the Holy Spirit undergirds our common fellowship with God and—therefore—with one another. The Spirit makes possible our obedience to Jesus' double commandment: "'You shall love the Lord your God with all your heart, and with all your soul, and with all your mind.' This is the greatest and first commandment. And a second is like it: 'You shall love your neighbor as yourself'" (Matt. 22:37-39).

So while the "tongues of fire" might strike us as more dramatic, they do not constitute the climax of Pentecost. The climax of Pentecost, the very point of Pentecost, is *the church*. Particular gifts like tongues provide one small (and relatively minor) window into how the church embodies and extends God's salvation in the world, in fulfillment of God's promise to "pour out my Spirit upon all flesh" (Acts 2:17; cf. 1 Corinthians 12–14). Therefore, in the pages that follow you will find a sustained focus on the mission of the church, a mission that is both internal (with respect to the fellowship of believers) and external (with respect to all of humanity). Obviously, that focus is easier to maintain with respect to the Epistles and the Gospels. Even when commenting on the Old Testament readings, however, I try to make connections to the New Testament readings with this focus in mind. While I do not always explicitly mention the Holy Spirit, it is assumed throughout that the Spirit empowers and sustains the church. At Pentecost we celebrate our communion with each other precisely because it is at once a communion with our Creator.

There is one constant in the lectionary readings that follow, and that is the Gospel readings from Mark. Understanding that most preachers focus on the Gospel readings in their sermons, I suggest for your consideration the theologically insightful commentaries of Eugene Boring (Westminster John Knox, 2006), Joel Marcus (2 vols; Yale University Press, 2002, 2009), and Francis Moloney (Hendrickson, 2002). For a concise and readable overview of Mark's basic theological plot, you may also consult Ira Brent Driggers, "Jesus' Atoning Life in the Gospel of Mark" (*The Lutheran* 44, no. 4 [2010]: 11–14).

June 3, 2012
Holy Trinity Sunday
First Sunday after Pentecost

Revised Common Lectionary (RCL)	Lectionary for Mass (LFM)
Isaiah 6:1-8	Deuteronomy 4:32-34, 39-40
Psalm 29	Psalm 33:4-9, 18-22
Romans 8:12-17	Romans 8:14-17
John 3:1-17	Matthew 28:16-20

The doctrine of the Trinity evolved over several centuries as a logical consequence of the conviction that Jesus was both fully human and fully God. It allows Christians to articulate a proper understanding of the incarnation without positing a second god alongside the God of Israel. Trinity Sunday is appropriately celebrated after Pentecost because Pentecost celebrates the Holy Spirit, the third "person" whom Augustine famously identified as the love shared between the Father and the Son. In fact, love is the perfect theme for anyone wishing to invoke Trinity Sunday in a sermon, for the fundamental claim of this doctrine is that "God is love" (1 John 4:8, 16). The Father and the Son love one another "before the foundation of the world" (John 17:24). There is no such thing as love, properly speaking, apart from this eternal Trinity. All human love is a reflection of, indeed a participation in, the love that is God.

This has implications for how we view ourselves as creatures, for if love is eternal in these trinitarian terms, then creation is, quite simply, *unnecessary*. In other words, creation is not God's compulsive quest to find an "other" to love, as if God needed us to be complete. Creation is, rather, a gracious spilling-over of the love God enjoys eternally, a love already and always complete. Love, then, does not ultimately originate from within creation. Rather, it is love that creates, so that we in turn might know love—that is, God, the source of all goodness, without whom we could not truly love one another, much less ourselves.

First Reading

Isaiah 6:1-8 (RCL)

The main purpose of a call narrative is to emphasize divine initiative, to illustrate the prophet's being set apart by God for a holy task (cf. Jer. 1:1-19; Ezek. 2:1—3:11; cf. Exod. 3:1-22). This in turn lends credibility to the mission of the prophet, which is typically speaking God's message to God's own people. In the case of this week's reading, God calls Isaiah through a vision of the temple's inner sanctuary (Isaiah is not physically in the temple), and God sets Isaiah apart through the cleansing of his lips (since his vocation consists primarily of speaking).

Interestingly, the fact that it is a vision seems not to lessen the reality of God's holy presence, as if it were "only a dream." It is precisely through the vision, in other words, that Isaiah is brought into the divine presence. He does not *imagine* the chorus of seraphs or the removal of his guilt. As Isaiah himself puts it, "My eyes have seen the King, the LORD of hosts!" (6:5). Neither has he imagined the climactic question: "Whom shall I send?" When the vision ends Isaiah is no longer walking his own path and speaking his own words. He is a prophet of God.

Christians generally do not receive visions of this clarity. But we are certainly called and commissioned, each in our own way. Some moments of commission we also hold in common: for example, baptism, confirmation, and even the concluding benediction of most traditional liturgies. It is equally true for all of us that we hear and discern our various vocations in relation to other members of Christ's body—the true temple of God (1 Cor. 3:16-17). As with Isaiah, those vocations will involve following God's path and speaking God's words. They will require our cleansing and our obedient response. Every profession must prove consistent with the pattern of Christian discipleship.

Deuteronomy 4:32-34, 39-40 (LFM)

The final verse of this passage emphasizes obedience, which is the main theme of Deuteronomy: "Keep his statutes and his commandments . . ." (4:40). Yet the preceding verses, which emphasize the greatness of God, remain crucial for understanding the *logic* of obedience. To put it simply, obedience stems from trust.

Consider the context of this passage. Deuteronomy begins by recounting the Israelites' journey from Mount Horeb (Sinai), emphasizing their faithless refusal to enter the promised land and the consequent penalty of extended wilderness wandering. Then at 2:26 the pace of the narration slows to describe key military victories. The point is not merely to reminisce but to foster a collective trust in God, "who fights for you" (3:22).

This context adds depth to the rhetorical questions that constitute 4:32-34. This is a God of mighty deeds *for* Israel. The very God who created humans is also the God who spoke to Moses from fire (alluding to Exod. 3:1-12) in order to "take a nation for himself" by bringing them out of slavery "by a mighty hand and an outstretched arm" (v. 34). Echoing the first commandment, verse 39 insists that Israel, though surrounded by other nations with other deities, has "no other" God than this one, the God of both "heaven above" and the "earth beneath." God claims Israel by loving Israel, delivering Israel, and defending Israel. Thus the logic of obedience: Israel obeys in thankful response to the gracious, saving acts of God.

A common Christian caricature of Old Testament law is that obedience earns salvation. But the unfolding of the scriptural narrative suggests otherwise. Exodus precedes law. Salvation draws Israel into covenant. We must admit that verse 40 presents obedience as a condition for prosperity in the land (a motif common to the historical books and many prophets). This verse requires special handling so as to avoid a "prosperity gospel" that undercuts the very heart of Christian theology (namely Christ's utter self-giving). By invoking the immediate context of verses 32-34, as well as the wider context of Deuteronomy 1–4, the preacher can present obedience as an occasion for joy, praise, and thanksgiving. Commandments are not merely compatible with Christianity. They are essential to it. They provide the concrete form of our thankful response to God's salvation. For there is no such thing as being thankful in the abstract.

Psalmody
Psalm 29 (RCL)

Following the reading from Isaiah, this psalm moves hearers from the confines of the temple to the larger creation. Verses 1-2 summon the "sons of God" (NRSV: "heavenly beings") to praise the Lord. Verses 3-10 justify this summons by describing the very glory that hearers should ascribe to God. We hear first of God's glory manifest at the creation, when the divine "voice" spoke light into existence and separated the primordial "waters" (vv. 3-4; cf. Gen. 1:1-8). The focus then shifts to God's authority within creation itself and over humanity in particular, as seen in God's enthronement within the holy temple (vv. 5-9). The repeated reference to "the voice of the LORD" seems to suggest that God's authority over peoples is simply an extension of God's role as Creator. Appropriately, God's people acknowledge this authority with their own collective voice: "Glory!" (v. 9). According to John's Gospel, Nicodemus hears this voice and beholds this glory, although he must journey gradually into that realization (see below).

Psalm 33:4-9, 18-22 (LFM)

Like the first reading, these verses describe the greatness and faithfulness of God, but in a more universal tone, with no explicit mention of Israel's unique history (save, perhaps, v. 19b). God's power and authority as Creator (vv. 5b-9) make God Lord over "all humankind" (v. 13). Likewise, the claim that God "loves righteousness and justice" (v. 5a) suggests an ethical mandate more inclusive than certain ritual commandments. The human response is equally universal: "Let all the earth fear the LORD" (v. 8). The concluding verses appear to turn this fear into a means of ensuring God's faithfulness rather than a response to it, again raising the problem of a "prosperity gospel" (see comments on the first reading). If the preacher invokes these verses, she could acknowledge the difficulty of the text's "plain sense" and provide a "spiritualized" interpretation, with death and famine (v. 19) understood as separation from God. The universal tone of this psalm accords well with the Great Commission in the Gospel reading.

Second Reading
Romans 8:12-17 (RCL)
Romans 8:14-17 (LFM)

The term "flesh" (*sarx*) is tricky in Pauline usage. Without clarification, parishioners can easily assume that Paul condemns our material fleshiness. Yet Paul is not a Gnostic who rejects physicality as such. He knows that the physical world is "good" by virtue of its having been created by God (Gen. 1:1—2:4a). In fact, immediately following these verses Paul makes clear that the salvation of humans—which includes "the redemption of our bodies" (v. 23) —is part of God's larger plan for the "whole creation" (v. 22).

For Paul, life "according to the flesh" (vv. 12-13) simply means life apart from the Spirit that "adopts" humans into God's reconciled family (v. 15). It is life reduced to "the [mere] deeds of the body" (v. 13), a bodily existence apart from *Christ's* body. By contrast, life "led by the Spirit" (v. 14) means bodily existence in communion with Christ's body. For Paul, this is the difference between slavery and freedom (cf. Galatians 3–5).

However, it is crucial to note that Paul does not lay out these forms of existence as options, asking for a human response ("Do not live according to the flesh"). Writing to baptized believers, he has already declared: "You are not in the flesh; you are in the Spirit, since the Spirit of God dwells in you" (v. 9). Thus a sermon that seeks to follow Paul's logic will not command human "decision" as much as it will describe divine action, and this for the purpose of assurance that inevitably shapes action (see my comments on "the logic of obedience" in the LFM's first reading, above). By virtue of this gracious spiritual adoption and fellowship, we now live with divine guidance and empowerment. Yes, as God's adopted children we can expect suffering (v. 17), just as Christ himself suffered in bearing witness to God in a not-yet-fully-redeemed world. More fundamentally, however, our adoption grounds our hope in a glorious redemption that ends suffering, just as Christ himself was raised and exalted.

Gospel
John 3:1-17 (RCL)

Nicodemus and other Pharisees have seen the signs (2:1-22), but they have not interpreted them accurately enough. Yes, Jesus comes "from God" and his mighty deeds reflect "the presence of God" (Greek: "God is with him"), but he is no mere "rabbi" or "teacher" (3:2). He is the eternal Word of God, the divine agent of creation, made flesh (1:1-18). Jesus does not simply teach. He saves. And his salvation expresses God's own love for the world (vv. 17-21). Accordingly, Jesus is not on his own individual mission. As the Son of God, he shares in and completes the single divine mission to "draw all people" to himself (12:32) so that they may "abide in" (15:1-11) the eternal love shared between him and the Father "before the foundation of the world" (17:24).

Of course, it would be silly to disparage Nicodemus for not getting all this. As a character in the Gospel, he has not been privileged with the narrator's commentary. He seems to be doing the best he can with what little he knows, even if Jesus does tease him for being a teacher himself (v. 10). While some characters seek to kill Jesus, Nicodemus at least seems to be moving in the right direction. In fact, he later defends Jesus in a gathering of Jerusalem authorities (7:45-52) and then, along with Joseph of Arimathea, brings spices to anoint Jesus' corpse for burial (19:38-42). For these reasons the church has traditionally held Nicodemus to be a disciple, even a saint.

I mention this journey to faith because the Gospel of John can lend itself to strict dichotomies of "us" versus "them." Jesus himself suggests this dichotomy in verse 11: "We speak of what we know and testify to what we have seen; yet you do not receive our testimony." Historically, this language suggests a time when believers were being ostracized from local synagogues in the late first century (see 9:22; 12:42). Tragically, the gospel proved a divisive message among Jesus' own people. Yet the Nicodemus story shows that no situation proves too polarizing for God. When Jesus speaks of drawing all people to himself, he does not merely mean all of "us," as opposed to "them." He really does mean *all* people—humanity. "For God so loved *the world* [Gk.: *ton kosmon*] that he gave his only Son, so that everyone [Gk.: *pas*] who believes in him may not perish but may have eternal life." It is a truly catholic mission, as the eventual discipleship of Nicodemus shows.

Finally, when it comes to the matter of eternal life, we can easily miss that the last phrase of verse 16 is in the present tense. That is because we are inclined to think of eternal life as some future existence requiring a movement from "earth" to "heaven." But this is not the evangelist's perspective. The word *eternal* does not describe a reality in future time but a reality *beyond* time. It is precisely because Jesus is the eternal Word made flesh—and thus made present to creation—that eternal life is, likewise, a present reality. More to the point, eternal life is a matter of fellowship with Jesus, which, as previously mentioned, is our "abiding" in the love shared eternally between Jesus and the Father.

Thus the NRSV captures the real import of Jesus' teaching on birth (vv. 3-10) when it translates "from above" rather than "again," even though the Greek word (*anōthen*, 3:3, 7) can mean both. Of course the evangelist means this as wordplay. Nicodemus hears "again" and thus thinks strictly in physical terms. Yet as Jesus points out, "what is born of the flesh is flesh, and what is born of the Spirit is spirit" (v. 6). To enter into fellowship with Jesus is to be born from above, from God who "is spirit" (4:24). It is to enter eternal life. With remarkable insight, the early church considered this birth the beginning of our journey toward "full humanity," since our fellowship with God is the very purpose of our having been created. To have flesh and bones, a beating heart, a functioning brain, and even an exciting life—this is not what it means to be human. To be human is to be born "of water and Spirit" (v. 5). It is to dwell, ever more deeply, in divine love, and to use our physical bodies to live out of that love.

Most Christians, if asked to describe the nature of salvation, will speak in strictly future terms. To be sure, salvation does have a future dimension. The state of creation is not yet as God would have it. But to imagine salvation only in future terms is to reduce it—indeed, it is to reduce God and what God has accomplished in Christ. It also reduces the ecclesial body of Christ, which sustains our fellowship with God in Christ through the Holy Spirit. Due largely to the Gospel of John, Christianity has viewed salvation—eternal life—as something to be presently enjoyed and not something for which we wait. "I came that they may have life, and have it abundantly" (10:10).

Matthew 28:16-20 (LFM)

Matthew's conclusion includes unique details intended to defend the claim that God had raised Jesus from the dead. It is the evangelist's response to an alternative theory about the empty tomb—the disciples had stolen the body (28:11-15). If this theory is true, then the gospel is most definitely a scam. So Matthew departs from the Markan script (in which the women find the unguarded tomb already open and the angelic messenger waiting inside) to describe an earthquake and the descent of the angel, all within full view of appointed guards (vv. 2-4). More than dramatic details, these verses "show" that God is the main actor. They provide cosmic support to the angel's claim that Jesus has been "raised from the dead" (v. 7)—not stolen, and not awakened (as if not truly dead), but raised by God (passive voice, *egerthē*) from death to life. Additionally, Matthew adds a scene intended to explain the very source of the opposing theory: the chief priests sought to cover up the truth (vv. 11-15). The very ones who bribed Judas Iscariot now bribe the guards, who have seen and reported "everything that had happened" (v. 11). This is little different from the false testimony those same priests brought against Jesus when he stood before the high priest (26:59), only now it is a matter of preempting the message of his disciples.

If there was in fact an opposing explanation for the empty tomb (and we have no reason to doubt this), we can understand why Matthew wanted to throw his own rhetorical counterpunch. It is important, however, that we understand these details precisely in this way, and not as historical "proofs" for the resurrection. In the ancient world, highly polemical contexts often involved exaggerated claims and counterclaims, including the demonization of one's enemy. Besides, by virtually every mainstream scholarly account, the Gospels were directed to Christian communities—people who already believed in the resurrection. Matthew, then, has used his narrative to reinforce that faith in response to an anti-Christian fabrication that, if left unaddressed, would have raised serious questions.

Along these lines, it is crucial to note that some of the disciples doubted *even when faced with the risen Jesus himself* (v. 17). This is a clear indication that the resurrection cannot be reduced to empirical or historical proofs. Nor is there any indication that these doubting disciples left Jesus, or that Jesus excluded them from his following. The narrator simply says that Jesus addressed "them" (v. 18)—presumably all of them—with the Great Commission to make disciples of the nations (vv. 18-20). At one level, this affirms the possibility of doubt for Jesus' followers. At a deeper level, it suggests that following Jesus is the very means of moving from doubt to worship. Doubt is temporary, provisional, in light of Jesus' abiding presence "to the end of the age" (v. 20). Jesus does not scold us when we doubt; but he also does not back down from the command to follow and obey. Doubting does not exempt us from discipleship, for it is precisely discipleship that leads us to an ever-deeper faithfulness to Jesus (see 24:9). We do not trust "before" following. Jesus himself leads us to trust.

In the life of the parish it is difficult to balance an openness to and acceptance of doubt, on the one hand, with the call to singular trust in Jesus, on the other hand. Too frequently we slip into the extremes of either over-embracing doubt at the expense of genuine discipleship (which leads us to a kind of relativism) or insisting on the lordship of Jesus to the utter exclusion of doubt (which reflects a kind of fundamentalism). Beneath Matthew's rhetoric we find an acknowledgment that Jesus embraces doubters, but not by letting them off the hook. In opening ourselves to Jesus' having been raised, and in committing ourselves to his path, we gradually find that he is risen indeed, and that he is in fact the Lord. To have doubted yet followed is to testify to this truth.

June 10, 2012
Lectionary 10 / Tenth Sunday in Ordinary Time / Proper 5
Second Sunday after Pentecost

Revised Common Lectionary (RCL)

Genesis 3:8-15 or 1 Sam. 8:4-11, (12-15), 16-20, (11:14-15)

Psalm 130 or 138

2 Corinthians 4:13—5:1

Mark 3:20-35

Lectionary for Mass (LFM)*

Genesis 3:9-15

Psalm 130:1-2, 3-4, 5-6, 7-8

2 Corinthians 4:13—5:1

Mark 3:20-35

First Reading
Genesis 3:8-15 (RCL)
Genesis 3:9-15 (LFM)

We commonly assume that Adam and Eve "discover" their nakedness, and that is because we reduce their situation to a physical predicament—not having clothes. That God later provides garments (3:21) reinforces this interpretation. Yet we must remember that God created Adam and Eve naked. So unless we wish to fault God with the original arrangement (the start of a very poor theological path), we should follow that church tradition which reads the physical predicament as symbolic of a spiritual predicament.

Adam claims to be hiding because he is naked. Yet the preceding scene tells us that he and Eve hide because they have *disobeyed God* (3:1-7). They have asserted their own will against the divine will; and this self-induced disharmony yields fear and further efforts at distancing. Hiding from God is less a calculated "response" to an "original" sin and more a continuation of the logic of rebellion, just as eating the fruit (or even *considering* it) is already a kind of hiding, that is, a removing of oneself from

---

*In Roman Catholic tradition, the Second Sunday after Pentecost is the Solemnity of Corpus Christi (Body and Blood of Christ). The texts for that day may be found in *New Proclamation Commentary on Feasts, Saints' Days, and Other Celebrations*, ed. David B. Lott (Fortress Press, 2007).

God's benevolent care. Likewise, passing on the blame—from Adam to Eve, and from Eve to the serpent (vv. 12-13)—does not differ substantively from either eating or hiding. It is all the same attempt to preserve a "self" apart from God.

The perpetuation of this cycle makes us increasingly resistant, even hostile, to God's presence. We prefer the mythical-autonomous self to the real, divinely fashioned and sustained self. Thus, when Jesus asserts God's will for the renewal of creation, it evokes various forms of opposition (see this week's Gospel reading). In many respects, Jesus' ministry is simply God's walking through the garden, seeking us in our rebellious hiding, and asking us, "Who told you that you were naked?" That is, "You are *not* naked! You are only naked insofar as you continue to hide from me. And there is no reason to hide." God breaks the cycle of "self"-preservation by "clothing" us with Christ (Gal. 3:27). In being clothed with Christ we reenter the divine presence (Heb. 10:19-23), realizing our true humanity as God intended it.

I Samuel 8:4-11, (12-15), 16-20, (11:14-15) (RCL alt.)

While the Israelites request a king so that they can be like other nations (8:5), that is not the whole story. The sons of Samuel have proven self-interested and unjust (8:1-3), unfit to rule God's people. What other options do the Israelites have for unification and protection? A king would certainly do the trick. The problem, however, is that they already have a king: the God who brought them out of slavery in Egypt (v. 8). Thus to request a human king is tantamount to rejecting God. Samuel warns the Israelites that whatever protection and stability a human king might bring will come at a cost, namely their own oppression to the king's personal benefit (in contrast to the God who liberates). While this is an entirely negative view of kingship, it is worth noting that more positive images emerge in the golden years of David's rule (2 Sam. 1:1—10:19), as well as in the figures of Hezekiah (2 Kings 18–20) and Josiah (2 Kings 22–23). The wider context suggests that a human king benefits the people to the extent that he remains faithful to God, serving as viceroy to the true, divine king. In the kingship of Jesus (the fully obedient Son), nationalistic concerns over land and conquest also dissolve, revealing the nature of true kingship (God's kingship) as absolute, self-giving love.

Psalmody
Psalm 130 (RCL)
Psalm 130:1-2, 3-4, 5-6, 7-8 (LFM)

The psalmist contends that no amount of human sin will prove too great for God. He does not petition God to "change his mind" in "reaction" to Israel's rebellion. Rather, he expresses hope in God's own nature as forgiving and redeeming. That is, he petitions God simply to be God. Note that this anticipation has, in the gospel of Jesus Christ, become a realization. For while there are clearly things for which Christians wait, forgiveness is not one of them. There is only our own hiding from the

God who seeks us out (see the first reading). The psalmist's desire has been fulfilled. Yet the profound longing of these verses can foster in us a greater appreciation of the forgiveness we have received and too easily take for granted.

Psalm 138 (RCL alt.)

This psalm makes some very important associations. The increasing of the strength of the speaker's soul (v. 3) is a matter of God's own love and faithfulness (v. 2a), which is at once the exaltation of God's own name and word (v. 2b). This suggests that the well-being of humans is wrapped up in the realization of God's own purposes in creation. For God to "fulfill his purpose" (v. 8) is for God to deliver the lowly (vv. 6-7), to penetrate the self-promoting facades of powerful earthly rulers (v. 4), even (we boldly claim) the enemies of Jesus and the church.

Second Reading
2 Corinthians 4:13—5:1 (RCL, LFM)

Like much of 2 Corinthians, this passage deals with Paul's apparent weakness. The letter opens with an emphasis on his (and Timothy's) recent affliction, in which they shared in the sufferings of Christ and through which they came to know the consolation of God. They were so "unbearably crushed" in Asia that their deliverance from the situation was nothing less than a deliverance from death itself, a miracle in keeping with the God who raised Jesus from the dead (1:1-11).

The argument of this week's passage stretches back at least as far as 4:1, where Paul first says "we do not lose heart" (repeated in v. 16). Paul's reason for not losing heart is the simple fact that God (and no human) has commissioned him and Timothy to proclaim the gospel that brings "the light of the knowledge of the glory of God in the face of Jesus Christ" (v. 6). In keeping with this commission, Paul and Timothy have been honest and truthful in their words and conduct (v. 2), reflecting God's own trustworthiness. Put simply, then, Paul does not lose heart because he knows that God is at work in his ministry, bringing light out of the darkness.

Paul picks up the issue of suffering in verse 7: "But we have this treasure in clay jars, so that it may be made clear that this extraordinary power belongs to God and does not come from us." That is, we hold and proclaim this life-giving gospel (the treasure) in mortal, ever-persecuted bodies (clay jars), making it clear that God is the one giving life, and not us weak apostles. Of course, this is consistent with the content of the gospel itself, since it is through an utterly self-emptying (Phil. 2:5-8) and shamefully crucified Messiah (1 Cor. 2:1-5) that God brings salvation, justifying sinners (Gal. 2:15-21; Rom. 3:21-26) and renewing the whole of creation (Rom. 8:18-25; 1 Cor. 15:20-28). It is not only "out of" death but *through* death that God brings life. Thus Paul boldly states that he and Timothy "are always being given up to death for Jesus' sake, so that the life of Jesus may be made visible in our mortal flesh" (v. 12). In this way they proclaim the gospel with their very lives, not simply in their words. By contrast, an apostle who skates comfortably around the sufferings of Christ actually hides the truth and power of the gospel. He or she takes over the spotlight, casting God into the shadows.

When we arrive at the beginning of this week's reading, Paul is very much in midthought, still explaining why he and Timothy do not lose heart. He invokes a portion of Psalm 115—"I believed, and so I spoke"—a verse that, interestingly, goes on to say, "but I was greatly humiliated" (v. 13, quoting LXX Ps. 115:1, 10). This is Paul's way of clarifying that his suffering stems from his proclamation, which in turn stems from his believing in the gospel itself. Moreover, Paul believes that the gospel is not simply about Jesus. Precisely because it is about Jesus, it is also about Paul, Timothy, and the Corinthians: "Because we know that the one who raised the Lord Jesus will raise us also with Jesus, and will bring us with you into his presence" (v. 14). The very truth that Paul preaches, resulting in his affliction, is the truth about God bringing life out of death. The God of Jesus Christ is a God of faithfulness and deliverance for all people. In a culture that might easily mistake human suffering for divine punishment, this is a crucial clarification. God does not "cause" Paul's suffering in any direct sense. In fact, if the Corinthians are paying attention, they will have noticed a profound subtext: Paul is actually suffering *for them*. After all, it is through Paul's ministry that they have been brought out of darkness and into the light, from death to life. "Everything is for your sake, so that grace, as it extends to more and more people, may increase thanksgiving, to the glory of God" (v. 15).

"So we do not lose heart" (v. 16), Paul continues. For things are not as they appear. The sufferings of Paul and Timothy are merely the "wasting away" of their "outer nature" (v. 16), a "slight momentary affliction preparing us for an eternal weight of glory" (v. 17). They gladly endure such hardship in order to make God known. But there is a future in which the hardship will end, and the gift of the Spirit is the divine "guarantee" of this outcome (5:5). The destruction of Paul's "earthly tent" (his physical body) is of no real concern in light of the "heavenly dwelling" that awaits (5:1; cf. 5:2-10).

In preaching from this passage, it is important to remember that Paul's suffering is of a very specific variety. He is not the victim of a natural disaster or a criminal justly sentenced to imprisonment. He is suffering for the sake of the gospel, suffering for Christ's sake. Paul lived every day knowing, and often experiencing, the worldly cycle of self-promotion by means of power and violence. Into this world he preached a self-emptying God, a God of eternal love and reconciliation. Through Paul, Jesus continued to break the worldly cycle and extend his body of fellowship. Like Jesus, Paul was persecuted for doing so.

In loving, we risk ourselves. Yet if God really is love, then our selves are already eternally safe and at home.

Gospel
Mark 3:20-35 (RCL, LFM)

Mark is fond of "sandwiching" originally independent traditions together so that one story interrupts another (see also 5:21-43; 11:12-25). In the standoff with his family, Jesus challenges and redefines the sacred ties of kinship. Because he speaks and acts in accordance with the divine will that transcends all blood ties, his true family consists of those who do likewise (3:35). Meanwhile, in responding to accusations from the Jerusalem scribes, Jesus challenges and threatens social institutions that have grown so blindly self-interested that they confuse the reign of God with the work of Satan (v. 22). But Satan, Jesus contends, is not stupid. The prince of demons would not be working through Jesus to cast out his own minions, since that would be self-defeating (vv. 23-26). To see Jesus clearly is to see him binding and plundering Satan, reclaiming the goods that Satan has stolen, things that rightly belong to God (v. 27).

Such is the basic "point" of each story in isolation. The point of the sandwich, however, is to have these stories shed light on each other. Notice, for instance, that when we focus only on the confrontation with the scribes, it is unclear what exactly Jesus plunders from Satan and reclaims for God. The other story provides the answer: it is the very group surrounding him in the house, those called to obey God's will as members of Jesus' true family. This makes sense when we consider the larger narrative context: Jesus' mission is to bring the "kingdom of God" through healing and reconciliation. Simply put, Jesus transforms creation in accordance with the divine will (see my discussion of "the kingdom of God" in connection with next week's Gospel reading, below). While Mark does not explicitly say it, we can imagine that many of those in the house with Jesus have also been healed by Jesus. Jesus has reclaimed them from satanic bondage and now gathers them for extending his own ministry, to be his "hands and feet" in the world.

Likewise, when read in isolation, Jesus' teaching about true family can easily become a lifeless and groundless call to mere obedience ("because I said so"). But his retort to the scribes gives a profound logic to the obedience: God's will is for *our deliverance*. To do God's will, to belong to Jesus' family, is to participate in God's own reign, the binding and conquering of Satan, and the healing of creation. We are freed in order to free others. Indeed, we are free only in freeing others. In the previous appointing of twelve apostles (vv. 13-19), Jesus' true family has already begun to take shape, even as it now continues to bring in new members. The extension of God's kingdom means the extension of Jesus' family.

I have known parents who call their own children "brother" and "sister" when they are passing the peace in Sunday worship. It is a powerful testament to God's transformative kingdom. It is not that such people relinquish their authority as parents. They simply wish to communicate to their children—and themselves— that there is a divine center to their everyday domestic affairs, that their common belonging to Jesus defines their family. Such reminders not only foster Jesus' healing and reconciliation within the household; they encourage us to spread that same healing and reconciliation outside the household, to our true family. Jesus will not settle for isolated family units coming and going on Sunday. While ministries that target family units can prove edifying, we too frequently emphasize them to the detriment of Jesus' truly catholic mission, which forms a single family out of all humanity. God pulls us out of our self-interested households, giving us the means of growing in faith and love through the gift of brothers and sisters we would have otherwise ignored.

June 17, 2012
Lectionary 11 / Eleventh Sunday in Ordinary Time / Proper 6
Third Sunday after Pentecost

Revised Common Lectionary (RCL)

Ezekiel 17:22-24 or 1 Samuel 15:34—
16:13

Psalm 92:1-4, 12-15 or Psalm 20

2 Corinthians 5:6-10, (11-13), 14-17

Mark 4:26-34

Lectionary for Mass (LFM)

Ezekiel 17:22-24

Psalm 92:2-3, 13-14, 15-16

2 Corinthians 5:6-10

Mark 4:26-34

First Reading
Ezekiel 17:22-24 (RCL, LFM)

In its original context, these verses symbolically pronounce the restoration of Judah from its Babylonian exile. The mountain (vv. 22, 23) likely refers to Jerusalem, while the "noble cedar" (v. 23) suggests the replanted Davidic kingdom. It is through the Davidic kingdom, then, that God will feed and provide a home for "every kind of bird" (v. 23) so that "all the trees in the field" (v. 24) will come to know God (see also 34:23-24; 37:24). Thus Ezekiel proclaims to a rebellious people that God's faithfulness, and not Judah's rebellion, is the final word in the covenant relationship: "I the LORD have spoken; I will accomplish it" (v. 24). Moreover, the restoration of Judah will make God known to the other nations: "All the trees of the field shall know that I am the LORD." The noble cedar of Davidic Israel will stand as a testament to God's power and mercy.

Jesus envisions something similar in today's Gospel reading (see below), although the cedar in his parable has become a lowly mustard bush. In both readings something small is planted and grows into something remarkably large, providing shelter for the birds of the air. More to the point, both readings use these symbols to describe God's kingdom. God asserts divine kingship, not through violent imposition, but by restoring a recalcitrant, self-serving people under a benevolent reign. For Mark, of course, that kingdom transcends any and all geographical loci. It is "located" instead in the healing ministry of Jesus, who sows God's final word of faithfulness.

I Samuel 15:34—16:13 (RCL alt.)

While God's rejection of Saul is now complete (15:10-33), he continues to function as king, even as Samuel works to anoint his replacement. That is why Samuel fears Saul's wrath (16:2), for the anointing of David poses a real threat to Saul's reign, no matter the fact that David is unusually young and (by all appearances) nonthreatening. Of course, David will eventually meet those human standards, becoming a mighty warrior and a shrewd politician. The dramatic scene among Jesse's sons does not, therefore, subvert human standards of kingship as much as it simply assures Samuel (and the readers) that God sees beyond present appearances. Somewhere in this ruddy, handsome shepherd boy there is a king waiting to reign, to protect the people on all sides, and to unify them around Jerusalem. The one truly countercultural element we find is the rejection of the elder sons on behalf of the youngest, a dynamic in keeping with the patriarchal narratives (Isaac, Jacob, Joseph). In this sense God truly does defy expectations. Much more substantial surprises come in David's royal descendant, the carpenter's son, who reigns through healing, forgiveness, and the conquering of death.

Psalmody
Psalm 92:1-4, 12-15 (RCL)
Psalm 92:2-3, 13-14, 15-16 (LFM)

This is a psalm of praise and thanksgiving in response to the works of God, works that are accomplished in the face of great opposition (92:7-9, omitted from the lectionary). So confident is the psalmist in God's "steadfast love" and "faithfulness" (v. 2) that, at the conclusion of the song, he sings of the opposition as already defeated (vv. 10-15). The promise of this victory parallels the basic message of Jesus' kingdom parables in Mark 4:1-34 (see the Gospel reading below). More specifically, the "planting" of the righteous like a tree in God's presence (vv. 12-14) parallels the harvest imagery of those parables, especially the final promise of a great shrub in which the birds of the air will nest. Our songs of thanksgiving and praise testify to God's reign having taken root in and among us.

Psalm 20 (RCL alt.)

Not until verse 5 does it become clear that this is a royal psalm, sung on behalf of the king of Israel. While addressed to the king, it is nonetheless a kind of indirect petition to God for the king's protection and victory, predicated on the king's own faithfulness to God. It is difficult for us in modern democratic countries to understand and appreciate how the king's own well-being (in times of war and peace) would have been tied to the well-being of the people over whom he ruled, how the king's victory would be "our" victory (not necessarily, but at least ideally). Yet in reading the psalm christologically—identifying the anointed king as Christ—congregations will see that they do in fact have a king ruling over them, a faithful king to whom God gives victory. And that victory is also ours.

Second Reading
2 Corinthians 5:6-10, (11-13), 14-17 (RCL)
2 Corinthians 5:6-10 (LFM)

This reading begins, somewhat awkwardly, with a conclusion based on previous points: "Therefore [NRSV: "so"] we are always confident; even though we know that while we are at home in the body we are away from the Lord" (v. 6). That is, our current bodily-mortal existence does not hinder God. This conclusion Paul draws "by faith, not by sight." Mere appearances (i.e., Paul suffering because of his service to God) would suggest a different conclusion, namely that our present "home" stands at odds with our future "home." It is true, of course, that verses 6-8 contrast our present existence "away from the Lord" with our future existence "with the Lord." But this can be misleading, since Paul believes firmly in our living in communion with Christ, here and now, through the gift of the Holy Spirit that creates and sustains the fellowship of the church. Paul would never say that our bodily-mortal existence stands at odds with God's plan for salvation, since it is precisely God who creates us bodily and mortal.

At the same time, however, the reality of suffering testifies to the brokenness of the creation that God has set out to redeem. To share in the suffering of Christ, which is the world's violent repulsion to divine love, is to experience the world's separation from the Lord in one's own body. So yes, things are not as they should be. But Christ's own resurrection, coupled with the "down payment" of the Spirit (v. 5), convinces Paul that salvation is well under way, not in some unseen heavenly sphere but in the bodily-mortal fellowship of the church. Thus the "afterlife" does not come through the erasure of this life, like a great divine do-over, but by means of this life, just as it was the same Jesus Christ whom God raised from the dead, his physical body being transformed into a spiritual body, not rejected and replaced (1 Corinthians 15; see my comments on the Gospel reading for Trinity Sunday, above). So while we no longer regard Jesus Christ "from a human point of view" (v. 16), we still regard *him*, the same Lord who broke bread with his disciples and was crucified on our behalf. Likewise, to be "in Christ" is to be a "new creation" (v. 17; cf. Gal. 6:15) in this transformed sense—or, more precisely, in the process-of-being-transformed sense.

Keep in mind that Paul says these things to explain why he even bothers with his apostolic ministry in and for the church. If the "afterlife" is at odds with this life, then the church would be, for Paul, pointless. We would be better off returning home to await death. We might even prefer to seek death (cf. Phil. 1:12-30). Precisely because of the continuity, however, Paul can write that "whether we are at home or away, we make it our aim to please him" (v. 9). Because the members of Christ's body are each a new creation, as well as participants in a new creation, they "live no longer for themselves" but for God (v. 15).

Gospel
Mark 4:26-34 (RCL, LFM)

These two parables conclude an extended series of parables that describe the kingdom of God (4:1-34). To best appreciate them, however, we need to retrace our narrative steps, for Mark has connected God's kingdom with Jesus' public ministry ever since that ministry began. Jesus first made the connection himself, upon emerging from his wilderness confrontation with Satan: "The time is fulfilled, and the kingdom of God has come near; repent, and believe in the good news" (1:15). Indeed, the entire story of Jesus is good news (1:1) precisely because it is the story of God's kingdom having come near.

But how should we understand the phrase "has come near"? It is not mere proximity, as if the kingdom were merely "close by" but not yet present. In my own classes I use the analogy of the sunrise: when the first rays of light pierce the night sky, we have grounds for saying it is now daytime, even as we continue to see some lingering darkness. Likewise, for Jesus, the kingdom of God is very much present. We will see it in his ministry. The fact that it does not immediately envelop the entire creation does not make this divine presence any less real. (This interpretation is also in keeping with the perfect tense of the verb in question: *éggiken*).

Along these lines, it will help to rid ourselves of strictly spatial connotations of "kingdom," as if Mark were referring to a geographical terrain with clearly defined boundaries. While the Greek noun *basileia* can carry such connotations, Mark seems not to intend them. The noun stems from the verb "to reign" or "to rule" (*basileuó*). In Markan usage, it denotes God's active lordship. So, in announcing the arrival of God's *basileia*, Jesus is not planting a flag in "this territory" as opposed to "that territory." After all, the entire creation already belongs to God. However, God's creation does not fully enjoy the benefits of God's loving reign. It is a creation marked by demonic influence, whereby people pursue their own agendas, lording it over others in conflict (10:42) rather than submitting to the Lord who alone brings peace and harmony. Creation stands in need of God's benevolent and healing reign.

Bearing this in mind, it is easier to see the correlation between God's reign and the ministry of Jesus. Jesus brings to creation God's peace and harmony—what the Hebrew Scriptures refer to as God's *shalom*—the wholeness intended for creation from the very beginning. Whether it is cleansing a leper, forgiving a sinner, feeding a hungry crowd, or accepting a culturally despised Gentile, Jesus creates wholeness where there had once been brokenness. Sometimes we can easily attribute the initial brokenness to human sinfulness. Sometimes the precise causes lie beyond our line of vision. But in every case the brokenness marks a deviation from the divine will for creation, and in every case the action of Jesus brings a restoration to that creative intent.

This brings us finally to the parables of chapter 4, which serve several purposes. First, they acknowledge that God's reign finds staunch resistance from a broken world, a world in which God's own creatures have turned in on themselves and away from the Creator. Notice what happens in the initial parable, when the sower indiscriminately casts the seed—the word—across the earth: Satan snatches it away. People let go of it for fear of persecution and out of desire for wealth and status (vv. 14-19). The kingdom of God is not a violent imposition that undermines the freedom of creation. This king does not pillage for himself but gives himself, riding lowly on a colt (11:1-11).

Second, the parables promise that the recalcitrance of creatures is not the final word in the matter. At the end of this unconventional harvest, the loving reign of the Creator envelops the creation. Even now, in fact, God's reign has begun to take root. There is "good earth" (NRSV: "good soil") to be found those who "hear the word and accept it and bear fruit" (v. 20). Interestingly, when we survey the Markan landscape, we find that this good earth consists mainly of the spiritually broken and socially oppressed recipients of Jesus' healing ministry, those so thoroughly crushed by life (and by others) that there is essentially no remaining "self" toward which they can turn selfishly. Being utterly open to Jesus' healing touch makes them good earth for his word. (By contrast, the disciples prove vulnerable to worldly cares [e.g., 9:33-41; 10:35-45] and flee from persecution [14:50, 66-72], although Jesus promises their restoration after his resurrection [13:9-11; 14:27-28]).

From a worldly perspective this good earth strikes us as small potatoes. But over time it yields a remarkable harvest: "thirty and sixty and a hundredfold" (v. 20). It is like the mustard seed that, beginning as "the smallest of all the seeds on earth," grows into "the greatest of all shrubs," providing shade for birds (vv. 31-32). The opposition to God is real, then, and it may strike us as disproportionate, especially at Golgotha. But things are not as they seem. And things are not as they will be. The reign of God is taking root, and it will eventually be seen by all. For "there is nothing hidden, except to be disclosed" (v. 22).

Finally, the parables make certain that the bounty of the harvest does not stem ultimately from the skill of human sowers and harvesters. It is fundamentally a divine act. Note that in today's reading Jesus has altered his use of terms. Initially the "earth" referred to the "good earth," those open to the word (v. 20). When we come to verses 26-29, however, the production of the earth suggests the mysterious way in which *God* brings the harvest. As humans we can, like Jesus, sow the word. Perhaps we can even provide water and a nice protective lattice. But we cannot actually make the seeds grow. The earth produces "automatically" (NRSV: "of itself"), and the farmer "does not know how" (vv. 27-28). It is something of a cooperative effort, the entire possibility and result of which is divine. Disciples have a participatory role in the subordination of creation to God's reign (3:14-16; 6:7-13), but they do not themselves reign. They do not "do" the actual healing.

Understood within its context, today's reading allows us to address shallow notions of "missions," to orient congregational ministries around the *single* mission of sharing (and sharing *in*) God's benevolent reign, a reign that brings wholeness and is thus continuous with God's role as self-giving Creator. One cannot read the Gospel of Mark and reduce God's kingdom to a strictly future, strictly spiritual, phenomenon. It is here, calling us to an awareness of physical, and not only spiritual, needs (as if the two could even be separated). These needs exist both "inside" and "outside" our church walls. At the same time, the reading does not dwell only on the present. It allows us to acknowledge evil in the world, but with a hope that the mustard seed will grow into the greatest of all shrubs. Whether we are sharing in God's reign or opposing it, this passage takes the ultimate power out of our hands. We are the farmer sowing (v. 26), and we are the birds of the air resting (v. 32).

June 24, 2012
Lectionary 12 / Twelfth Sunday in Ordinary Time / Proper 7
Fourth Sunday after Pentecost

First Reading
Job 38:1-11 (RCL)
Job 38:1, 8-11 (LFM)

This passage is part of the divine response to Job, who dares to question God's justice. Job has experienced tremendous suffering, the loss of virtually everything—and all of it unjustly. Initially, Job's allegiance to God remains unswerving. His suffering does not lead him to question God's goodness but to rely upon it. But then his "friends" begin to insist, in varying ways, that someone must be to blame, whether Job or members of his family. The friends cannot imagine anyone suffering unjustly; therefore God, in their view, must be punishing someone. Job insists that they are wrong, that no one is to blame. Yet with the escalation of tension and with all the talk of blame, Job's righteous anger toward his suffering slowly slips into a more resentful and accusatory view of God. He insinuates that God is unjust. He wants to question God, and he wants God to answer for the injustice.

Job 38 commences God's great theophanic response. It is a barrage of rhetorical questions intended to put Job in his place. The first question sets the stage: Job has presumed to provide counsel out of ignorance (v. 2). The ensuing command turns the tables: God will question Job, and Job will answer God (v. 3). The remaining questions then expose Job's ignorance, indeed his mortality, vis-à-vis the magnificent acts of God. Job was not there when God laid the earth's foundation (v. 4). He did not determine its measurements (v. 5) or its bases (v. 6). Finally, he did not shut in the sea, setting its limits so that life on earth might flourish (vv. 8-11). God is the one Creator. Job is but a creature. While it comes later on, Job's response is worth noting: "I am of small account. . . . I lay my hand on my mouth" (40:4).

When the smoke clears, we do not have a neat and tidy solution to "the problem of evil." But we know that one thing is off-limits: God's goodness. Job does not incite God's response by insisting on his own righteousness (which is a given) or by complaining angrily about his affliction. He is not even to blame for demanding a divine response. He crosses the line when he *accuses* God of injustice.

The lectionary has placed these verses alongside the Gospel reading because Jesus, in calming the sea, manifests God's own authority as Creator. His act on behalf of the disciples continues the divine "shutting in" of the sea for the well-being of creation. When interpreted on its own, however, this reading speaks more to our mortal limitations vis-à-vis an all-knowing Creator (we are *all* "of small account") and of the theological dangers inherent in challenging the goodness and justice of God. However we explain the tragedy of human suffering, it cannot be "caused" by God in any direct sense (see the helpful discussion by David Bentley Hart, *The Doors of the Sea: Where Was God in the Tsunami?* [Grand Rapids: Eerdmans, 2005]).

1 Samuel 17:(1a, 4-11, 19-23), 32-49 or 17:57—18:5, 10-16 (RCL alt.)

This week the new king begins to emerge. The shepherd boy's finely honed skills with the sling win the Israelites a monumental victory against the Philistines. It is the first of several steps by which the already anointed David effectively replaces Saul as king. That David tries, but refuses, to wear Saul's armor suggests that his "power" is of a different sort: "The Lord does not save by sword and spear," he exclaims to Goliath, "for the battle is the Lord's and he will give you into our hand" (v. 47). The world scoffs (with Goliath) at the proposition of defeating the seemingly unbeatable giant with a single smooth stone, just as it scoffs at the proposition of defeating sin and death through a singular, incarnate love. The Christian story here is not one of violence and bloodshed but trusting that God works within the creation (and in unexpected ways, through a shepherd boy or a carpenter's son) to realize the divine will for creation.

The second alternative reading continues David's rise. His military prowess earns him the favor, and then the wrath, of an increasingly demented Saul. In contrast to this volatility, the friendship with Jonathan proves constant. Significantly, the one who refused to wear the armor of the king (see above) does wear the armor of the king's son; for David, and not Jonathan, will replace Saul. Yet it is Jonathan who exhibits the power of love to set aside potential worldly rivalry for the benefit of God's people. David does not take Jonathan's armor; Jonathan gives it willingly. Indeed, Jonathan's faithfulness to David will later save him from Saul's villainy (1 Samuel 20). It is yet another unexpected means by which divine promises are realized.

Psalmody
Psalm 107:1-3, 23-32 (RCL)
Psalm 107:23-24, 25-26, 28-29, 30-31 (LFM)

This psalm celebrates God's steadfast love, particularly insofar as it delivers people from various forms of oppression: homeless desert wanderers who hunger and thirst (vv. 4-9), prisoners sitting miserably in darkness and gloom (vv. 10-16), the sick drawing near to death's gates (vv. 17-22), and sailors endangered by stormy seas (vv. 23-32). The lectionary focuses on verses 23-32 because of the obvious parallel to the Gospel reading. In fact, Mark may have intended to invoke verses 27-29, in which the sailors stagger at "their wit's end" and cry out to God, who responds by "stilling" the storm and "hushing" the waves. Yet the psalm as a whole reminds us that God's steadfast love cannot be confined to a particular group, however much we would like to restrict it to the boat of followers. God proves faithful to all and seeks the deliverance of all.

Psalm 9:9-20 (RCL alt.)

These selected verses highlight God's faithfulness in delivering the oppressed and afflicted, as well as God's judgment against their oppressors. This judgment is essentially a matter of the wicked being "snared in the work of their own hands" (v. 16). We might say that to oppress others is actually, in reality, a form of oppression. The repeated reference to "nations" (*goyim*, vv. 15, 17, 19, 20) can lend itself to a perverse nationalistic Christianity, as if the fate of the United States, for example, depended on a kind of wholesale political "conversion" (see especially v. 17). We must not forget, however, that Christianity's catholicity depends on its transnational character. First and foremost, the followers of Christ seek the building up of Christ's body, the church, more than of any particular nation-state. They may (and should) participate in the politics of the nation-state, always acting in accordance with Christ's mission of love, but always with the understanding that the church, and not a particular country, is ultimately commissioned with magnifying God's name on earth.

Psalm 133 (RCL alt.)

This beautifully succinct psalm celebrates the "dwelling together" of kindred, by which the psalmist means blood relatives, the traditional clan. With the modern fracturing of the extended clan into the "nuclear family," often quite removed from other relatives, we miss the beauty of this togetherness, how it benefits children and parents and ensures the provision of all members. It is all the more important, therefore, to remember that Christians find their true kindred in the body of Christ, that the gospel transcends and reorients traditional blood relations. With this in mind the psalm celebrates the unity of the church and all that Christ accomplishes through his members, for the benefit of those members and the entire creation. "For there the LORD ordained his blessing" (v. 3).

Second Reading
2 Corinthians 6:1-13 (RCL)

This week's passage is largely an elaboration on the preceding verse: "So we are ambassadors for Christ, since God consoles [NRSV: 'is making his appeal'] through us; we entreat you on behalf of Christ, be reconciled to God" (5:20). Understanding this context helps us make sense of the seemingly awkward transition from verse 2 to verse 3: How does the urgency of accepting God's grace (vv. 1-2) relate to the lengthy description of Paul's faultless ministry (vv. 3-10)? They are related insofar as it is precisely in Paul's ministry that the Corinthians encounter God's gracious work of reconciliation. Communion with Paul is therefore essential. Yet this is no apostolic egotism. For Paul knows that some so-called apostles conveniently avoid any sharing in Christ's suffering and, not coincidentally, find Paul's suffering evidence of his inferior authority (see 2 Corinthians 10–12). Paul, by contrast, believes that the ambassador of Christ does not merely preach "about" the gospel but embodies the self-emptying love that *is* the gospel, risking exposure to the same violent repulsion that Christ faced. Only then can Paul say that he is "putting no obstacle in anyone's way, so that no fault may be found with our ministry" (v. 3).

The ensuing description of this faultless ministry contains what outsiders will only see as a litany of contradictions: the virtues of verses 6-7 (purity, knowledge, patience, etc.) stand alongside the horrors of verses 4-5 (calamities, beatings, imprisonments, etc.). From Paul's perspective, however, the sufferings substantiate the virtues, and this *not* because suffering is inherently virtuous, but rather because creation is caught in a cycle of solipsistic rebellion against the Creator. Paul's afflictions, then, affirm that God continues to reconcile the world through Christ (5:19) . . . through Paul. "We are treated as impostors, and yet are true" (v. 8).

Modern suspicion of all authority and hierarchy encourages us to understand Paul's self-commendation as also a self-promotion, a desperate attempt to assert his authority among the Corinthians simply for the sake of preserving his own power. But in reality his self-promotion is a Christ-promotion. Paul's apostolic "self" has been completely absorbed by and reshaped into the image of Christ. Had he wanted to secure power, he would have asserted power. As it is, he asserts his sufferings in order to assert Christ's own lordship. Note, however, that Paul does not exhort the Corinthians to *seek* hardship from the world. He simply exhorts them to embrace his ministry as a sharing in God's reconciling love. Communing with a self-promoting apostle fosters a self-promoting community (or, better, a noncommunity) by means of "another Jesus" (11:4). At stake is not merely the acceptance of Paul's words and life but the church's own salvific participation in Christ. When it comes to the Corinthians' fellowship with Paul, "now is the day of salvation!" (v. 2).

2 Corinthians 5:14-17 (LFM)

For comments on this lection, see the second reading (RCL) for Proper 6, above.

Gospel
Mark 4:35-41 (RCL, LFM)

The primary opponent is this passage is the stormy sea. But the real danger is not weather related. Jesus engages in spiritual warfare, with creation itself at stake.

Within the typical ancient Hebrew cosmology, God held back primordial waters by means of a firmament, thus providing a space for life to exist and flourish (so Gen. 1:6-8). Those waters were believed to represent chaos, standing at odds with God's benevolent ordering of creation. The profound theological implication (despite the scientific inaccuracies) is that creation is not a singular event but a constant divine sustaining. Take God out of the equation, and creation at once dissolves into nothing. Or, to use another image from Genesis, creation becomes chaotically flooded to the point of ultimate annihilation (Genesis 7). Anyone who has experienced a storm at sea knows that it is very much like creation running in reverse. You are no longer floating peacefully and harmoniously with nature but fighting against it.

So it is easy to see why ancient Jews commonly attributed storms to demonic spirits. Likewise, we can see how Jesus, in calming the stormy sea, manifests a divine authority over the creation—or any force that would seek to jeopardize its harmonious integrity. The immediate effect of Jesus' command—"'Peace! Be still!' Then the wind ceased, and there was a dead calm" (v. 39)—reminds us of his exorcisms (e.g., 1:25-26). Indeed, this *is* an exorcism, not of an individual person but of creation itself. So don't be fooled by commentaries that speculate on the historical possibility (whether likely or unlikely) of such a severe storm on a relatively small lake. Such speculation misses Mark's theological point. Mark uses the term *sea* (*thalassa*, v. 39) symbolically, to push us beyond questions of historicity, invoking images of Genesis, the primordial waters, and the divine taming of chaos. No wonder the disciples are filled with awe! Their only response is to wonder at Jesus' identity: "Who then is this, that even the wind and the sea obey him?" (v. 41; cf. Ps. 107:28-29). Indeed, the disciples have witnessed not only an exorcism but a kind of theophany (see my comments on the first reading, above).

At the same time, this passage is not a biblical "proof" for Jesus' divinity. In the first place, Mark seems not to have conceived of Jesus as "divine" in the sense that we do, indebted as we are to John's Gospel and the later creedal traditions. In fact, Jesus sleeping in the boat seems to suggest his own trust in God (following Job 11:18-19; Pss. 3:5; 4:8). Wielding a divine authority is not precisely the same thing as *being* God. In the second place, if Mark had intended this story as such a proof, then it surely would have ended with a much clearer recognition on the part of the disciples. In other words, we would have an "Aha!" moment instead of the question "Who is this?" The church hears this story as a theophany precisely because it stands on this side of Easter, having encountered the risen Lord and having discerned his divinity retrospectively. By contrast, a biblical "proof" attempts to move one from disbelief to belief without this necessary encounter and retrospection, which is why it generally results in a deepening of disbelief. None of this is to deny Jesus' divinity for Christians. It is simply to help us focus more clearly on what Mark is trying to do, and not do, through this narrative.

Consider, for instance, the role of "faith" (*pistis*) in this very passage. When Jesus asks, "Why are you afraid? Have you still no faith?" he is not demanding intellectual assent to doctrinal propositions (although that does become an important and necessary part of Christianity's theological tradition). For Mark, the Greek noun *pistis* means "trust." As the disciples journey with Jesus, they are expected to grow in their trust of him. They have witnessed, and will soon take part in (6:7-13), a ministry dedicated to the healing of a broken creation. Admitting a certain degree of mystery in the unfolding of that ministry (4:10-13), Jesus nonetheless has given them every reason to trust him, and no reason at all to distrust him. So if we hear a tone of frustration in Jesus' voice, it is not because he wishes to remain separate from their distress, as if his sleep mattered more to him than the lives of his friends. Rather, he is frustrated because he knows their distrust. Note that the disciples themselves reveal this to him. For while the typical petitioner would exclaim, "Help me!" the disciples ask, "*Do you not care* that we are perishing?" Fear has overwhelmed them to the point that they question Jesus' concern (note also the juxtaposition of fear and trust at 5:36). They have questioned his trustworthiness. So Jesus would be remiss to save them without also challenging them in this regard. For, unlike the typical petitioner, the disciples have been called to follow Jesus and extend his ministry of *shalom*. Whatever Christology the early church may have developed after Easter, it is predicated on a fundamental trust in Jesus as the one who seeks our well-being, brings about our well-being, and, in so doing, reveals to us the very nature of God.

The juxtaposition between fear and trust will bear much homiletic fruit. The world gives us a whole litany of reasons to fear and question God's reliability and "motivation," but this passage reminds us that the reign of God is never only for others—it is always also for us—for we are a part of the creation God sustains and loves. It is precisely because God has freely brought us into existence, and continually sustains our existence, that we trust God (see also my introductory comments for Trinity Sunday). Take away God's role as our creator and sustainer and we have every reason to fear the chaotic waters that surround us and threaten us. As it is, however, we are God's own possession, just as surely as the disciples sit in the boat with Jesus. Of course, we do not typically experience healing with the immediacy found in the Gospels. And we do not explain weather patterns in terms of evil spirits. But we do know brokenness, we have grounds for implicating unseen evil forces in that brokenness, and we grow afraid when those forces appear to gain the upper hand. Mark assures us that God, through Jesus, delivers us from such forces, just as God tamed the chaos in the beginning.

The homiletic challenge is to engender trust in God's gracious and merciful self-giving, but without limiting it to particular "moments" of fear and distrust.

For one does not want to reduce faith to a self-serving utilitarianism. Until the full consummation of God's reign, the voyage of life *is* at once the voyage of trust. Some moments may be more frightening than others, but that is precisely why we nurture trust throughout the journey, and not just when we appear to "need" it the most.

July 1, 2012
Lectionary 13 / Thirteenth Sunday in Ordinary Time / Proper 8
Fifth Sunday after Pentecost

Revised Common Lectionary (RCL)
Lamentations 3:23-33 or
  Wisdom of Solomon 1:13-15; 2:23-24
  or 2 Samuel 1:1, 17-27
Psalm 30 or 130
2 Corinthians 8:7-15
Mark 5:21-43

Lectionary for Mass (LFM)
Wisdom of Solomon 1:13-15; 2:23-24

Psalm 30:2 + 4, 5-6, 11-12a + 13b
2 Corinthians 8:7, 9, 13-15
Mark 5:21-43 or 5:21-24, 35-43

First Reading
Lamentations 3:23-33 (RCL alt.)

The book of Lamentations mourns the destruction of Jerusalem by the Babylonians in the sixth century BCE. Like the historical books and many of the prophets, the writer interprets this disaster as God's punishment upon Judah for its transgressions (e.g., 1:8-18; 2:1-9). In today's reading we see only a glimpse of this perspective, when God is said to "cause grief" (3:32).

The direct attribution of human suffering to God creates problems for Christians insofar as the gospel of Jesus Christ leads us to the rather different conclusion that God is eternally loving and self-emptying, not "reacting" to sinful humans, but rather healing them in accordance with the eternal, creative will. This hardly precludes the reality of judgment and damnation, but it does relativize them as the inevitable consequence of our own continued self-delusional, solipsistic resistance to the Creator as the beginning and end of our lives. To borrow the language of John, judgment is simply loving the darkness rather than the light (John 3:19). While this may seem an excessive explanation (or dismissal!) of a small phrase in this week's reading, the potential theological dangers warrant it. At any rate, there is a reason the lectionary focuses on the writer's unwavering hope in God, as this is more conducive to what is revealed in Christ.

In many respects this hope is the heart of the writer's message. It brings a redemptive quality to the prolonged lamentation. God may "punish," but God never rejects (v. 31). God's steadfast love and mercy never cease (v. 22). The saving end of this mercy is rarely realized immediately—it requires waiting quietly (v. 26), sitting alone in silence (vv. 28-29), sometimes even enduring of insults (v. 30). But the passage of time is natural to our mortal, time-bound existence as creatures. Time is the arena for cultivating virtues that open us ever more to the Creator who can always be trusted to redeem. The hemorrhaging woman in today's Gospel reading comes quickly to mind: for *twelve years* she waited for God, enduring great hardship, perhaps even at the hands of fellow humans (Mark 5:26). We can imagine her praying to God without ceasing, lamenting her condition. Yet regardless of how much hope she might have lost along the way, she certainly regained it in the presence of Jesus. If God is revealed in Jesus Christ, then the passage of time is hardly a reason to lose hope. It is precisely the opportunity to hope, to ready ourselves for salvation.

Wisdom of Solomon 1:13-15; 2:23-24 (RCL alt., LFM)

The lectionary extracts these verses from an extended discourse about righteousness (here synonymous with wisdom) and those who conform to her (Wisdom of Solomon 1–3). This discourse begins with an exhortation to love righteousness, which is simply seeking God "with sincerity of heart" (1:1-2). Chapter 1 promotes righteousness through a description of the ungodly, whom God will "convict" due to their "lawless deeds" (v. 9). The first set of lectionary verses (vv. 13-15) asserts that such unrighteousness leads inevitably to "death," by which the writer seems to mean a permanent separation from God (not mere physical mortality). God "did not make" this death and "does not delight" in it (v. 13). Rather, God as Creator wills only life. In accordance with this creative will, the very origins (*geneseis*; NRSV: "generative forces") of the world are salvific and life giving (*sotérioi*; NRSV: "wholesome," v. 14). The climactic conclusion to these verses is that "righteousness is immortal" (v. 15). The second set of verses (2:23-24) states the corollary to this: those who love righteousness and conform to her are likewise immortal. This indeed is God's eternal will, "for God created humanity [*ton anthrópon*; NRSV: 'us'] for incorruption" (v. 23). By contrast, the unrighteous are blind to this mystery (*mystéria*; NRSV: "secret purposes"), the tragic consequence of their own wickedness (vv. 21-22). The final reference to the devil explains the origins of this "death," but without exonerating the wicked (cf. 1:12, 16).

In a culture plagued with and infatuated by human-induced death (real and fictionalized), there is never a bad time to proclaim God's eternal, creative will for life. We see this especially in the story of the hemorrhaging woman, who "endured much under many physicians" and "spent all that she had" for their pointless services (Mark 5:26). Jesus overcomes their exploitive endeavors, restoring her to the will of the life-giving Creator.

2 Samuel 1:1, 17-27 (RCL alt.)

Saul, the first and once-mighty king of Israel, has been slain by the Philistines and finished off (mercifully) by one of his own men. Because David's divinely ordained ascendancy has gained such momentum, and because Saul had become David's enemy, the death of Saul might seem a cause for celebration (the messenger who reports to David in vv. 2-16 evidently thinks so). But David's mournful response to this news reminds us that the fall of Saul is truly tragic. After all, he was the Lord's own anointed king who brought safety and prosperity to Israel. We might expect any appreciation for the enemy Saul to stem from the fact that he was the father of David's beloved friend, Jonathan. But David sings about Jonathan only after praising Saul, acknowledging that "in life and in death they were not divided" (v. 23). At the very moment he receives royal power, David sees beyond himself to the larger story of God and God's people. Sin and hostility do not cloud his vision, even in the case of his relentless enemy.

Psalmody
Psalm 30 (RCL)
Psalm 30:2 + 4, 5-6, 11-12a + 13b (LFM)

The verses complement the RCL first reading from Lamentations quite well (see above), for while the lamenter hopes in God's salvation, the psalmist has experienced it and now gives God thanks and praise. God has answered his cry with healing, having delivered his soul from death (Sheol, the Pit; vv. 2-3). Weeping has turned to joy (v. 5) and mourning to dancing (v. 11). We can imagine both of the petitioners in this week's Gospel reading—the hemorrhaging woman and the synagogue leader—singing this song at the top of their lungs. In fact, it would not be inappropriate to recite this song even in the midst of suffering as an expression of hope, anticipating God's promised deliverance.

Psalm 130 (RCL alt.)

For commentary on this text, see the psalmody for Proper 5, above.

Second Reading
2 Corinthians 8:7-15 (RCL)
2 Corinthians 8:7, 9, 13-15 (LFM)

Second Corinthians 8–9 is an extended appeal by Paul to the Corinthians requesting their generous contribution to a monetary collection intended for the poor Christians in Jerusalem (see Rom. 15:25-32; 1 Cor. 16:1-4; Gal. 2:10). Paul intended this collection not only as a means of financial assistance but as an expression of Christian unity, through which his predominantly Gentile converts (like the Corinthians) would acknowledge their indebtedness to Jewish believers (concentrated in Jerusalem). "For if the Gentiles have come to share in their spiritual blessings, they ought also to be of service to them in material things" (Rom. 15:27). After all, the salvation of the Gentiles consists in their entering into communion with the God of Israel, the one Creator, making the body of Christ the realization of God's creative will for "one new humanity" (Eph. 2:15).

Paul had already instructed the Corinthians about the collection in a previous letter (1 Cor. 16:1-4), and they have had a year to set things in motion (8:10). So this is more of a reminder of their obligation, which is also a voluntarily gracious giving (*charis*, v. 4; NRSV: "privilege") to which they had previously agreed and even desired to carry through (vv. 10-11). In fact, Paul notes that the churches in neighboring Macedonia have already proven faithful to this mission despite their "severe ordeal of affliction" (v. 2). Now the Corinthians, who "excel in everything" (v. 7), are expected to follow suit. Paul has boasted about them and expects them to show the churches "proof of [their] love" (v. 24). That is why he insists on calling the collection a "testing" rather than a "command" (v. 8). It is about *their faithfulness* to Christ and his body more than it is about Paul's reputation.

More specifically, the collection is an opportunity for the Corinthians to share in Christ's own self-giving. In providing for the poor saints in Jerusalem, they reciprocate the grace (*charis*; NRSV: "generous act") of Christ, whose own impoverishment enriched others, including the Corinthians themselves (v. 9). Paul assures them that this provision need not exceed their means (v. 12). One cannot give what one does not have. At the same time, however, the Corinthians should not give based simply on what is comfortable to them. They should rather seek an "equality" (*isotés*; NRSV: "fair balance"), so that the Gentile abundance might fill what is lacking among the Jerusalem brethren. If the need is not met, then some will be seen to have "too much" and others "too little" (v. 15). Paul is not keeping a ledger, taking names, and counting pennies. He is drawing the Corinthians into the unity of Christ's body, apart from which they have no life. This is their opportunity to give life, just as they have been given life.

Gospel
Mark 5:21-43 (RCL)
Mark 5:21-43 or 5:21-24, 35-43 (LFM)

In discussing last week's Gospel reading, I mentioned the importance of trusting Jesus (Gk.: *pistis, pisteuó*). That was a story about Jesus and his disciples. In this week's reading we find trust exhibited by two minor characters.

The hemorrhaging woman exhibits trust by pushing through a crowd to reach Jesus, convinced that she will be healed simply by touching his clothes (vv. 27-28). As a woman, she puts herself at great social risk, venturing into public unaccompanied and initiating contact with a male (her ritually unclean status might have ostracized her further). We can imagine the incredulous hush sweeping over the crowd after Jesus asks, "Who touched me?" only to have a lowly and sickly woman step forward. From the perspective of bystanders, the woman's reverent posture—"falling down" before Jesus in "fear and trembling" (v. 33)—would not have hidden her scandalous overstepping of social boundaries. She seems to have shamed both herself and the man she presumed to touch.

Yet the story does not unfold as society would have it. Jesus does not shame the woman, and he does not contract her uncleanness. Rather, he spreads to her the wholeness of God's reign, and he applauds her scandalous actions: "Daughter, your trust [*pistis*; NRSV: 'faith'] has made you well; go in peace, and be healed of your disease" (v. 34). His acknowledgment of the woman's trust affirms the cooperative nature of this healing. Jesus has healed her, of course, but only because she ventured forth to touch him. She trusts Jesus—that he seeks her well-being and can realize it for her—more than she fears the society that has shamed her at the *expense* of her well-being (v. 26). What looks like only a bold disregard for accepted social mores is, more fundamentally, an irresistible attraction to the in-breaking reign of God. From the Markan perspective, the mission of bringing *shalom* to creation overrides a culture's preestablished rules of order. Ideally, it is precisely the mission of *shalom* that gives rise to *godly* rules of order. Under God's reign, this woman is not an outcast subject to oppression but a "daughter" of Abraham for whom God intends "peace" (v. 34).

The story of Jairus has clear differences. As a male, he would have been granted considerably more social status. As a synagogue leader, he would have been well respected enough to oversee (and perhaps host) community gatherings. Finally, he approaches Jesus on behalf of someone else—his daughter. The honorable, socially empowered Jairus stands in stark contrast to the shameful and solitary hemorrhaging woman. Yet they have this in common: a desperation for Jesus' healing, and a trust that Jesus has their well-being in mind (or, in Jairus's case, the well-being of his daughter).

It is true that the language of trust does not surface at the time of Jairus's initial petition. We hear only that he fell at Jesus' feet and begged him to heal his dying daughter (vv. 22-23). However, once Jesus names the actions of the hemorrhaging woman as trust, we can retrospectively consider Jairus in a similar light. So when, upon hearing of the daughter's death, Jesus exhorts Jairus, "Do not fear, only trust" (NRSV: "believe"), he does not insinuate that Jairus previously did not trust. He is asking Jairus to *continue* trusting. Along these lines, note that Jesus does not even await a response from Jairus, as if he needed to say, "Okay, Jesus, I still trust you." Jesus evidently is bent on healing his daughter regardless of the new circumstances. Jairus's trust has already set Jesus on his way, and Jesus will not be deterred, even by death.

In fact, I am inclined to think that Jairus *loses* trust at precisely this point. After all, nothing in the story has given him grounds for thinking that Jesus could raise someone from the dead. He would naturally conclude that Jesus was now *too late* to save his daughter. The messengers say it quite well: "Why trouble the teacher any further?" (v. 35). If the little girl is beyond saving, then trusting Jesus becomes a moot point. How odd and disorienting it must have been, then, to hear Jesus' summons to continued trust, pressing on to Jairus's house.

This brings us to an often-overlooked social predicament. Jesus has stopped dead in his tracks for an outcast woman, making the honorable male synagogue leader *wait*. And in the process of waiting, Jairus's daughter dies! We can imagine Jairus thinking something similar to Martha, the brother of Lazarus, in the Gospel of John: "Lord, if you had been here, my brother would not have died" (11:21). How can you trust someone who fails to accomplish what he promised to do, who even appears to play favorites against you? Jairus cannot dwell on these questions very long, for as the story unfolds Jesus proves his trustworthiness. He restores the little girl to wholeness. This requires what seems to us a more awe-inspiring miracle, but the end result is the same. The reign of God takes residence in Jairus's home, and if he had lost trust on the way, he surely regains it in the face of his healthy daughter. As it turns out, Jesus was not playing favorites.

Finally, it would be a mistake to read Jesus' words in verse 39 literally: "The child is not dead but sleeping." Sleep was a euphemism for death, and Jesus plays on that euphemism in anticipation of his healing. The mourners know full well that the girl is dead, which is precisely why they laugh scoffingly. Since Jesus forces them outside, however, with the result that they do not witness the miracle, they are led to believe that the girl was asleep after all. Only the child's parents, along with the three disciples, witness the event firsthand. It is a secrecy in keeping with Mark's Jesus, who does not want the glory of powerful deeds overshadowing his mission of humble self-giving.

Jesus does not cater to the demands of the socially privileged at the expense of the destitute. It is worth driving this home in a sermon, not only with respect to society at large, but also with respect to the church, which inevitably exhibits its own social hierarchies. At the same time, Jesus does not reverse the hierarchy, placing the outcasts "on top" and the privileged "on the bottom." This would be merely to perpetuate the same oppression over against the reign of God. At the end of the day, there is sufficient time for everyone to find healing. Jesus is never late. No one stands beyond his reach, even the dead. We may trust him in all circumstances.

July 8, 2012
Lectionary 14 / Fourteenth Sunday in Ordinary Time / Proper 9
Sixth Sunday after Pentecost

Revised Common Lectionary (RCL)	**Lectionary for Mass (LFM)**
Ezekiel 2:1-5 or 2 Samuel 5:1-5, 9-10	Ezekiel 2:2-5
Psalm 123 or 48	Psalm 123:1-2a, 2bc, 3-4
2 Corinthians 12:2-10	2 Corinthians 12:7-10
Mark 6:1-13	Mark 6:1-6

First Reading
Ezekiel 2:1-5 (RCL)
Ezekiel 2:2-5 (LFM)

These verses are part of Ezekiel's call narrative (on the purpose of a call narrative, see my comments on the RCL first reading for Trinity Sunday, above). God has appeared to Ezekiel in a vision of a heavenly throne-chariot (chap. 1), an anticipation of the divine presence "moving" out of the temple (chap. 10) so as to allow its destruction (chaps. 4–5, 7). The continued rebellion of Israel has driven God away (2:3). Now Ezekiel, a mere mortal, must speak a divine word of judgment to his own people. The time for repentance has come and gone. Israel has grown so "impudent" and "stubborn" (v. 4) that it can no longer discern and follow God's will. In fact, it will not even be able to hear Ezekiel's word of judgment (v. 5). Its rebellion against God will extend to a rebellion against God's messenger. Thus Ezekiel will live among "briers," "thorns," and "scorpions" (v. 6). Yet despite this opposition, Ezekiel must not fear (v. 6). He will not be caught off-guard. Indeed, God soon assures him of divine empowerment: "I have made your face hard against their faces, and your forehead hard against their foreheads" (3:8). The prophet of God must be hardheaded.

This is a helpful backdrop for Jesus' saying in the Gospel reading: "Prophets are not without honor, except in their hometown, and among their own kin, and in their own house" (Mark 6:4). Ezekiel was hardly the only prophet to face rejection from his own people. It is difficult to hear the truth when it challenges us and calls us to change. When that truth deals directly with God, it is all the more threatening; and with the stakes so raised we can lash out at God's messenger, confusing him or her as the enemy (one thinks especially of Jeremiah, even Martin Luther King Jr.). Jesus, of course, is more than a prophetic messenger. Yet the hostility he meets repeats the cycle that many prophets experienced before him (Mark 12:1-12). Jesus' hardheadedness, however, takes the form of self-giving. He refuses to compromise the mission of God's reign for the healing of creation. He moves on from Nazareth (Mark 6:6b), unfazed by the thorns and scorpions.

2 Samuel 5:1-5, 9-10 (RCL alt.)

David has already been anointed king of the southern tribes of Judah, ruling them from the city of Hebron. Now, seven years later, he is anointed king of the northern tribes of Israel. The journey of "all the tribes of Israel" (v. 1) to Hebron is surely hyperbole. Verse 3 is more realistic when it says that all the *elders* of Israel came to Hebron. Still, the hyperbole communicates an important point, namely that David's kingship stemmed from the unanimous consent of the people (see an identical hyperbole in 2:4), who recognized God's will in the political ascendancy of this Bethlehemite shepherd boy: "It is you who shall be shepherd of my people Israel" (v. 2). Indeed, we know that God had already anointed David for this very purpose, while he was still a young shepherd of sheep (1 Sam. 16:1-13). So the subsequent anointing in Judah and Israel serves only to confirm for the people what God has already brought about.

In conquering the city of Zion (Jerusalem) and making it his capital, David moves the seat of political power slightly north, a symbolic gesture intended to assuage whatever anxiety the northern tribes might have about a Judean king (these divisions reemerge after David's death in 1 Kings. 12:1-19). It is this unification of the people—and not his military might—that makes David a true prefiguration of the Messiah. He rules not by means of sheer power, but rather as a shepherd leading sheep, and this in accordance with the will of God, the transcendent and true Shepherd (see Psalm 23).

Psalmody
Psalm 123 (RCL)
Psalm 123:1-2a, 2bc, 3-4 (LFM)

The psalmist speaks on behalf of the congregation that has had "more than its fill" of scorn and contempt cast upon it (v. 4). His petition is for merciful deliverance (v. 3), and his anticipation is like that of the most attentive servant (v. 2). The psalm fits well with the first reading, in which God sends Ezekiel against the rebellious house of Israel, and with the Gospel reading, in which Jesus faces hostility from his fellow Nazarenes. While it cuts against the grain of the psalm's "original" intent, one might consider turning the tables, so to speak, so as to emphasize our need for divine deliverance from *our own contempt of God* (the Hebrew of verse 3b is actually amenable to this interpretation; see the KJV, NAS). It depends, of course, on the kind of bondage from which one needs deliverance.

Psalm 48 (RCL alt.)

This psalm celebrates not only the splendor and magnificence of Jerusalem (Zion) but, more fundamentally, its holiness as the city of God, who dwells in its temple. Zion is the Lord's "holy mountain" (v. 1), which is why the assembled kings (preparing to lay siege) take flight in panic (vv. 4-7). Because Christianity does not "locate" or centralize the divine presence in a specific place (and, to be fair, neither does the Old Testament when all its voices are heard), but rather in the person of Christ, this psalm presents itself as an allegory for Christ and his ecclesial body. When the church fulfills its mission as Christ's body, visitors (whether hostile or peaceful) can only recognize the divine presence, ponder God's steadfast love (v. 9), and seek their own residence within its borders.

Second Reading
2 Corinthians 12:2-10 (RCL)
2 Corinthians 12:7-10 (LFM)

Few passages in the Pauline corpus are as opaque as this one. We know it describes an ecstatic experience, fourteen years prior to this letter, in which an unnamed person was snatched up "as far as the third heaven" (v. 2). Paul does not know whether the experience was in the body or out of the body. Nor does he state what precisely was seen or heard.

It is fairly clear, however, the unnamed person is Paul himself. While the beginning of verse 5 might seem to suggest otherwise, verses 6-7 clarify that Paul distances himself from the "person" only to call attention to the revelations themselves. That is, he does not want to take credit for them. He boasts about them, but not as something produced of his own power or merit. He seems to want the Corinthians to know that he could provide more detail—particularly about what he heard (v. 4)—but in doing so he risks appearing to boast about himself (v. 6).

Yet Paul wants to emphasize that the experience was real and that he is not afraid to boast about it. Here context is crucial. For what the Corinthians have normally "seen" in Paul and "heard" from him (v. 6) is not an ecstatic, this-worldly spirituality, but rather a crucified Lord who reveals a self-emptying God and brings them into communion with this God through a bodily fellowship of self-giving members. The letter as a whole deals mainly with the nature of this scandalous gospel as it pertains to life in relationship with other members of Christ's body, including especially Paul himself. By contrast, the Corinthians have a tendency to become enamored with their own spiritual gifts (1 Corinthians 12–15) and with self-promoting "apostles" who conveniently avoid Christ's sufferings (2 Corinthians 11; cf. 1 Corinthians 1–4). Over against these worldly tendencies, Paul has pointed to his own afflictions as evidence of his authority, for he has met the same violent repulsion to divine love that Christ himself experienced. Thus, in the passage immediately preceding this one, Paul "boasts" in a litany of persecutions testifying to the power of God who raised Jesus from the dead (11:16-33).

So Paul allows himself to boast in this experience, however briefly, because it gives God glory and because it underscores his own apostolic authority in terms that the Corinthians—perhaps to their shame—can more easily understand. Yet even this brief personal aside must include an equally vague acknowledgment of personal weakness: the "thorn" in Paul's "flesh," the messenger from Satan who torments him and keeps him from being "too elated" about his visions (v. 7). Paul does not identify this torment, and it is pointless for us to try. We need only understand that it exposes a weakness in Paul and that God's grace suffices in dealing with it. As with Paul's other afflictions, this torment would utterly destroy him without God's empowering support. That is why the answer to Paul's prayer encapsulates the gospel itself: "Power is made perfect in weakness." God does not inflict suffering. Rather, God brings life in the face of suffering. At the end of the day, then, Paul will boast more in his weakness, "so that the power of Christ may dwell in me" (v. 9). If the Corinthians desire to commune with God, they should commune with this apostle.

Gospel
Mark 6:1-13 (RCL)
Mark 6:1-6 (LFM)

It might seem as if Jesus has exceeded the expectations of his fellow Nazarenes. It would be more accurate, however, to say that the expectations of his fellow Nazarenes have blinded them to the validity of Jesus' ministry. To exceed expectations is simply a matter of degree: *We thought you'd be a fine carpenter, but you've really outdone yourself. You're the best carpenter we've ever seen!* Mark, however, describes a difference in kind. Rather than exceeding expectations, Jesus has completely jumped the track. He moves in an altogether different direction, a direction so different that his neighbors can only "take offense" at him (*skandalizó*, v. 3). The Greek verb literally refers to the placing of a "stumbling block" that impedes movement. In the parable of the sower, for instance, trouble and persecution prove to be stumbling blocks (NRSV: "they fall away," 4:17). Later, Jesus warns the disciples to avoid stumbling blocks and to keep themselves from being stumbling blocks to others (9:42, 43, 45, 47). We encounter the verb again when Jesus predicts the "desertion" of his followers (14:27, 29), suggesting that the passion itself functions as a stumbling block for discipleship—at least on *this* side of Easter.

In the case of his fellow Nazarenes, Jesus' own ministry is a stumbling block. It is not the kind of vocation one expects from the son of a carpenter. Given what they know about Jesus and his upbringing, the "wisdom" and the "deeds of power" are virtually incomprehensible: "Where did this man get all this?" (vv. 2-3). The answer, of course, is God. But it is all so incredible in relation to their previous conceptions of Jesus that acceptance proves impossible. So, having taken offense at Jesus, the villagers do not find Jesus a trustworthy source of healing. Jesus likens this to the way Israel historically rejects the prophets: "Prophets are not without honor, except in their hometown, and among their own kin, and in their own house" (v. 4). This seems to suggest that his teaching in Nazareth (v. 2) focused on repentance, which was a typical prophetic message that often led to the prophet's own rejection (see the first reading, above). Repentance was also a component of Jesus' first preaching in 1:15.

At any rate, this helps to clarify the seemingly troublesome conclusion to the passage: "And he could do no deed of power there, except that he laid his hands on a few sick people and cured them" (vv. 5-6). It is not that Jesus has actually become powerless but that the Nazarenes, restricted by their own expectations, cannot see their own well-being realized in his ministry. Stated simply, Jesus cannot heal those who do not approach him for healing. If there was a small exception—a few people healed—that is because a minority trusted Jesus in this regard. Jesus healed the few who trusted him, despite their preconceptions. Otherwise he was "amazed at their lack of trust" (*apistia*, v. 6; NRSV: "unbelief").

Thus we find further evidence of the "cooperative" nature of Jesus' ministry. Last week's Gospel reading gave us a positive glimpse into this theme. The hemorrhaging woman would not have been healed had she not pushed through the crowd to touch Jesus; and she would not have pushed through the crowd had she not trusted him: "Daughter, your trust [*pistis*; NRSV: 'faith'] has made you well" (5:34; contrast Zacchaeus in Luke 19:1-10). Unlike the physicians who have drained her resources (5:26), this physician truly had the woman's well-being in mind, along with the authority and power to bring it about.

Jesus' affirmation of the woman gives words to what Mark's hearers have seen all along. For while Jesus at times targets specific people for healing (e.g., 3:1-6), the more dominant pattern is for people to target him. As soon as the word of his ministry gets out (1:28), crowds flock to him, gathering around the houses in which he stays (1:32-34; cf. 1:37). Some go so far as to dig through rooftops to reach him (2:1-12). Elsewhere, Jesus sits in a boat on the lake so that the crowd will not "crush" him (3:9). The point is that people in need of healing go to great lengths to reach Jesus. And the corollary is this: unless we need healing, Jesus will probably not register on our radars. Furthermore, unless we trust that Jesus can and will heal us—that he has our well-being in mind—we will not venture out of our comfortable home to get to him. Finally, we will not trust Jesus for healing, much less go out of our way to find him, if we have already decided what he can and cannot be for us.

Some Christians may find talk of "cooperation" and "venturing forth" theologically problematic. Does it undermine the primacy of divine grace? Only if we read these passages in isolation, without reference to the larger narrative. We must keep in mind that Jesus' ministry is itself a matter of divine initiative, as the Gospel's opening verses make clear (1:2-3; cf. John 3:16). No one in Mark's Gospel heals themselves. Jesus heals them. He has been graciously sent, without our prompting or compulsion, for the healing of creation. Generally speaking, however, Jesus does not heal those who do not trustingly place their well-being in his hands. There is no such thing as abstract, disembodied trust as far as Jesus is concerned. As we are bodily creatures, trust must take a bodily form, whether pushing through a crowd, digging through a roof, or even simply kneeling at an altar.

This brings us to one last observation: the people who exhibit trust in this Gospel are desperate. That is, they realize their brokenness and are all but forced by that brokenness to seek healing in Jesus. It is easy for us to see their brokenness. It is more difficult for us—or at least most of us (Western Christians)—to see our own brokenness. In this sense we are no different from the majority of the Nazarenes who apparently recognize Jesus' power but wish to confine him to a healer for *others*. Every person, every congregation, has its stumbling blocks. And every person and congregation stands in need of healing. Whether we come to Jesus for healing, or whether we need him to show us our brokenness first—in both cases we are putting our trust in Jesus. We always want to uphold God's gracious initiative and even empowerment, from creation to redemption. But we also want to be ever seeking Jesus, actively removing the impediments, placing our entire well-being—and not just certain "parts" of us—trustingly in his healing hands.

(Commentary on the remainder of the RCL Gospel, Mark 6:7-13, can be found under the LFM Gospel for Proper 10, below.)

July 15, 2012
Lectionary 15 / Fifteenth Sunday in Ordinary Time / Proper 10
Seventh Sunday after Pentecost

Revised Common Lectionary (RCL)

Amos 7:7-15 or 2 Samuel 6:1-5, 12b-19
Psalm 85:8-13 or Psalm 24
Ephesians 1:3-14
Mark 6:14-29

Lectionary for Mass (LFM)

Amos 7:12-15
Psalm 85:9ab-10, 11-12, 13-14
Ephesians 1:3-14 or 1:3-10
Mark 6:7-13

First Reading
Amos 7:7-15 (RCL)
Amos 7:12-15 (LFM)

Although hailing from the Southern Kingdom of Judah, Amos spoke a message of divine judgment to the Northern Kingdom of Israel (eighth century BCE). It was a period of political peace and great prosperity within Israel, yet the prosperity was remarkably disproportionate. God's judgment targeted the social injustice of gaining wealth through the oppression of the poor.

This reading focuses on the opposition Amos meets from the authorities in Israel. The royal priest Amaziah perceives the message as a political threat. And rightly so: Amos has promised the destruction of Israel and King Jeroboam himself (vv. 8-9). Amaziah reports this to the king (v. 11), but we hear nothing of Jeroboam's response. We hear only Amaziah's tacit accusation that Amos is meddling in other people's business. He should go back to Judah and earn his prophetic bread there, never to return to the prestigious courts of Bethel (vv. 12-13). The command to "flee" suggests that Amos's life is now in danger (v. 12).

Amos does not back down. He contends that he is not a career prophet, as Amaziah imagines, but rather a lowly herdsman chosen by God to speak against the injustices in Israel. His motivation is not to earn bread (an accusation more revealing of Amaziah than Amos) but to remain faithful to his vocation, no matter where it takes him.

The royal opposition to Amos ties in nicely with the RCL Gospel reading about John the Baptizer. That God sends Amos to a foreign land anticipates the sending of the Twelve in the LFM reading. Like Amos, the Twelve come from humble origins, and Jesus tells them to expect their share of rejection.

2 Samuel 6:1-5, 12b-19 (RCL alt.)

The changing of David's capital, from Hebron to Jerusalem, is only one step toward the consolidation of royal authority and the unification of the people. Next—and more theologically significant—is the acquisition of the ark of the covenant to be housed in the new capital. The ark served as both the throne of God and the container of God's covenant with Israel. It was no mere relic from the past. Rather, from the time of its construction in the wilderness (Exodus 25–31, 35–40), it guaranteed God's own presence among the people (as the omitted tale of Uzzah, in vv. 6-12a, disturbingly conveys). Prior to the rise of the monarchy, the ark had been captured by the Philistines but eventually returned to the town of Kiriath-jearim (1 Sam. 4:2—7:3), here referred to as Baale-judah (v. 2). In retrieving the ark, David exhibits a wisdom that was lacking in Saul. His priorities—at least in the early stages of his reign—are certainly in order. One would expect this kind of celebratory procession for a victorious earthly king returning from war; but David reserves it for God, Israel's true king (it may be that Michal fails to appreciate David's priorities in this regard). The ensuing blessing and feast, in which "all the people" (v. 19) participate, show that David refuses to restrict the benefits of the divine presence to his royal household. He is not an autonomous ruler but a viceroy for God, fulfilling his role as king precisely in his praise, obedience, and provision. In this way he shepherds God's sheep (see 5:2). He will no doubt struggle with consistency (2 Samuel 11–12), but for now he gives us an important glimpse into the nature of Christian ministry and, more fundamentally, the ministry of the Good Shepherd himself (John 10:1-21).

Psalmody
Psalm 85:8-13 (RCL)
Psalm 85:9ab-10, 11-12, 13-14 (LFM)

These verses give assurance that the word of God is always peace for those who "turn to him" and "fear him" and that this peace is nothing less than God's own glorious dwelling among them (vv. 8-9). The remaining stanzas elaborate upon this claim, with a particular emphasis on righteousness. The assurance of God's peace is appropriate in light of the conflicts described in this week's first reading and Gospel readings. It is what the Gentile recipients of Ephesians were called to recognize in their own churches.

Psalm 24 (RCL alt.)

The psalmist not only celebrates God's entrance into the holy temple (vv. 7-10) but also commemorates the entrance of the people. That would explain the concern, expressed in verses 3-6, with "who shall ascend the hill of the Lᴏʀᴅ" (that is, the mountain of Jerusalem, upon which the temple sat). From a Christian perspective, these middle verses do not mean to preclude God's love and compassion for sinners, but rather to emphasize the holiness of God's presence and the necessity for repentance (much the way confession and absolution traditionally precede the Lord's Supper). Significantly, the psalm opens on a cosmic note: the God of Jacob (v. 6) is also Lord of all the earth (vv. 1-2). This is not some strictly tribal deity who enters the sanctuary but, more fundamentally, the "Lᴏʀᴅ of [heavenly] hosts" (v. 10).

Second Reading
Ephesians 1:3-14 (RCL, LFM)
Ephesians 1:3-10 (LFM alt.)

The letter to the Ephesians was originally a circular letter intended for wide distribution among Gentile churches in various cities. More specifically, it served as a kind of catechesis for Gentile converts, describing their salvation as an incorporation into the promises of Israel, the creation of "one new humanity" by the one Creator (2:11-22).

This context helps explain why this week's reading (which is the letter's introduction) emphasizes predestination, that is, the unfolding in time of God's eternal, unchanging will. An uncatechized former pagan might think the God of Israel had "changed his mind" about the Gentiles (they should now be included) as well as the Jews (they should no longer be included). But this thinking creates problems with regard to God's trustworthiness, for if the divine will can change, what grounds do we have for trusting God? Who is to say that God's mind will not change again? More to the point, if God's faithfulness to humans is dependent upon human faithfulness to God, there is little ground for hope.

That is why the letter's introduction insists that Gentile inclusion is not a new idea with respect to God (God's faithfulness to Israel is implied in 2:11-22; see also Romans 11). Their present spiritual blessings originate in God's choosing them "before the foundation of the world," that is, eternally and not in time (1:4). God "destined us for adoption" out of the "good pleasure of his [equally eternal] will" (v. 5). This adoption, experienced in time as redemption and forgiveness, is not an alteration of the divine mind but a "mystery" now being "made known to us" (vv. 7-9). It is in Christ that God has "set forth" this eternal plan in time, which makes the revelation, and humanity's ecclesial participation in it, an indication of "the fullness of time" (vv. 9-10). "All things," both in heaven and earth—including Gentiles—are no longer separated from God but rather are being "gathered up" in Christ (v. 10). Likewise, the Christian life of holiness and praise has been "inherited" and "destined" according to God's eternal purpose and will (vv. 11-12). The gift of the Spirit is a "down payment" (*arrabón*; NRSV: "pledge") of this redemptive inheritance, the full completion of which we may now confidently expect (vv. 13-14).

It should be clear that such predestination is not God "deciding" before the fact which humans will be "saved" and not "saved." For the Pauline school the will of God does not undermine our own wills but rather transforms them through our participation in Christ, a participation made possible by the Holy Spirit at work in the body of Christ. This life "in Christ" is the definition of *true* freedom (see Gal. 5:2-15). Gentile Christians—such as most of us!—are not the lucky beneficiaries of a mind-changing God, much less chess pieces moved at a divine whim. Rather, we are God's eternal "possession" (NRSV: "God's own people," 1:14), and this by virtue of our having been fashioned by a trustworthy Creator who eternally wills to commune with us, who actually does commune with us, and who brings our true "selves" into existence precisely in that communion.

Gospel
Mark 6:14-29 (RCL)

This is the only passage in Mark where Jesus is absent, although it is still very much "about" him and the mission of God's reign. Verses 17-29 form a flashback. In the narrative's present time, the twelve apostles are out in the world, extending Jesus' healing ministry and making his name known (v. 14; see discussion of 6:1-7 under the Gospel reading for Proper 9, above). All the buzz over Jesus and his powers makes Herod Antipas (tetrarch of Galilee and Perea, son of Herod the Great) think that John the Baptizer has been raised from the dead. The narrative then flashes back to the prophet's execution by Herod.

This flashback is no meaningless interruption. Mark *could* have reported John's martyrdom at any point in the narrative (the arrest was reported all the way back in 1:14). He reports it here to draw parallels between John and the Twelve. In the first place, both John and the Twelve participate in Jesus' mission, the in-breaking of God's healing reign. John participates by way of anticipation (with a ritual cleansing of preparation) and the Twelve by way of extension (having received authority to heal and cast out demons). In the second place, both ministries face opposition from worldly powers entrenched in a status quo that preserves their own (merely human) authority. The powers opposing John occupy the bulk of this passage, so they merit further explanation.

The impetus to kill John comes not from Herod but from his wife, Herodias, who resents the prophet's condemnation of their marriage (cf. 10:10-12). This condemnation may have led to John's arrest. Once John is in custody, however, Herod recognizes his holiness and enjoys listening to him. The ruler's fearful reverence keeps the prophet alive. To eliminate John, Herodias manipulates her husband's self-serving tendencies at his own birthday banquet, a high-profile affair intended to enhance his reputation as powerful tetrarch. There is a strong interpretive tradition that reads sexual innuendo into this scene—as if women could only exert influence by means of sexual temptation, as if a manly pleasure could only be erotic. And so we assume that Herodias has planned everything out. But we arrive at this interpretation largely through our presuppositions about women and men. The text suggests neither that the mother orders the girl to dance nor that the mother demands to be consulted afterward. It seems more likely that Herod becomes enraptured by the innocent beauty of his own daughter, that he delights in the thought of her one day ruling in his stead, and that he makes a promise to that effect. The promise is rash (if not also unrealistic for a first-century female) and is clearly worded too openly. Herod thinks in terms of territory (v. 23), but the phrase "whatever you wish" (v. 22) gives Herodias the opening she needs once the daughter approaches her. The life of the Baptizer was not what Herod had in mind. Yet he is bound by his word before an audience of public officials. He can keep that word and display his power (and what better way to display power than to kill a nobody?), or he can negotiate with a girl in order to spare the life of a nobody. The choice is tragically easy. "Out of regard for his oaths and for his guests" (v. 26), Herod suppresses his grief to save his public "self." His self-aggrandizing cares (see 4:19!) lead to a gruesome (but politically beneficial) final course to the banquet: John's head on a platter. Ironically, when the flashback ends, the Twelve surround Jesus in the desert (not a palace), where Jesus will selflessly feed a large crowd of nobodies. No fancy platters required.

While the Twelve parallel John both in their participation in Jesus' ministry and in the opposition they meet in response to that ministry, Mark does not explicitly narrate any opposition to the Twelve in this passage. In fact, the passage is bracketed by apostolic success (vv. 13, 30). It is precisely the flashback—the martyrdom of John—that suggests the parallel. Mark recalls John's martyrdom here, while the Twelve extend God's reign, in order to "warn" his audience (both ancient and modern) about the inevitable consequences of following Jesus. Jesus later spells out those consequences on his way to Jerusalem: "Those who want to save their life will lose it, and those who lose their life for my sake, and for the sake of the gospel, will save it" (8:34-35; see also 9:33-37; 10:42-45).

With the battle lines so clearly drawn, we easily identify with John and the Twelve in their support of Jesus. There is nothing wrong with that. But keep in mind the relative complexity of Herod's character: there is an opening for the message of John to enter, but it is closed off by the ungodly desire to preserve his own "self" vis-à-vis God. Likewise, the apostles (especially in Mark) do not truly fulfill their calling until they have fallen victim to the same desire for self-preservation—in their case by abandoning Jesus (14:50). The battle lines are blurrier than they might first appear. Mark shows us our own inclinations toward self-preservation and Jesus' power to fashion our *true* selves under the gracious and merciful reign of the Creator. The narrative encourages us to identify with Herod even as we define ourselves as disciples. For preaching purposes, that requires a precise naming of the worldly desires that kill us, a clear call to lose the so-called life fabricated by those desires, a bold embracing of the potentially violent consequences that await Jesus' followers, and a joyful proclamation that, in facing those consequences, we really do find life. For unlike John, Jesus' corpse is nowhere to be found.

Mark 6:7-13 (LFM)

When interpreted in its immediate context, this passage repeats an important Markan pattern: opposition to Jesus followed by the further extension of Jesus' ministry. The pattern first surfaces at Mark 3:1-19, when a public challenge from Pharisees about the sabbath law, culminating in a conspiracy to kill Jesus (3:6), segues into Jesus' boldly spreading God's reign into Gentile regions and then appointing twelve apostles to extend his ministry even further. The sower parable (4:1-10) tells the same basic story: despite various obstacles to seeds taking root, some seed does find good earth, and from it grows a disproportionately grand harvest. The pattern implicitly assures us that no opposition to the reign of God, however substantial, will ultimately prove successful.

This week's reading falls within the same pattern. Jesus has just met opposition from his own hometown (6:1-6; see last week's Gospel reading, above). Yet it is precisely at this point that he chooses to dispatch the Twelve (evidently waiting in the wings since 3:14-19). At a moment of heightened conflict they will expand the mission through a message of repentance, exorcisms, and healings (vv. 7, 12-13). None of them have any basis for claiming this as "my" ministry, for they all participate in *Jesus'* ministry, having received *Jesus'* authority. They are dispatched in different directions, but the geographical distance in no way lessens the common fellowship centered around Jesus and on behalf of God's reign. Because it is truly a reign of *shalom*—wholeness—it is not to be partitioned into various apostolic pieces. Appropriately, Jesus arranges them in pairs so as to preclude such partitioning and to prevent isolation, sustaining the fellowship they have enjoyed as a larger group.

Jesus also retains the ministry's current ascetic form, lest "the cares of the world . . . choke the word, and it yields nothing" (4:19). The danger here pertains not only to the apostles but to the ones they will encounter, since the priorities of the minister inform the priorities of the ministered. Because the reign of God seeks the restoration of creation and, therefore, the well-being of all creatures, the apostles must strip themselves of all self-promotion. They extend God's reign, not their own personalities or agendas. So only the essentials: sandals, one tunic, and a staff. No bread, bag, or money. They rely on the hospitality of others, particularly those who prove open to God's *shalom* (cf. 2:13-17; 15:40-41). If an entire village proves inhospitable, they will shake off the dust from their sandals to symbolize the burning of the bridge. This implies both shame and judgment.

I doubt this asceticism is drastically different from "normal" life on the road with Jesus. It is more like a reinforcing of that arrangement for the purpose of extending Jesus' ministry. In bringing God's reign, Jesus takes the form of a servant, bringing wholeness to the broken, freeing creation from a demonic stranglehold. The Son of Man came not to be served but to serve (10:45). To extend Jesus' self-giving means to give one's own self on behalf of Jesus. Christian discipleship is a cooperative affair, not only in terms of our trusting openness to his healing, but also in terms of our evangelism in the world.

The mission of the Twelve proves effective (vv. 7, 30). It is a fleeting but important glimpse into what the future holds for them, especially given their impending struggles to understand the *extent* of Jesus' self-giving . . . unto death. Later on, Jesus promises the continuation of their mission: "They will hand you over to councils; and you will be beaten in synagogues; and you will stand before governors and kings because of me, as a testimony to them. And the good news must first be proclaimed to all nations" (13:9-10). It is the same pattern writ large: even the crucifixion of the Messiah cannot slow his ministry. The harvest of God's reign is ensured.

July 22, 2012
Lectionary 16 / Sixteenth Sunday in Ordinary Time / Proper 11
Eighth Sunday after Pentecost

Revised Common Lectionary (RCL)

Jeremiah 23:1-6 or 2 Samuel 7:1-14a

Psalm 23 or 89:20-37

Ephesians 2:11-22

Mark 6:30-34, 53-56

Lectionary for Mass (LFM)

Jeremiah 23:1-6

Psalm 23:1-3a, 3b-4, 5, 6

Ephesians 2:13-18

Mark 6:30-34

First Reading
Jeremiah 23:1-6 (RCL, LFM)

The prophet Jeremiah ministered in Judah during the time of the Babylonian crisis (sixth century BCE). He condemned Judah's idolatry and social injustices, predicted its conquest and exile into Babylon, yet also assured it of a merciful restoration after the days of punishment. In many respects this week's reading encapsulates that message in all its variety. We find a denunciation of transgressions and a vow of punishment; but we also find a promise of "gathering" those who have been scattered (v. 3). As is usually the case with the Old Testament prophets, restoration, not punishment, is the final word.

What distinguishes this passage is its clear focus on the leaders of Judah. Jeremiah attributes the transgressions of the sheep to the folly of the shepherds. In this sense the shepherds are to blame for the exile itself: "It is you [emphasized in the Hebrew] who have scattered my flock, and have driven them away, and you have not attended [Heb.: *faqad*] to them. So I will attend [Heb.: *faqad*] to you for your evil doings" (v. 2). The promised restoration is the gathering, as well as the flourishing, of the scattered sheep under new shepherds (vv. 3-4). In verses 5-6 Jeremiah grounds his hope for restoration in God's faithfulness to the house of David, a common theme in the prophets and historical books (based on 2 Samuel 7:8-16).

Jesus was not encountering a new problem when he saw that the crowds were like sheep without a shepherd (Mark 6:34; see below); and we would be lying if we claimed that the problem has gone away with the advent of Christianity. This week's arrangement of lectionary texts encourages us to see Jesus as both the true Shepherd who gathers his sheep under his care, instructing and nourishing them, as well the righteous Branch of David who reigns with wisdom and justice, for the good of our salvation.

This passage should elicit in church leaders an awed appreciation of their calling as shepherds of *God's* sheep (not their own sheep). It is also, more importantly, an opportunity for congregations to hear that *they are God's sheep*. Sheep do not naturally cohere or travel uniformly without a wise and attentive shepherd. Likewise we are, apart from God's own prodding and guidance, inclined to move in our own individual directions, and this under the assumption that our freedom lies apart from the group. Jeremiah reminds us that our communion as God's flock hardly means submitting to a "herd mentality." Quite the opposite, it is our returning home, to the place of flourishing. Spend some time thinking about all the different "directions" in which Christians are pulled away from God and each other, not only by society but also the church. Against that disorienting and anxiety-producing backdrop, affirm that as God's sheep we are never wandering aimlessly but always exactly where we are supposed to be (no matter where we are!). The Christian pilgrimage is a labyrinth, not a maze.

2 Samuel 7:1-14a (RCL alt.)

In keeping with his religious priorities in elevating God's presence among the people, David wishes to build a temple for God (recall that the ark of the covenant represents God's presence). In David's view, it is not proper for the ark to remain in a tent—tattered from its wilderness journey and holy wars—while the king lives in a strong and magnificent house of cedar. We must empathize with David's desire to "magnify the LORD" in this regard. We must also admit that God does, in fact, implicitly concede David's point, albeit for the next generation: it is David's son Solomon who will build the temple (v. 13; see 1 Kings 5–8). It is easy to interpret God's retort (vv. 4-7) as meaning that David has his priorities all wrong; and of course it is true that God does not "need" a magnificent temple. God is still God even in the old, worn-out tabernacle. But the real debate is not over the *what* but the *when*. For David to build the temple is not in keeping with God's timing. The covenant with David must precede the temple. While we are not explicitly told why this is the case (perhaps it is simply the writer making sense of historical facts), I am inclined to say that God's order, as opposed to David's, better accentuates the priority of divine grace in Israel's covenant relationship. For the temple to precede the Davidic covenant could easily suggest that God had rewarded David. As it is, however, God pledges faithfulness to David first, while Solomon constructs the temple in response to that covenant (1 Kgs. 8:22-26). Thus, in a play on the Hebrew word *bet* ("house"), God promises to build a house for David rather than David building a house for God (v. 12). That is, God will secure the royal *household* of David, giving him a son and therefore a dynasty for future generations: "I will establish the throne of his kingdom forever" (v. 13; see also v. 16; 1 Kgs. 8:25). This is the very covenant that gives Israel hope in times of destruction and exile (e.g., Isa. 55:3-5; Jer. 23:5-8), and it is of course a significant component in the church's interpretation of Jesus as a Davidic Messiah. Christianity will have to reinterpret, in light of Christ, the Old Testament's tendency to associate prosperity with obedience/reward and misfortune with disobedience/punishment; but it will find in the Davidic covenant (as with the Abrahamic covenant) a concept around which it can orient itself, namely divine faithfulness. God remains true to God's own promises. Well beyond the return from Babylonian exile, the salvation graciously bestowed in the person of Jesus marks—in an ultimate sense—God's faithfulness to the Davidic covenant.

Psalmody
Psalm 23 (RCL)
Psalm 23:1-3a, 3b-4, 5, 6 (LFM)

The first four verses of this well-known psalm depict God as the trustworthy Shepherd, guiding the speaker (the sheep) to restful pastures and restorative waters, leading her down right paths both for her own well-being and "for his name's sake" (v. 3). Because of this trustworthiness, the sheep does not need to fear, even when traversing the most dangerous and frightening of terrains. The staff of the LORD comforts. It does not threaten.

Verses 5-6 shift the metaphor, casting God as the gracious host who provides shelter from the speaker's enemies. The shelter is at once the place of feasting, with God treating the speaker as the guest of honor. Even more, this shelter, with its bountiful feast, does not end: "I shall dwell in the house of the LORD my whole life long" (v. 6).

Both metaphors (shepherd and host) emphasize God's constant, benevolent provision and protection. The psalm functions as an elaboration upon Jeremiah's promise of good shepherds—to be a good shepherd is to emulate the divine Shepherd. When coupled with this week's Gospel reading, it is, more specifically, a christological elaboration, as Jesus himself emulates the divine Shepherd (cf. John 10:1-21).

Psalm 89:20-37 (RCL alt.)

These selected verses reiterate the main theme of the semicontinuous Old Testament reading (2 Sam. 7:1-14a), in which God promises David a perpetual royal lineage: "I will establish his line forever, and his throne as long as the heavens endure" (v. 29). This reading, however, gives a fuller description of the "Davidic covenant," taking into account the possibility of Davidic kings disobeying God (corresponding to 2 Sam. 7:14b-15, verses omitted from the Old Testament reading). In those circumstances the kings will receive the necessary punishment, but the disobedience will not be grounds for divine rejection. "Forever I will keep my steadfast love for him" (v. 28). (See my comments on the RCL alternative first reading, 2 Sam. 7:1-4a, above.)

Second Reading
Ephesians 2:11-22 (RCL)
Ephesians 2:13-18 (LFM)

Last week's reading from Ephesians emphasized how the salvation of the Gentiles does not imply change in the divine will for humanity. However, with respect to the Gentile religious experience—not to mention human history in general—there is certainly a radical change. One can imagine a Gentile convert, familiar with the basics of the Christian gospel but still quite accustomed to pagan traditions, thinking: "What have I gotten myself into?" Paul's answer, stated simply, is "one new humanity" (v. 15). Being a Christian is not strictly a matter of one's individual life. It is grander than any particular Christian community or local culture. It is nothing short of God's will for all humans, the transcending (but without the abolishing) of contingent cultural differences through a common, unifying participation in the "one body" (v. 16) of Christ.

As with Christians today, it would have been difficult for ancient believers, separated by vast geographical space and innumerable cultural differences, to conceive of "the church" beyond their local gatherings. For pagan converts in particular, it would have been difficult to conceive of their religious experience—indeed their salvation—communally, and not simply individually. It might also have seemed to them like they had joined a "new" religious movement. Paul corrects these misconceptions in just a few powerful sentences.

In the first place, he clarifies that Gentile converts have not joined some new community. Perhaps there had been no Christian "church" in the entire world until recently; but the church has its roots in ancient covenants established within "the commonwealth of Israel" (v. 12). Gentiles have come to know promises to which they had previously been strangers. Being once "far off," they have now been "brought near" through the flesh of Christ (v. 13). That is, they have been brought into communion with the one Creator whom they did not previously know.

Moreover, the Gentiles' reconciled communion with God includes their reconciled communion with the original covenant people. From the Jewish perspective, humanity consisted of the chosen people of Israel, on the one hand, and all the other "nations," the Gentiles, on the other hand. There was a built-in "hostility" (v. 14) to this arrangement insofar as the ritual commandments of the Torah created various degrees of separation from Gentiles. Verse 11 summarizes this separation in the way it contrasts "the uncircumcision" (Gentiles) with "the circumcision" (Jews). However, through the flesh of Christ God draws both groups into a single communion—"he is our peace" (v. 14)—resulting in the abolishment of those particular "commandments and ordinances" that had previously separated them (vv. 15-16). In fact, the implication of verse 18 is that even the Jews, while previously much "nearer" to God than the Gentiles, did not have the kind of "access" now available through the one Spirit of Christ.

It is easy to reduce the "one holy catholic church" to our merely agreeing to a specific set of doctrines or moral agendas. Paul insists that the church is more real than that. It is nothing short of a divine act. It is God who "builds" the single "household" upon the "foundation of the apostles and prophets," with Christ as the "cornerstone" (v. 20). It is in Christ, God's own historical self-emptying (Phil. 2:6-8), and not in our own whimsical consensus, that we are "joined together" into one "holy temple . . . a dwelling place for God" (vv. 21-22). In the life of the church, even within single parishes, we find innumerable reasons to disagree. Apart from our common fellowship with Christ, we are inclined to foster division and hostility rather than peace. Ephesians points us to single, unifying divine will for the salvation of humanity. More specifically, it points us to a single, unifying Messiah in whom all of humanity is saved. It does not say that we will always agree about everything, but it does remind us that God has *already* joined us together and *continues* to hold us together. Christ is our fundamental peace.

Gospel
Mark 6:30-34, 53-56 (RCL)
Mark 6:30-34 (LFM)

The RCL skips a great deal of text. The opening verse of this passage concludes the mission of the Twelve (6:7-13), while verses 31-34 set the stage for Jesus' feeding the five thousand in the wilderness (6:35-44). Jesus and the disciples then venture across the lake, where Jesus walks on the water (vv. 45-52). The RCL picks up the narrative at verses 53-56, which summarize Jesus' ministry in Gennesaret.

The gathering of the Twelve around Jesus reminds us that their journeys have been part of a single ministry—Jesus' ministry—that spreads God's healing reign for the restoration of creation. There are no grounds, in other words, for anyone to speak in terms of "my" ministry. We are also reminded of their initial appointment, which included not only the imparting of authority to preach and exorcize but also the expectation that they would "be with him" (3:14). So while Jesus regularly seeks prayerful isolation (1:35; 6:46; 14:32-42), he never separates himself from the ongoing fellowship of disciples. The healing of creation requires the participation of creatures, and in this sense even the Messiah cannot go it alone.

Nor can the Twelve go it alone. Since the ministry depends on their sharing in the authority of Jesus (3:15; 6:7), it also depends on their continued fellowship with Jesus. That is why Jesus takes them into the wilderness on a kind of apostolic retreat: "Come away to a deserted place all by yourselves and rest awhile." Why? Because "many were coming and going, and they had no leisure even to eat" (v. 31). Pastors can easily identify with the need to get away from the demands of ministry, recovering personal sanity through solitude (or any temporary fleeing from the parish "crowds"). Sometimes—regularly—the cell phone must be turned off, the laptop closed, and the office door shut. Sometimes even a nice vacation is in order. But note that in fleeing the crowds the disciples never separate themselves from the Master. The phrase "by yourselves" (literally "alone," *kat' idian*) does not mean "without Jesus." The point is that doing Christ's work requires one's personal fellowship with Christ and that this personal fellowship requires deliberate acts of cultivating friendship quite apart from the "work" itself.

At the same time, insofar as all Christians are called to be ministers, we must also interpret the apostolic retreat in terms of the church itself. This affords preachers the opportunity to identify all the reasons (both good and bad) that congregants go to church and to center those reasons around a single purpose: fellowship with one Lord. For Mark, and for the Christian tradition in general, discipleship is not about getting into heaven, mechanistically obeying God ("just because" God commanded), or even learning the Bible. It is about realizing the very purpose of our existence—communing with God through a communion with God's Son (cf. John 15:1-17). For too many Christians the demands of work and family weigh so heavily that the deliberate cultivation of friendship with Jesus seems like extra "work," when in fact that friendship (whether cultivated in solitude or among others) lightens those demands by putting them in the right perspective. The deeper the friendship with Jesus, the lighter the weight of the world: "Come to me, all you that are weary and are carrying heavy burdens, and I will give you rest. Take my yoke upon you, and learn from me; for I am gentle and humble in heart, and you will find rest for your souls" (Matt. 11:28-29). In this friendship we are healed.

Likewise, in this friendship we are empowered to heal. Obedience does not open the door to communion with Christ. Rather, the communion fosters obedience, inspiring us ("in-spiriting" us) to love as God loves—indeed, as God is. Note that when the crowds arrive, abruptly ending the retreat, the fellowship turns outward in compassion toward them (vv. 35-44). Never mind that the Twelve struggle to anticipate Jesus' miraculous actions. Jesus still employs them to feed those who "were like sheep without a shepherd" (v. 34). Apart from the guidance of Jesus, the people would have been sent away hungry, having heard Jesus' wisdom in the abstract, but without receiving the physical, material love that necessarily complements that wisdom. Without some mention of the feeding, the preacher risks distorting the holistic nature of Jesus' shepherdly provision.

The summary in 6:53-56 continues this theme of compassionate shepherding. Like other summaries (1:32-34, 39; 3:7-12; 6:12-13), it encapsulates the nature of Jesus' public ministry.

Time after Pentecost / Ordinary Time
Lectionary 17 / Proper 12 through Lectionary 26 / Proper 21

Susan E. Hylen

It is midsummer, and the pews are filled with familiar faces. A number of people are away on vacation, and a few others are visiting from out of town. But by and large, those who gather for worship are "the regulars." Most of them were present for Christmas, Easter, and Pentecost. Many can recite the Apostles' Creed and the Lord's Prayer and Psalm 23. Yet knowing about Jesus and living as his followers are two different things. After the din of Easter alleluias and the rushing wind of Pentecost die down, those who remain are left with the mundane and difficult task of understanding this faith and putting it into action.

The Time after Pentecost, often called Ordinary Time, is a time to reflect on the daily difficulties of discipleship. The lectionary passages of the ninth through eighteenth Sundays after Pentecost, provide a fertile ground for cultivating knowledge of God and reflection on how that knowledge should shape the life of the individual and the life of the church. The first set of Gospel lessons is from John 6, one long story parceled out over the course of five Sundays. John tells of Jesus' miraculous feeding of the crowd and their refusal to accept his words, and he does so in a way that evokes the story of the Israelites in the wilderness. This crowd is like the Israelites: they murmur, though they have seen what God has done. Without losing the exodus connections, the preacher may also choose to tell this story as the story of every disciple. Those who follow Jesus do so because they have experienced the wonders he has done. Yet even those who have seen such signs struggle to understand them and to let the claim of Jesus' teachings bear fruit in their lives.

The second set of Gospel readings comes from the central chapters of Mark. They are stories of Jesus' miracles, and also of the disciples' resistance to Jesus' teaching about the true nature of his mission. As in the Gospel of John, the disciples and others who follow have experienced his great acts of power. Yet Jesus' claims about his own identity—and the way that identity should be reflected in the lives of his followers—are difficult for the disciples to grasp.

The Old Testament texts paired with the Gospel lessons provide a context for Jesus' acts. In them, the reader sees acts of healing and provision, prophetic vision, and conflict with worldly powers. All of these are similar to what we see in Jesus. Yet these are powerful stories and are worth preaching in their own right, for they establish the long tradition of God's healing power and communication through prophets. It is this same tradition that allowed the early Christians to recognize Jesus as one who came from God and who spoke God's word. The echoes we hear of these Old Testament stories in the Gospel lessons are a reminder of the endurance of the love of God, and of human resistance to it.

The semicontinuous Old Testament texts of the Revised Common Lectionary provide their own rich source of discipleship stories. They begin with the story of David's sin and its aftermath, the continuation of the Davidic line in Solomon, and the establishment of the temple. This is a story of the faithfulness of God, whose promises to David are fulfilled despite his own failings. The later group of semicontinuous texts focuses on the teachings of Wisdom. Wisdom calls out to all who would hear, inviting them to a life of abundance. Yet her teachings are difficult and many turn to other paths.

The epistle lessons, from Ephesians and James, bring insight to specific problems disciples encounter as they seek to live out the gospel. Some of these are the difficulties of a diverse group seeking to live together. Others are individual questions of faithful action and practice. In each case, the letters show the way some early Christians understood the transformation of life in Christ, and the roadblocks they identified along the way.

Although these passages will be familiar to many, the church returns to them again and again because cultivating the wisdom of these texts is a process much more difficult than simply learning the characters and events. Like the crowd of followers in the Gospel stories, the listener knows something already about Jesus—that is, that he gives bread (John 6:34) or that he is the Messiah (Mark 8:29). Yet allowing one's life to be shaped by this knowledge is a lifelong process.

The texts of Ordinary Time provide the preacher a way of engaging and addressing this process. Too often contemporary worship can project a picture of "the regulars" as people who have no problems: their faith established, they apparently have everything together, with no physical or spiritual needs. Prayers are offered for "others" as if no one present is lonely, sick, or grieving. The biblical texts for these Sundays make no room for this picture of Christian life. The Israelites' murmuring in the wilderness, David's adultery and murder, Jesus' rejection by those closest to him: repeatedly, the faithful misunderstand God and turn away.

Yet this does not make them any less a people chosen by God. A common theological mistake presents discipleship as an all-or-nothing affair. Those who are outside the church have no hope, while those who are in already exhibit the flourishing of the kingdom of God. The passages of this portion of the lectionary offer a different picture, one that is at once more difficult and more hopeful than the all-or-nothing approach. It is difficult because it requires believers to confront their continued inability to live as God asks. They have both knowledge and faith. Yet in big and small ways, they struggle to act in ways that manifest that knowledge and faith. Although acknowledging the sinful reality of human life is difficult, these passages also offer hope because they claim God's love and salvation even for such as these.

Preaching in Ordinary Time is a means of cultivating a tree, like the tree of Psalm 1:3. Planted next to the word of God, its roots reach down a little further each year. As a result of this nourishment, the tree grows, weathers difficult times, and bears fruit.

July 29, 2012
Lectionary 17 / Seventeenth Sunday in Ordinary Time / Proper 12
Ninth Sunday after Pentecost

Revised Common Lectionary (RCL)
2 Kings 4:42-44 or 2 Samuel 11:1-15
Psalm 145:10-18 or Psalm 14
Ephesians 3:14-21
John 6:1-21

Lectionary for Mass (LFM)
2 Kings 4:42-44
Psalm 145:10-11, 15-16, 17-18
Ephesians 4:1-6
John 6:1-15

First Reading
2 Kings 4:42-44 (RCL, LFM)

In 2 Kings 4, Elisha performs a series of miracles. The last, verses 42-44, involves a provision of food from seemingly small resources. Elisha's actions here echo those of Elijah, who provided meal and oil to the widow of Zarephath according to the word of the Lord (1 Kgs. 17:8-16). Both prophets display the power of God for the sake of those in need.

Central to this miracle is the prophet's ability to communicate God's word. Elisha repeats his instructions to his doubting servant, followed by an oracle of God: "They shall eat and have some left" (v. 43). The narration is brief, but the repetition of the same words, "They ate, and had some left" (v. 44), suggests that events proceed exactly as Elisha has indicated in his communication of God's word. The story emphasizes the prophet's power in understanding the divine will.

The Gospel story for this Sunday echoes the Elisha passage: food is provided from an outside source, others question its adequacy, yet there is much left over. Yet Elisha's story is not simply a precursor of Jesus' acts, but has meaning in its own right. God's faithfulness and care for God's people are seen in the abundant provision of bread in each of these stories. The prophets were God's messengers regarding this abundance, and thus it is not surprising to find the Gospel authors drawing on this tradition to characterize Jesus as one sent by God to perform signs of God's power and care for humankind.

2 Samuel 11:1-15 (RCL alt.)

This is a powerful and well-known story of David's decision to take another man's wife. Although many interpreters have placed blame on Bathsheba, the author tells the story from beginning to end as one of David's poor choices. From the outset, David does not go out to battle himself, as kings are expected to do. The opening of the story sets the scene in "the spring of the year, the time when kings go out to battle." Yet David "remained at Jerusalem" (v. 1). He does not fulfill the expected kingly role but sends others in his place while he enjoys the luxuries of home. Overwhelmed by his desire for Bathsheba, he sends messengers to get her and lies with her (v. 4). Bathsheba conceives (v. 5).[1]

Finally, David sets an elaborate trap to cover up his actions. He brings Uriah home, expecting him to have sex with Bathsheba and thus legitimize her pregnancy. Yet Uriah the Hittite proves himself more faithful than God's anointed, David. He refuses sex with his wife (v. 9), even after David plots to get him drunk (v. 13). Uriah proclaims his loyalty to the ark, Israel, and Judah, underscoring the contrast with David's own treachery (v. 11). When David's trap fails, he plots to kill Uriah (vv. 14-15).

David's story is a rich entry point into the depth of human sin. His acts reflect a degree of intentional plotting to do evil, and they also underscore the way that sin can become a trap from which it is difficult to escape. David's initial choice leads to abominable acts. Yet in all this, David remains God's chosen king. His sin does not invalidate God's anointing but exists in tension alongside the expectations of one who has received the spirit of the Lord (1 Sam. 16:13). David's story presents a challenge to our modern tendency to categorize others (and ourselves) as good and bad, deserving and undeserving.

Psalmody
Psalm 145:10-18 (RCL)
Psalm 145:10-11, 15-16, 17-18 (LFM)

This psalm speaks eloquently of the power and goodness of God. God is portrayed as a powerful king (vv. 11-13) who graciously supplies for the needs of his subjects. The king satisfies physical needs (vv. 15-16), judges rightly (v. 18; cf. v. 20), and saves those in distress (v. 14; cf. v. 19). God is faithful and righteous (v. 13b), just and kind (v. 17).

As a result of the identity of God, the faithful proclaim God's goodness to the whole world. The language of the psalm implies that God's goodness exists independent of human experience (v. 13), yet it becomes known within the realm of human experience. God intervenes in human affairs, acting to protect the vulnerable and to provide for human needs. Those who experience such goodness proclaim it to others. God's protection and nurture of the people are the basis for praising God, praise that echoes out to "all flesh" (v. 21).

Psalm 14 (RCL alt.)

The psalm introduces a tension by expressing two differing views of humanity. One affirms that all people fail to recognize the implications of God's lordship: "There is no one who does good, no, not one" (v. 3). Although the opening line identifies those who deny God as fools (Heb.: *nabal*, v. 1), the remainder of the verse underscores that these fools are not a small group of unwise people, but all people. By failing to "do good" (v. 1), humans display denial of God. Such actions convey the belief that God is absent or powerless, and will not respond to unrighteous deeds.[2]

However, the closing verses (vv. 5-7) identify some—the "righteous" (v. 5) and the "poor" (v. 6)—as separate from the evildoers and protected by God. God promises deliverance and restoration to those who suffer from the "abominable deeds" (v. 1) of others. Here, the lowly appear to be a distinct group from the evildoers, and the evildoers do not comprise all of humanity.[3]

The tension may be viewed as theologically productive. The psalmist addresses the tendency of all people to act as if we exist independent of God's righteousness and mercy. At the same time, God's promise of restoration is for those who are harmed by the abominable acts that proceed from this worldview. The psalm serves as a reminder that "God is with the company of the righteous" (v. 5), that God is the refuge of the poor (v. 6). The wise will shape their actions to this foundational reality.

Second Reading
Ephesians 3:14-21 (RCL)
Ephesians 4:1-6 (LFM)

Both passages are a hinge between the theological framework of Ephesians (chaps. 1–3) and the exhortations for behavior (chaps. 4–6). The opening words in each case, "for this reason" (3:14) and "therefore" (4:1), provide the causal link between the two sections of the letter. The work of reconciliation, which God has accomplished through Christ by putting to death the hostility between Jews and Gentiles (cf. 2:13-18), is the foundation for the teachings regarding the Christian life.

The combination of Jew and Gentile within one body that shared religious practices was a difficult step, as many of the New Testament writings attest. The church today faces similar challenges in gathering together across divisions of race, sexuality, class, and gender to worship and share in the Lord's Supper. The language of Ephesians is a useful reminder that the various differences within churches do not disappear as a result of God's reconciliation. Instead, the author sees the diversity within the church as a manifestation of the "wisdom of God in its rich variety" (3:10). The church's struggle to bear with one another may lead to greater comprehension of God's wisdom through the encounter of differences that are not erased by Christian unity.

In 3:14-21 Paul prays that God may enable the church to grasp the depth of what God has accomplished in Christ. He makes two parallel petitions: that "you may be strengthened in your inner being with power through his Spirit" (v. 16), and that "Christ may dwell in your hearts through faith" (v. 17). Both phrases suggest an inner transformation enabled by both God's Spirit and the believer's faith. The result of the transformation is comprehension of the magnitude of the love of Christ and the fullness of God (vv. 18-19).

Ephesians 4:1-6 emphasizes the unity God has brought about through reconciliation. Hearers should respond to this message with humility, patience, and love (v. 2), making an effort to maintain unity. Since God has shown grace and kindness (2:4-9), creating one new humanity (2:14-16), humans must make an effort to maintain this unity. The word *one* appears six times in verses 4-6, and the word *all* appears four times, underscoring the call to understand the complex church as one unified body. Such unity is maintained intentionally by "bearing with one another" and "making an effort" (vv. 2-3).

Gospel
John 6:1-21 (RCL)
John 6:1-15 (LFM)

The feeding of the five thousand is the only miracle story told in all four Gospels. John shapes the story in such a way that the feeding miracle evokes the exodus from Egypt as an act of God's liberating and transforming power.

John sets the story at the time of the festival of Passover (6:4). John is alone among the Gospels in narrating more than one Passover festival within the story of Jesus' ministry. He uses the festivals as a backdrop against which the reader may understand events that follow (cf. 2:13; 7:2; 13:1; 19:42). The arc of the narrative in John 6 reinforces the invocation of Passover: first there is a miraculous meal (vv. 1-14; cf. Exodus 12), followed by an experience of God's power during a sea crossing (vv. 16-21; cf. Exodus 14), followed by a conversation about manna (vv. 31-58; cf. Exodus 16). The explicit allusion to Passover and the repeated elements of the exodus story suggest that John wants the reader to interpret the events of Jesus' life in light of the exodus story.

John characterizes Jesus as Moses through the explicit allusion to Passover and a number of other clues. The crowd follows Jesus because of his "signs" (v. 2; cf. v. 14). The same word identifies Moses' acts to convince Pharaoh to let God's people go (e.g., Exod. 4:8-9; 8:23; 10:1). The location of the story on a mountain (vv. 3, 15) evokes Moses' association with Mount Sinai (e.g., Exod. 19:12, 14; 24:1-2; 32:1; 34:2-4). Finally, for John's audience, the crowd's identification of Jesus as "the prophet who is to come into the world" would likely have brought Moses to mind. Understanding Moses as a prophet was common in Jewish tradition of the time. Some messianic expectations drew on the idea of a "prophet like Moses" (cf. Deut. 18:18) who would speak God's word and lead the people into the eschatological age. John's language of the "prophet who is to come into the world" (v. 14) shares this eschatological tone.

Although these Old Testament echoes may appear faint to the modern reader, Moses was such a well-known and highly discussed figure in Jewish antiquity that it is likely John's first readers would recognize Moses in these verses.

The sea-crossing story (vv. 16-21, RCL) continues the exodus theme, although Moses fades from view. Here Jesus takes on qualities of God, whose power became visible in the Red Sea crossing. Unlike in the Synoptic Gospels, Jesus' disciples do not mistake him for a ghost (cf. Matt. 14:26; Mark 6:49). Instead, "they saw Jesus walking on the sea" (v. 19). In the context of the Synoptic accounts, Jesus' words, *egō eimi*, are appropriately translated "It is I." That is, Jesus reassures his disciples that he is real and not a ghost. However, John's use of these Greek words suggests more is at stake. The words still retain the more mundane meaning "It is I," yet at the same time they recall the divine name, "I AM" (Exod. 3:14). Placing the divine name on the lips of Jesus suggests that John tells this story as a theophany: the disciples see and experience God. The disciples' terror (v. 19) and Jesus' reassurance ("Do not be afraid," v. 20) are conventional elements of theophany stories (e.g., Luke 1:12-13, 30).[4] Jesus exhibits the same power the Israelites knew in the God of the exodus.

Framed in this way, the feeding of the five thousand is told as a story that exhibits God's salvific power displayed in the Passover meal and delivery from Egypt. The exodus imagery is extended in the conversation that follows, especially verses 30-58 (see the entries below for the Tenth, Eleventh, and Twelfth Sundays after Pentecost). John portrays Jesus first as taking on elements of Moses' role in the exodus, and then as taking on elements of God's role.

It is tempting for modern readers to diminish the relationship between Jesus and Moses because the metaphor of Jesus as God corresponds to our notions of orthodox faith. It may help when reading the Gospel to think of John as using resources available to him from Jewish tradition to articulate different aspects of Jesus' identity. Jesus is clearly a multifaceted and complex character, and John is one of the first Christians to attempt to synthesize his understanding of Jesus. That John is unacquainted with creedal language (like that of the Apostles' Creed) is a resource for the contemporary preacher, because John gives us unique ways to think about Jesus' identity. Each element of John's characterization of Jesus may contribute something meaningful to the reader's understanding of Jesus.

Here Jesus is portrayed both as Moses and as God. Like Moses, Jesus is sent by God to perform miraculous signs. He is a prophet whose return ushers in the eschatological age. The connections to Moses shed light on some of Jesus' actions in the Gospel story and help the reader to understand their importance. John also likens Jesus to God, but that does not invalidate the ways Jesus is Moses. In fact, much of the Gospel's language is difficult to understand without the connection between Jesus and Moses.

John's portrayal of Jesus as God also provides meaningful content for the reader's understanding of Jesus. This is not simply a point of doctrine for John, identifying

Jesus as one person of the Trinity. Instead, John's use of the exodus story provides important content to help the reader understand the ways in which Jesus is God. Like God, Jesus has power over the waters. He frees humankind from slavery to sin (cf. John 8:34-36). John does not simply portray Jesus as a powerful heavenly being, but as the God who set Israel free.

A good approach to preaching John 6 is to invite the congregation to see themselves as the Israelites and to understand Jesus in the various roles he takes on: here, as Moses and as God (and, later in John 6, as manna). John's language is metaphorical, and thus the preacher's approach should also be metaphorical. The point is not to translate the metaphors to propositional language. That is, the idea is not to translate "Jesus is Moses" into "Jesus is a leader sent by God." Instead, these metaphors provide an opening for the preacher to step into John's worldview and see Jesus as John sees him. John creates a connection between Jesus and Moses and the preacher can explore the meaning of the metaphor without exhausting its possibilities. The congregation may come to see themselves as the Israelites to whom God, through Jesus, offers freedom from slavery.

Notes

1. See the discussion by Walter Brueggemann, *First and Second Samuel*, Interpretation: A Bible Commentary for Teaching and Preaching (Louisville: John Knox, 1990), 273.
2. See Patrick D. Miller, *Interpreting the Psalms* (Philadelphia: Fortress Press, 1986), 97.
3. For a discussion, see James Luther Mays, *Psalms*, Interpretation: A Bible Commentary for Teaching and Preaching (Louisville: John Knox, 1994), 81–82.
4. For further exploration of the theophany motif, see Gail R. O'Day, "John 6:15-21: Jesus Walking on Water as Narrative Embodiment of Johannine Christology," in *Critical Readings of John 6*, ed. R. Alan Culpepper, Biblical Interpretation Series 22 (Leiden: Brill, 1997), 149–59.

August 5, 2012
Lectionary 18 / Eighteenth Sunday in Ordinary Time / Proper 13
Tenth Sunday after Pentecost

Revised Common Lectionary (RCL)

Exodus 16:2-4, 9-15 or 2 Samuel
  11:26—12:13a
Psalm 78:23-29 or 51:1-12
Ephesians 4:1-16
John 6:24-35

Lectionary for Mass (LFM)

Exodus 16:2-4, 12-15

Psalm 78:3-4, 23-24, 25 + 54
Ephesians 4:17, 20-24
John 6:24-35

First Reading
Exodus 16:2-4, 9-15 (RCL)
Exodus 16:2-4, 12-15 (LFM)

The exodus out of Egypt is followed by rejoicing and belief (Exod. 14:31—15:21) that turns quickly to complaining and disbelief. An earlier complaint already occurred because of a lack of potable water (15:23-24), followed by the complaint about hunger in 16:2. The shift from rejoicing to complaining is abrupt and suggests a lack of real comprehension by the people. In the face of continuing adversity, they seem not to understand that the God who "triumphed gloriously" (15:1, 21) at the Red Sea still intends to care for and lead them. Instead, the people accuse Moses and Aaron: "You have brought us out into this wilderness to kill this whole assembly with hunger" (16:3).

God responds (v. 4) by providing manna for Israel during its forty-year sojourn in the wilderness (v. 35). God hears their complaining (vv. 9, 12) and sends both quail and manna. Manna was an unfamiliar substance that the Israelites discovered on the ground when the dew lifted. Their question in verse 15, "What is it?" (Heb.: *man hu*), is one explanation of the origin of the word *manna* (Heb.: *man*, v. 31).

The miracle of the manna is remembered as a story of God's abundant provision and care for God's people. The gift of "bread from heaven" is remembered in story and psalm (cf. Neh. 9:15; Pss. 78:24; 105:40; Wis. 16:20). In Jewish tradition, the manna also becomes an example of the importance of following God's command. The instructions for gathering the manna (vv. 16, 19, 23) are an essential part of the story: following God's commands resulted in being fed. As the story is told and retold, the manna becomes a lesson that God provides for those who attend to God's word (see Deut. 8:2-6).

2 Samuel 11:26—12:13a (RCL alt.)

The opening verses are a reminder of the previous story (see the discussion of 2 Sam. 11:1-15 in the Ninth Sunday after Pentecost, above). David has killed Uriah the Hittite to cover his adultery with Uriah's wife. He now takes Bathsheba and makes her his wife.

God views David's treachery as evil. Verse 27 literally reads, "The thing David did was evil in the eyes of the LORD." God communicates this through the prophet Nathan.

Nathan's parable allows David to reinterpret his actions and understand them as sinful. The poor man is Uriah; the lamb, Bathsheba. David is the rich man, who has wives already, yet takes from Uriah to satisfy his desires. The narration positions the reader to see the parallels clearly, but David is blind to the trap Nathan sets for him. He immediately sees the injustice of the poor man's situation, but he has not understood his own actions in this light.

The climax of the story is beautifully constructed, as David pronounces judgment upon the rich man, and thus upon himself. Nathan's denunciation of David is direct and places blame squarely on his shoulders. He has "despised the word of the LORD" (12:9).

Perhaps the only positive characteristic of David in this sequence comes with his response to Nathan. He immediately acknowledges his responsibility and the gravity of the situation. He states simply: "I have sinned against the LORD" (12:13). Previously, David worked hard to cover up the evidence of his deceit. Yet faced with this straightforward accusation, he admits his guilt.

A difficulty in preaching this story is allowing the congregation to experience what David experiences in coming to identify himself with Nathan's story. Many will not relate to the extremity of David's sin: adultery and murder. Yet the story conveys a human propensity to take from others in order to preserve one's own wealth. One strategy for preaching this passage would be to employ Nathan's tactic, developing a story that rings true to the hearers in which they can identify their own sinfulness before God.

Psalmody
Psalm 78:23-29 (RCL)
Psalm 78:3-4, 23-24, 25 + 54 (LCM)

Psalm 78 is a meditation on God's signs in the exodus story, Israel's rebellion, and God's anger and compassion. Verses 23-29 focus on the gift of manna and quail, and

God's continued response in spite of the people's faithlessness. God is angry because people do not trust God (v. 21). Nevertheless, God commands food to rain down (vv. 23-24) in response to their complaint.

The psalm retells Israel's early history as a parable (v. 2). The stories should be told and retold so that those who come later can learn not to be rebellious (vv. 1-8). Israel's complaints result from forgetting God's acts of power (v. 42), which thus should be recounted (vv. 12-16, 42-55). The lectionary verses emphasize an instance when God responded with compassion (see also vv. 38-39). The psalm also includes reference to God's punishment of Israel's rebellion (vv. 30-31, 58-64).

Psalm 51:1-12 (RCL alt.)

Tradition ascribes these words to David: "When the prophet Nathan came to him, after he had gone in to Bathsheba" (Psalm 51, inscription; vv. 1-2 Masoretic Text). Imagined in this way, the psalm is an apt companion for the first reading from 2 Samuel (RCL alt.). David's sin is grave. He has committed adultery and then murdered Uriah when he could not conceal the consequences. David's sin does not go unpunished, yet God ultimately forgives. The psalm expresses awareness of sin and the need for God's transforming grace.

Although appropriate to David's situation, the psalm expresses something of the common experience of human sinfulness and need for forgiveness. Because of this it is frequently used in corporate worship. Although David's story may prove a useful example of common traits of human sin, the preacher should prepare the hearer to identify herself or himself with the speaker of the psalm.

Second Reading
Ephesians 4:1-16 (RCL)

Earlier in the letter, the author established the metaphor of Christ as the head of his body, the church (1:22-23). God has reconciled Jews and Gentiles through the body of Christ on the cross (2:16), forming one group out of the two. The unity of the body is maintained with effort (4:3), however, and the remainder of the letter provides guidelines for maintaining unity. (For more on 4:1-6, see the second reading for the Ninth Sunday after Pentecost, above.)

The author understands church leadership as a gift from Christ, for the purpose of building up the body. Church leaders are not separate from the body but are part of it, and thus are included as part of the "all" that is growing to maturity (v. 13). All of the leadership functions that are mentioned in verse 11 are important for the growth of the body, and none is housed within one individual. Thus the metaphor of the body's growth is apt, as the whole body must grow together, with each part "working properly" (v. 16), or exercising the function that is uniquely its own.

The church is already the body of Christ (1:23; 4:4, 12), yet is also growing into this role. The metaphor creates a peculiar picture in that it presents the church as a body that does not yet fit its head, Christ: "We must grow up in every way into him who is the head, into Christ" (v. 15). The metaphor of Christ's body does not suggest perfect correspondence between Christ and the church. It expresses the unity of the church with Christ and the necessary leadership of Christ. Yet the church is still portrayed as a body striving for maturity.

Ephesians 4:17, 20-24 (LFM)

Believers are to seek the unity of the church (4:1-6) by attending to their own behavior. A transformation has occurred, one that necessitates a change from the former (Gentile) way of life to one oriented toward God.

The transformation began when the believer "learned Christ" (v. 20). The Greek conveys an intimate sense of learning directly from Christ. Verse 21 reads literally, "If indeed you heard him and were taught by him." The author is not speaking to people who experienced Christ directly during his life, but instead speaks metaphorically of the believer's conversion as hearing and learning directly from Christ.

The teachings of Christ are threefold: to lay aside former conduct, to be restored in the spirit of one's mind, and to clothe the new self in righteousness and holiness (vv. 22-24). The wording contrasts the "old self" (v. 22), corrupted by the deceit of passion, with the "new self" (v. 24), created in the likeness of God. The former self is already "old." Yet the believer must continue to reject the conduct associated with the old self. Likewise, the believer does not create the "new self"; God has already created it. Instead, the focus for action is on "clothing" the new self with behavior that reflects "true righteousness and holiness" (v. 24).

Gospel
John 6:24-35 (RCL, LFM)

These central verses of John 6 are important for understanding the whole chapter. The Scripture quotation in verses 30-31 introduces the story of the manna. John places the story of the manna and the story of Jesus in parallel, so that the reader may come to understand Jesus as manna.

There are two common mistakes made in interpreting this passage. One is to render a harsh verdict on the crowd's comprehension of Jesus' identity and purpose. The second is to contrast Jesus with the manna.

1. *John portrays the crowd in both negative and positive ways.* Jesus' words in verse 26 identify a problem: the crowd has not "seen signs," which is to say, they have not understood the meaning of Jesus' acts. Instead, they are simply impressed by the provision of bread and seek more of the same, focusing only on "food that perishes" (v. 27). The crowd's request for a sign so that they may believe (v. 30) underscores Jesus' point. They have not understood the signs that he has already done in their midst.

Yet the crowd understands a good deal about Jesus, and they eagerly pursue him and question him further. They understand enough to be curious about the mysterious sea crossing (vv. 24-25). Their questions in verses 28 and 30, and their citation of Scripture in verse 31, move the conversation forward, and their request for bread in verse 34 shows some real comprehension of what Jesus has said. They seem to accept that Jesus can provide them with "bread from heaven."

Recognizing the positive elements of John's portrayal of the crowd contributes to an understanding of one of John's unique contributions. Over the course of the chapter, John develops a connection between the crowd and the Israelites of the exodus story. These are the people who have seen what Jesus has done. They have experienced God's deliverance, yet they turn quickly to grumbling and disbelief (see the discussion of the first reading, above). Similarly, the crowd is not a wholly positive character, but neither is it wholly negative, and preachers would do well to maintain the richness of John's portrait.

Presenting the crowd as having both positive and negative elements can help prepare the reader to identify with the crowd. When the crowd only misunderstands, the reader has a tendency to distance herself from them, as one whom John has prepared to know better than the crowd. Yet if the crowd understands some important things about Jesus, the reader may begin to see herself in the portrayal of the crowd. Like the Israelites, they do not fully trust God, even though they have seen God's miraculous signs. The crowd needs the sustenance of God's provision of manna.

2. Most interpreters develop a contrast between Jesus and manna. They read the language of verse 32 as a rejection of Moses and his manna. For example, Rudolf Bultmann's influential reading of John saw the manna as a symbol of false expectations for the Messiah. Jesus "rejects the deluded view of the Jews that the bread once given by Moses could be the true 'bread from heaven.'"[1] Jesus, and not the manna, is true bread.

A better option for understanding the passage is that John draws on the manna story as a way of understanding the importance of Jesus.[2] In verse 32 Jesus begins to interpret the Scripture cited in verse 31. The Greek is awkward to translate, but may best be understood as defining the subject and verb tense of the Scripture. Taking the words "he gave them bread from heaven to eat," Jesus indicates that "he" refers to "my Father." Similarly, the verb tense is not in the past ("gave"), but is present ("gives").[3] That is, the gift of manna is not something confined to the past, but is something God continues to give in the present. This interpretation is not a rejection of Jewish tradition, for that tradition already understood God as the ultimate giver of manna, and the manna as a metaphor for following God's word (see the discussion of the first reading, above). What is new about Jesus' interpretation of the manna story is that he identifies himself with this important and ongoing gift of God.

This metaphor has enormous potential for preaching. A problem with reading the text in a way that rejects the manna story is that the metaphor of Jesus as bread can have only a vague meaning: Jesus is some kind of spiritual nourishment. Instead, if the words "I am the bread of life" create a connection between Jesus and the manna story, then Jesus shares the significance of the manna. Just as the manna came down from heaven and gave life to the Israelites for all of those precarious years in the desert, so also Jesus gives life to the world. Just as eating manna required that people follow God's command, so also coming to Jesus involves following God's word (cf. 6:45). Connecting Jesus' words, "I am the bread of life," with the manna tradition gives more specific content to these verses.

The metaphor of Jesus as manna is a rich resource for theological reflection and Christian self-understanding. Preachers may invite hearers to imagine their own lives as being enriched by God's ongoing gift of manna. Just as God gave manna to the Israelites, so God is still giving manna, even today. This present-day manna is located in Jesus, who nourishes and sustains the grumbling people of God.

Notes

1. Rudolf Bultmann, *The Gospel of John: A Commentary*, trans. G. R. Beasley-Murray (Philadelphia: Westminster, 1971), 228.
2. Susan Hylen, *Allusion and Meaning in John 6* (Berlin: Walter de Gruyter, 2005).
3. Peder Borgen, *Bread from Heaven: An Exegetical Study of the Concept of Manna in the Gospel of John and the Writings of Philo* (Leiden: Brill, 1965), 61–66.

August 12, 2012
Lectionary 19 / Nineteenth Sunday in Ordinary Time / Proper 14
Eleventh Sunday after Pentecost

Revised Common Lectionary (RCL)

1 Kings 19:4-8 or 2 Samuel 18:5-9, 15, 31-33

Psalm 34:1-8 or Psalm 130

Ephesians 4:25—5:2

John 6:35, 41-51

Lectionary for Mass (LFM)

1 Kings 19:4-8

Psalm 34:2-3, 4-5, 6-7, 8-9

Ephesians 4:30—5:2

John 6:41-51

First Reading
1 Kings 19:4-8 (RCL, LFM)

Throughout 1 Kings 17–18, God has provided for Elijah and proven the powerlessness of Baal. Yet Jezebel is not persuaded and seeks to kill Elijah (19:1-3). He flees south to Beer-sheba, and then further out into the wilderness beyond. Elijah appears at the end of his rope. He has done as God commanded. Yet he still encounters obstacles and hardship. He is fearful and despairing (19:3-4).

God provides what Elijah needs. Twice the angel of the Lord provides a cake baked on hot stones and a jar of water. The angel's words show awareness of Elijah's human weakness: "Get up and eat, otherwise the journey will be too much for you" (v. 7). Just as God has provided for others in need through Elijah (see 1 Kgs. 17:8-16, 17-24), so now God provides for Elijah's needs (cf. 17:1-6).

But the journey is not over. The angel indicates that the food is to strengthen Elijah for a journey. Elijah departs, going forty days and forty nights to Horeb (v. 8). The length of the journey and its destination recall Moses' journey with the Israelites. Like Moses, Elijah struggles as a leader in what seems a hopeless situation. God provides what Elijah needs to continue his leadership and deliver God's word.

Elijah's story speaks to the difficult journey encountered by many political and spiritual leaders. The obstacles to the proclamation of God's word are serious, and the stakes can be high. Yet, like Elijah, many leaders experience God's direct care in moments of deepest hardship. The story contains a message of hope that God will equip and invigorate those God calls.

2 Samuel 18:5-9, 15, 31-33 (RCL alt.)

This story forms the finale of the tragedy that began with David's own deception and sexual aggression (2 Samuel 11–12). The intervening chapters are a complex story of rape, ambition, and pride. Following Amnon's rape of his sister, Tamar (13:1-22), David's son Absalom kills his half-brother, Amnon, heir to David's throne (13:23-33). Absalom flees and later conspires to take David's throne.

David appears as a father who both mourns Absalom and cannot forgive him. He brings Absalom home but will not see him (14:21-28). He sends his army to fight against Absalom but asks them to "deal gently for my sake with the young man Absalom" (18:5). The story is set to end tragically—as it turns out, with the death of Absalom and David's lament for his son.

David's inability to respond appropriately to the crisis in his family does not make his grief less real. The story is poignantly told. David's cry for his son's death (v. 33) has the ring of a true lament. Yet Absalom's death was the only likely good outcome for David, who otherwise stood to be deposed. The situation, which David himself had helped to create, was one in which there was no possibility of a simple victory.

Thus there is a deep moral complexity to this story. Absalom acts to avenge his sister, yet also certainly to advance his career. Acting out of grief for one son, David estranges another and contributes directly to his death. David's own ability to feel the tragic nature of his situation is a testimony to his character. He is not willing to sacrifice his kingdom, yet neither can he be jubilant in victory. As Walter Brueggemann writes, "Victory and grief, power and defeat are left in unresolved tension."[1]

The story of David is one that evokes an experience of this tragedy for the reader. Preaching the text may be conceived as an exercise in moral formation. The story resists our attempts to flatten it, to define characters or their actions as purely good or evil. The good news of the story may lie in David's inability to celebrate his son's demise.

Psalmody
Psalm 34:1-8 (RCL)
Psalm 34:2-3, 4-5, 6-7, 8-9 (LFM)

The inscription attributes the psalm to David on the occasion of his release by King Abimelech (or King Achish; see 1 Sam. 21:12-15). The psalm fits the scenario of David's story, but also applies more generally to all who call on God in distress. As such, it is also a fitting companion to both the Elijah story and the Gospel reading.

The psalmist praises God, who fulfills every need. God hears the humble or poor (vv. 2, 6) and answers them. God acts to remove distress (vv. 4, 7; cf. v. 17). The psalm employs a number of metaphors that may become the focus of preaching. First, those who look toward God will be radiant. The Hebrew word *nahar*, "shine," suggests that those who look to God will reflect God's glory. As a result, they will not have reason for shame.

139

A second metaphor is that of the angel of the Lord encamping around those who fear God (v. 7). Those within the camp are "delivered." Here, "deliver" translates the Hebrew word *chalatz*, which conveys that the angel equips or invigorates the camp for battle. Those who fear God are thus envisioned as protected and prepared by God to combat the troubles that lie outside the camp.

A third metaphor suggests that God's goodness is tangible and tactile: "O taste and see that the LORD is good; happy are those who take refuge in him" (v. 8). Those who seek divine shelter experience real protection from God. The language is of invitation: try it for yourself. Those who seek God's help will find concrete evidence of God's goodness.

Psalm 130 (RCL alt.)

This psalm expresses hope for redemption. The psalmist addresses God from the depths of human experience (v. 1) and hopes for God's response (v. 2). The speaker acknowledges sinfulness (v. 3), although it is not clear that the psalm attributes the speaker's current state in the depths to sin. It may be that verses 3-4 recognize that the speaker has no special claim to righteousness that would justify God's action on his or her behalf. Nonetheless, the speaker petitions God with hope of a gracious response, for God is forgiving. The source of this hope is not the righteousness of the speaker but the mercy of God.

The psalm is a fitting companion to the alternate first reading, above. David's cry of lament over Absalom is surely a cry "out of the depths." David's own sin has certainly contributed to his situation, yet hope remains, both for David and for Israel. The hope of Israel that God will restore the Davidic lineage results from the steadfast love and power of God (v. 7).

Second Reading
Ephesians 4:25—5:2 (RCL)
Ephesians 4:30—5:2 (LFM)

Christian behavior is presented here as a response to and reflection of Christ's gift. Having reminded the reader of Christ's teaching to clothe the new self with righteousness and holiness, the author describes actions that are fitting for the transformed Christian life.

The instructions reflect the theological framework of the letter in two important ways. First, actions are directed toward the corporate good of the church. Instead of stealing, people should work in order to have something to share with the needy (v. 28). Christians should not speak a "rotten word" (NRSV: "evil talk," v. 29), but instead "what is useful for building up." The exhortations are thus directly related to the preceding metaphor of the church "body," as examples of how the body is built up (cf. 4:12, 16).

Second, the author views Christian behavior as a response to the gracious gift of God in Christ, described in Ephesians 1–2. Readers are called to "be imitators of God, as beloved children, and live in love, as Christ loved us" (5:1-2). Adoption by God (1:5) forms the basis for the transformed Christian life. God's children can expect an inheritance, and the seal of the Holy Spirit is a sign of the promise of inheritance (1:13-14). Thus behavior that does not imitate God is a betrayal of the status bestowed in adoption, and thus "grieves the Holy Spirit" (cf. v. 30).

Adoption was made possible through the offering of Christ, which results in forgiveness (1:5-8; 4:32; 5:2). The actions of believers should reflect the self-giving love of Christ. As with Christ's sacrifice, Christian behavior actively seeks the good of the body. It involves speaking truth (v. 25), being angry without sin (v. 26), giving to the needy (v. 28), and edifying others (v. 29).

Gospel
John 6:35, 41-51 (RCL)
John 6:41-51 (LFM)

These verses are the central section of a long conversation between Jesus and the crowd (John 6:25-58; see the Tenth and Twelfth Sundays after Pentecost for a discussion of the context of these verses). John continues to develop the connections between the crowd and the Israelites of the exodus story, and between Jesus and manna.

As with the Gospel reading for the Tenth Sunday, above, interpreters of this passage often render two unfortunate judgments. The first portrays the crowd, which in verse 41 is first called "the Jews," as completely uncomprehending. The second suggests that Jesus critiques manna, which he replaces with a superior, spiritual "bread."

1. *John has already begun to identify the crowd with the Israelites of the exodus story* (see also the Gospel readings for the Ninth and Tenth Sundays after Pentecost, above). Now this connection becomes more explicit. The word *complain* (NRSV) or *grumble* (Gk.: *gonguzō*) is also used to describe the Israelites' complaint against Moses and God in the wilderness (e.g., Exod. 16:2, 7-9; the LXX uses the related Greek word *diagonguzō*). John also explicitly calls the crowd "the Jews" (v. 41), underscoring the crowd's connection with this group. Back in verse 4, John indicated that "the Passover, the festival of the Jews, was near." The crowd with whom Jesus speaks is now identified explicitly as "the Jews," those to whom the Passover tradition belongs.

The identification of the crowd as "the Jews" leads many interpreters to characterize this group negatively. Most scholars understand John as sharply critical of the Jews, and that overall view of the Gospel is imported wherever the group appears. It is important not to prejudge this character, however. John certainly characterizes the Jews negatively at times: they seek to kill Jesus (5:18; 8:59). Yet the Jews are also characterized as believing in Jesus (8:31; 11:45; 12:11). Indeed, it is their belief in large numbers following the raising of Lazarus that leads the authorities to plot to kill Jesus (11:45-53). The Jews are a complex character in John's Gospel. The negative and positive attributes of their character seem to exist side by side. Thus it may be useful in John 6 not to assume that the Jews are disbelievers and enemies of Jesus.

Like the Israelites in the wilderness period, the Jews of this story show both comprehension and disbelief. Their understanding of what Jesus has said is seen in their summary statement, "I am the bread that came down from heaven" (v. 41; cf. v. 42). Jesus has not said exactly these words, but their ability to restate his claims shows comprehension of what Jesus has said. Nevertheless, they complain about his teaching, questioning in what sense Jesus has come from heaven.

Like the Israelites, the Jews understand some things but are reluctant to trust God's word. Jesus' listeners initially understood his interpretation of the Scripture about the manna (v. 31). In verses 32-33 Jesus pointed to the manna as an ongoing gift of God in the present, and the crowd was quick to respond: "Sir, give us this bread always" (v. 34). They understand this is a present gift, and they even seem to accept Jesus' role as a new Moses, the giver of manna (see the discussion in the Ninth Sunday after Pentecost, above). Their disbelief surfaces, however, as they begin to understand what Jesus says next. Without distancing him from Moses, John goes on to identify Jesus with the manna itself (v. 35). The crowd has been willing to accept the idea that Jesus is Moses, but balks at the notion that Jesus is the bread from heaven.

2. *Verses 41-51 continue to interpret the Scripture quoted in verse 31, developing the metaphor of Jesus as manna* (see the Gospel reading for the Tenth Sunday after Pentecost, above). John draws on the tradition that associated the manna with God's word. Israel collected manna according to God's instructions (see Exodus 16 and the discussion of the first reading for the Tenth Sunday after Pentecost, above). Similarly, those who learn from God come to Jesus (John 6:45). Here John expresses something similar to 5:39-47, where the Scriptures testify to Jesus. In each case, John establishes a connection between Jesus and the Scripture, so that the one who understands Scripture comes to believe in Jesus. Just as the Israelites who followed God's word were fed with manna, so now those who listen and learn come to Jesus.

John suggests that Jesus is even better than manna in one sense: he gives eternal life (vv. 47-51). Jesus' words in verses 49-50 contrast his bread with the manna, and thus are often interpreted as a rejection of the manna. However, what Jesus says about the manna is a well-established part of the wilderness tradition. The manna God gave to the Israelites was a miraculous, life-sustaining food. Nevertheless, the first generation of Israelites died in the wilderness (cf. Num. 27:13-14; Deut. 34:4-5). The implication of Jesus' speech, then, is not that the former manna was bad, for John still understands it as life-giving, both in a physical sense and as something that orients Israel toward God. However, Jesus' manna is different on this count: those who eat this bread "live forever" (v. 51).

Throughout the Gospel, John uses the phrase "eternal life" metaphorically, to suggest a quality of life offered to believers. Although the Synoptic writers use this phrase in reference to a future, heavenly life (e.g., Matt. 25:46; Mark 10:30), for John, "eternal life" is something Jesus offers in the present. The verbs in verse 47, for example, are present tense. John understands Jesus' gift of life to have a future aspect, and makes this clear through the language of the "last day" (vv. 39-40, 44). Yet his more common phrasing of "eternal life" indicates that it is not limited to the future, but speaks of the believer's experience, both in life and in death.[2] "Eternal" is a quality that belongs to God alone. Thus, by partaking of Jesus as manna, believers "have eternal life": that is, they share in the life that belongs solely to God.[3]

Notes

1. Walter Brueggemann, *First and Second Samuel*, Interpretation: A Bible Commentary for Teaching and Preaching (Louisville: John Knox, 1990), 318.
2. See Gail O'Day's discussion of this concept in the context of John 11:25-26 in *John*, New Interpreter's Bible (Nashville: Abingdon, 1995), 9:688–89.
3. For an extended discussion, see Gail R. O'Day and Susan Hylen, *John*, Westminster Bible Companion (Louisville: Westminster John Knox, 2006), 45.

August 19, 2012
Lectionary 20 / Twentieth Sunday in Ordinary Time / Proper 15
Twelfth Sunday after Pentecost

<table>
<tr><td>Revised Common Lectionary (RCL)</td><td>Lectionary for Mass (LFM)</td></tr>
<tr><td>Proverbs 9:1-6 or 1 Kings 2:10-12; 3:3-14</td><td>Proverbs 9:1-6</td></tr>
<tr><td>Psalm 34:9-14 or Psalm 111</td><td>Psalm 34:2-3, 4-5, 6-7</td></tr>
<tr><td>Ephesians 5:15-20</td><td>Ephesians 5:15-20</td></tr>
<tr><td>John 6:51-58</td><td>John 6:51-58</td></tr>
</table>

First Reading
Proverbs 9:1-6 (RCL, LFM)

God's Wisdom prepares a lavish feast and invites humans to partake. The initial verses focus on the effort Wisdom has already expended in preparation for her guests. First, she builds her house (9:1). Its seven pillars suggest a grand and stable edifice. Then Wisdom prepares a feast: slaughtering animals, mixing spices with wine, and arranging a table (v. 2), all acts of hospitality. The metaphor of eating and drinking in Wisdom's house suggests that wisdom is a lavish gift supplied by God and that humans may partake of it as a gift. It is a banquet that brings life (v. 6). The life of wisdom is appealing and abundant. It is open to all who seek it.

Wisdom's call to the "simple" (v. 4) invites those who are naïve or immature to feast at her table. The table is often a metaphor for learning in the ancient world, as it was a gathering place around which ideas were shared.[1] Physical hunger is also a metaphor expressing the human need for God (e.g., Isa. 55:1-3). Thus the feast laid out for the simple is an opportunity for learning, as well as an opportunity to satisfy the needs that only God can fill.

Wisdom's call to learn insight is open for hearers to accept or reject. Humans must choose whether to partake. The choice is not easy because there are many competing calls, including imitations of Wisdom's call (see 9:13-18). Much of the language of Proverbs is meant to persuade the listener to abandon other ways and to value the rich life available by feasting on God's Wisdom.

I Kings 2:10-12; 3:3-14 (RCL alt.)

Solomon is established as the successor to his father, King David. The period of succession is often one of uncertainty, and this was certainly so for David's conflicted family. Solomon's older brother, Abishag, also vied for the throne (1 Kings 1–2), and Solomon had some difficulty attaining the throne. These verses show Solomon's establishment as king and the validation of his reign by God's gift.

In the selected verses, Solomon begins his reign on the right foot by seeking God's wisdom. God appears to Solomon in a dream at Gibeon, offering to do whatever Solomon asks (3:5). Solomon's answer suggests he will seek to walk in the ways of the Lord (cf. 1 Kgs. 2:1-4).

Solomon recognizes that his kingship results from God's "steadfast love" (*khesed*, v. 6) toward David. Solomon's words portray David in an idealized manner, as a servant who followed God faithfully. In overlooking David's many shortcomings, Solomon nevertheless articulates virtues he seeks to emulate: faithfulness, righteousness, and uprightness of heart (v. 6).

Solomon asks God for "an understanding mind to govern your people" (v. 9). The Hebrew words translated "understanding mind" may also be rendered literally as "a hearing heart" (*lev shomea'*). Solomon asks for wisdom that is God-given and that rests in the ability to hear rightly. The purpose of the wisdom is to govern God's people. Solomon does not claim the people as "his," as a king might do, but recognizes that he leads God's people.

Solomon requests wisdom for the benefit of all God's people. God's response to Solomon is repetitive, a feature that is somewhat lost in the NRSV translation. More literally rendered, verse 11 reads, "God said to him, 'Because you have asked this thing and have not asked for yourself long life, and have not asked for yourself riches, and have not asked for the life of your enemies, and have asked for yourself to understand and to hear justice.'" The repetition draws attention to many things Solomon might have requested for himself. Solomon's request for wisdom is not self-serving, but leads to understanding and justice.

The famous example of Solomon's wisdom in judging between two women's claim to one child follows immediately on the heels of his dream (vv. 16-28). It is an example of wisdom that listens carefully, not only to the women's words but also to their intentions. And it is an example of wisdom that does not serve Solomon's personal interests, but those of the whole community.

Psalmody
Psalm 34:9-14 (RCL)
Psalm 34:2-3, 4-5, 6-7 (LFM)

For an introduction to the psalm, and for the LFM verses, see the Eleventh Sunday after Pentecost, above.

In verses 9-14 the psalmist continues to identify benefits granted to those who seek God. The verses also include teaching about what it means to fear or seek God. In doing so, the latter verses in the passage reflect the language and style of Wisdom literature.

As was true of verses 1-8, the benefits God provides are for those who fear (vv. 9, 11; cf. v. 7) or seek God (v. 10; cf. v. 4). These will not lack any good thing. They will not be poor or hungry (vv. 10-11).

The invitation of verse 11 is to learn the fear of the Lord that results in such benefits. The instructions that follow focus on concrete actions: not speaking evil (v. 13) and doing good (v. 14). Thus the teachings indicate that fear of the Lord is seen through one's actions toward others. The instructions are meant for those who "delight in" life (NRSV: "desire"; Heb.: *chaphetz*). Fear of the Lord is thus not seen as a frightening or oppressive force, but as something that leads one toward greater happiness.

Psalm 111 (RCL alt.)

Psalm 111 is a psalm of praise, the appropriate response of Israel to God's acts. The psalmist characterizes these acts as "full of honor and majesty" (v. 3), "faithful and just" (v. 7). The details evoke the exodus and wilderness stories of Israel: God's "redemption" of the people (v. 9); God's feeding the hungry (v. 5); the promise of land and its fulfillment (vv. 5-6); the giving of the law (vv. 7-9).

The acts of God are both past and present. Indeed, the word *forever* echoes throughout this psalm. It describes the endurance of God's righteousness (v. 3) and precepts (v. 8), God's command of the covenant (v. 9), and God's remembrance of it (v. 5). The use of the present tense in verse 5 ("He provides food for those who fear him") is one example of how the psalm evokes the history of God's gracious gifts while also asserting their availability in the present.

Second Reading
Ephesians 5:15-20 (RCL, LFM)

The author of Ephesians continues to give instructions regarding the transformed Christian life. The previous verses (5:8-14) describe this transformation as movement from darkness to light. The Christian life of verses 15-20 is one that shuns the "unfruitful works of darkness" (v. 11) and lives in the light of Christ.

The opening phrase, "Be careful how you live" (v. 15), sets the theme of the passage. Three parallel instructions follow: do not be unwise but wise (v. 15); do not be foolish but understand (v. 17); do not be drunk but filled with the Spirit (v. 18). The teaching reflects the content of the rest of the letter. The wisdom of God has led to the disclosure of God's plan for redemption (1:7-10), and believers are meant to live in response to God's blessing. The letter repeatedly contrasts the believer's former and current states (e.g., 2:1-4, 11-13; 4:22-24). Sin, corruption, falsehood, and darkness are set aside as one embraces life in the body of Christ.

The Christian life is essentially one of thanksgiving and praise to God. "Psalms," "hymns," and "spiritual songs" (v. 19) are synonyms, not specific types of songs. The repetition suggests a state of constant praise, "at all times and for everything" (v. 20), the believer's response to the gift of God in Christ. The author is clearly aware of the potential for conflict, both within the Christian community (hence the "effort" required by 4:2-3) and in society at large (reflected in the language of 5:16: "the days are evil"). The exhortation to singing exists alongside such difficulties, a response that proclaims the magnitude of God's gift and the power it has to shape Christian life even in the midst of hardship.

Gospel
John 6:51-58 (RCL, LFM)

These verses give us John's insight into the later Christian practice of the Eucharist. The phrase "eat his flesh and drink his blood," or a variation of it, is repeated in every verse. For readers of the Gospel, these words evoke the practice of the Lord's Supper.

Placing this language at this point in the Gospel is one of John's unique contributions to Christian understanding of the Eucharist. The Synoptic Gospels all situate the Last Supper at the time of Passover and narrate Jesus' institution of the Lord's Supper (Matt. 26:17-39; Mark 14:12-25; Luke 22:7-23). John's final meal happens on the day before Passover and focuses on the foot washing, not on the meal itself (13:1-20). John has no institution of the Lord's Supper. Instead, John places his eucharistic language here, in the context of Jesus' discourse on the manna.

By locating these verses within Jesus' discussion of manna (vv. 31-58), John relates the meaning of the Eucharist to the story of the manna. For many contemporary readers, the passage evokes the Reformation-era debates about the presence of Christ in the Eucharist. The echoes of those theological controversies still influence the way many readers hear these words. Because of this, it may help to reframe the text as part of the interpretation of the manna story that began back in 6:31.

Verse 51 is a continuation of the discussion Jesus has been having with the crowd about the manna story. Yet this verse begins a new phase in Jesus' interpretation. The earlier portion of Jesus' interpretation affirmed that manna is not a story of Israel's past, but remains an ongoing gift provided by God. Jesus identified himself as that gift (vv. 32-35; see the Tenth Sunday after Pentecost, above). To arrive at that interpretation, Jesus defined the subject, verb tense, and direct object of the Scripture verse. He said that the Scripture "He gave them bread from heaven to eat" (v. 31; cf. Exod. 16:4) essentially means, "My Father is giving bread: Jesus" (vv. 32-35). In verse 51 Jesus changes the subject, verb tense, and direct object again.

Subject	Verb	Direct Object		
He	gave	them	bread from heaven to eat.	(v. 31)
My Father	gives	you	the true bread from heaven.	(v. 32)
I	will give	for the life of the world	my flesh.	(v. 51)

147

In verse 51 Jesus interprets the same elements of the Scripture to arrive at yet another way of understanding the manna. Here the subject is Jesus, the verb tense is future, and the direct object is Jesus' flesh: "The bread I will give for the life of the world is my flesh." Jesus is still interpreting the story of the manna. He points forward to a time when God will feed people with manna through the eucharistic meal.

Jesus' manner of interpretation, which seems to redefine the wording of the Scripture, may surprise modern readers. This interpretive style was common in antiquity, however, especially among Jewish interpreters of Scripture. It stems in part from a careful appreciation of the words of the Scripture, and attention to each. It also represents an attempt to relate the words of Scripture to the interpreter's context, something that present-day interpreters also do.

In the Gospel lections for the previous two Sundays, I proposed an alternative to the most common reading of these verses. Many interpreters fall into a pattern of contrasting the manna and the bread of life. The manna is portrayed as something less important than what Jesus offers. Sometimes manna is even portrayed negatively. From this perspective, the manna was something God gave to the Jews, but it was only a piecemeal solution and is superceded by Jesus' bread.

A better approach instead claims the full importance of the manna and appreciates that story as a paradigmatic example of God's long-suffering faithfulness. Instead of rejecting the manna in favor of Jesus, John's claim is that Jesus is something as wonderful and powerful as manna. Jesus is manna. He was manna during his life and he continues to be manna for those who eat the eucharistic meal. Just as God fed the Israelites and sustained them with manna in the wilderness, just as Wisdom lays a lavish feast for the simple, so God continues to feed believers through the bread of Jesus.

John's language provides a theologically rich and largely untapped resource for enlivening Christian experience of the Eucharist today. While exodus imagery enters into the Catholic and Anglican eucharistic liturgies, the dominant eucharistic metaphor in the imaginations of most Christians is not of manna, but of ritual sacrifice. Here John offers a different view: God feeds participants with manna. Just as God faithfully sustained the grumbling Israelites with manna and with water from the rock, so God continues to sustain grumbling believers through the body and blood of Christ. The point is not to deny or diminish sacrificial understandings of the Eucharist, but to give voice to John's unique expression as a resource for the life of the church. Through Jesus' body and blood, God continues to provide manna for those who will come and eat.

Note

1. See Christine Roy Yoder, *Proverbs*, Abingdon Old Testament Commentaries (Nashville: Abingdon, 2009), 105.

August 26, 2012
Lectionary 21 / Twenty-First Sunday in Ordinary Time / Proper 16
Thirteenth Sunday after Pentecost

Revised Common Lectionary (RCL)

Joshua 24:1-2a, 14-18 or 1 Kings 8:(1, 6, 10-11), 22-30, 41-43

Psalm 34:15-22 or Psalm 84

Ephesians 6:10-20

John 6:56-69

Lectionary for Mass (LFM)

Joshua 24:1-2a, 15-17, 18b

Psalm 34:2-3, 16-17, 18-19, 20-21

Ephesians 5:21-32 or 5:2a, 25-32

John 6:60-69

First Reading
Joshua 24:1-2a, 14-18 (RCL)
Joshua 24:1-2a, 15-17, 18b (LFM)

It is a time of uncertainty: Israel's leader is aged, and the social context offers many alternative gods. In this situation, Joshua gathers the Israelites to renew their covenant with the Lord. He reviews the history of God's faithfulness to Israel, ending with the present situation of Israel's possession of the land (vv. 2b-13). He calls the people to a moment of decision: "Choose this day whom you will serve" (v. 15).

The language of "service" is repeated throughout the passage. The word *serve* (Heb.: *'abad*) occurs eight times in verses 14-18. The word is closely related to the word *slavery* (v. 17; Heb: *'abadim*). It is used metaphorically to convey devotion to God, but also connotes work and obedience to a master. The Israelites may choose whom to serve, but that service still requires commitment and labor.

Having been freed by God from their slavery to the Egyptians (v. 17), the Israelites now have a choice, to serve God or to serve other gods. The language makes it clear that both Israel's ancestors and the local Amorites have served other gods. The review of Israel's history reminds the people of God's prior acts of redemption and also of poor choices made by ancestors who were not faithful in their service of God. This passage offers an important counterweight to those stories, a day when Israel was wholehearted in its devotion to God.

This text is useful for reflection in a wide variety of contemporary contexts. The uncertainty of modern life and the pull of many other "gods" continue. "Choose this day" is a reminder for listeners to rededicate their lives in the service of God.

I Kings 8:(I, 6, 10-II), 22-30, 41-43 (RCL alt.)

Solomon dedicates the temple and petitions God to establish the place as a focal point for communication between God and the people. Verses 28-30 show the actions of both God and humans. God regards or looks toward the temple (vv. 28-29) while God's servant either prays there (v. 28) or prays elsewhere, facing toward the temple (vv. 29, 30; cf. v. 42). Christians today may think of the temple primarily as a place where sacrifices were made. However, this passage clearly focuses on the temple as a place of prayer.

Solomon's prayer begins with a recognition of God's greatness (v. 23). Although the temple is sometimes spoken of as a dwelling place of God (e.g., v. 13), in the prayer Solomon recognizes that the temple cannot contain God (v. 27).[1] God dwells in heaven, and the temple is that place which bears God's name (v. 29; cf. vv. 16, 41-43).

Solomon petitions God to heed a variety of prayers made in or toward the temple. Verses 31-40 and 44-53 focus on the prayers of Israel, yet in verses 41-43 the prayers of the foreigner come into view. The foreigner is said to approach the temple because God's name is already known elsewhere (vv. 41-42). God's response to the foreigner spreads the word about God's name, and the temple as the place that bears that name (v. 43). This is a prayer that others will come to know and fear the Lord as Israel does.

Psalmody
Psalm 34:15-22 (RCL)
Psalm 34:2-3, 16-17, 18-19, 20-21 (LFM)

In these verses the psalmist continues to describe the Lord's protection of those who seek God. This protection is described in various ways: God hears and sees the distress of the righteous (vv. 15, 17); God is near (v. 18); God "keeps all their bones" (v. 20). As James Limburg points out, God is the subject of every verse except verse 21.[2] These verses teach the reader about God.

Although God protects the righteous, they are not free from distress. Their afflictions are many (v. 19). The word *afflictions* or *evil* (Heb.: *ra'a*) echoes the word translated "evildoers" in verse 16. Because the face of God is against evil (v. 16), the evils experienced by the righteous cannot prevail (v. 19). The final verses contrast the fates of those who do not follow God. The wicked die and are found guilty (v. 21), yet the servants of God are redeemed and are not condemned (v. 22). The psalm holds out the hope that those who seek God are ultimately rewarded.

Psalm 84 (RCL alt.)

The psalmist declares the blessings given to the one who seeks God in the temple. The psalm has both literal and metaphorical meanings. The language of longing (v. 2) and of a journey (vv. 5-7) suggests pilgrimage to the temple, God's "dwelling place" (v. 1). Those who travel to the temple bring blessings with them (v. 6). A day in the Temple is much to be desired (v. 10).

Metaphorically, presence in the temple is likened to trust in God. Read in parallel, the three beatitudes of the psalm connect physical presence in the temple and trust: "Happy are those who live in your house" (v. 4); "Happy are those whose strength is in you" (v. 5); "Happy is everyone who trusts in you" (v. 12). The psalmist builds on the experience of pilgrimage and presence in the temple as a way of imagining an orientation of trust and security in relationship with God.

Two of the psalm's metaphors shed light on the benefits of seeking God in the temple. First, the seeker is compared indirectly to the birds that nest and bear their young in the temple courts. The image is one of the safety provided by God for the vulnerable. Second, the psalmist prefers "standing on the threshold" of God's house (NRSV: "be a doorkeeper," v. 10) to dwelling in tents of wickedness. Even one who exists on the fringes of the temple benefits from the "favor and honor" (v. 11) God gives. Such a position is preferred to having a secure dwelling elsewhere.

Second Reading
Ephesians 6:10-20 (RCL)

These verses form a fitting conclusion to the ethical exhortations of Ephesians 4–6. Although that material centers on seemingly mundane topics, the conclusion reframes these issues as part of the spiritual battle in which Christians are engaged. The Christian life, transformed by the reconciliation of God in Christ, which has been the focus of the letter, is depicted here as having cosmic implications.

The author borrows the metaphor of God's armor from Isaiah 59:15b-19. Instead of God being dressed as a divine warrior (Isa. 59:17), the church is to put on the armor of God. The transformation of the imagery suggests that the everyday virtues of church members described in 4:29—6:9 are seen as elements of engaging the battle of the heavenly realms against "spiritual forces of evil" (6:12). Faith, righteousness, truth, salvation, and God's word: all these prepare the body for the battle against spiritual authorities.

Christians may thus envision their efforts to speak in ways that build up the body (4:29) or to "bear with one another in love" (cf. 4:2) as means of participation in a heavenly battle. Because the power of God and the authority given to Christ are apparent in the letter (see 1:20-23), the one so clothed in God's armor does not undertake great risk. Powers that threaten the individual Christian are no match for the body of Christ adorned with the armor of God.

Ephesians 5:21-32 or 5:2a, 25-32 (LFM)

Ephesians 5:21-32 is a difficult text to preach today. We have a tendency to read the passage as a list of instructions for behavior, and these are difficult to translate into modern terms, for our values and norms have shifted a great deal regarding the gendered virtues under discussion here. Following are two possible options for understanding this text as Scripture for the church today.

1. The first option focuses on the rhetorical function of the text and looks for a contemporary parallel. The text states what it meant to be a person of integrity in the first century. People had a hierarchical view of society and placed much less emphasis on individual fulfillment. To be virtuous was to fulfill one's role within the hierarchy and thus contribute to society. The author reminds the readers that they should adhere to conventional gendered virtues as a way of building up the body of Christ.

However, Roman virtues left a good deal of room for variation in behavior. Although the language here may conjure an image for the modern reader of a woman who stays at home and defers to her husband in everything, in reality Roman women were much more complex. They owned property, managed households, and served their communities in official capacities. If such women were viewed as people of integrity, they were also described as exhibiting domestic virtues like those described here. So, for example, a woman who held the highest magistracy of her city might be praised for her "modesty." The domestic virtues function to identify her as a person of integrity.

Thus the wifely submission described here is not a set of particular behaviors to which readers were expected to conform, but rather is a shorthand for acting with integrity, according to norms that were widespread at the time. In the context of the letter, the author describes the transformed Christian life. Christians are instructed to view themselves as part of the social system of the period, and should contribute as productive members of it.

Today, most Christians in the United States would define integrity differently, although there are still conventions associated with the term. A person of integrity is one who treats others well, whether they are of greater or lesser social status and power, who follows through on promises made, and who seeks the good of the community. People of integrity have a wide variety of social and household roles. They have diverse views. They are important to the functioning of the church because of their leadership and wisdom. When a person of integrity speaks out on an issue, people are inclined to listen. The author of Ephesians seeks to cultivate such Christians.

2. The preacher may also find it fruitful to focus on the metaphor of marriage as a way of understanding the relationship between Christ and the church. (The second option within the LFM highlights these verses.) The author of Ephesians interprets Genesis 2:24 as a statement about the relationship of Christ and the church. The union of Christ and the church as "one flesh" is a mystery (5:32) worthy of the preacher's attention. As married people are two and yet metaphorically become "one," so also Christ and the church are separate and yet also one. The language of the church as Christ's body elsewhere in the letter points to a similar tension (see Eph. 1:22-23; 4:15-16; and the discussion in the Tenth Sunday after Pentecost, above).

Focusing a sermon in this way may be difficult without also reinforcing a hierarchical view of marriage that does not correspond with the experience or expectation of the listeners. The metaphor translates to the modern context more easily as a message about the love of Christ for the church than one about the sacrament of marriage. However, it may be possible to avoid discussing gender roles within marriage and instead to focus on the ideal of marriage as a reflection of the love between Christ and the church.[3]

Gospel
John 6:56-69 (RCL)
John 6:60-69 (LFM)

Jesus' teachings about the future gift of manna (vv. 51-58; see the Twelfth Sunday after Pentecost, above) prove too much for many of his disciples, who turn away. Like the Jews, the disciples are portrayed as the Israelites of the exodus (for a discussion of the characterization of the Jews in John 6, see the Eleventh Sunday after Pentecost, above). Although they have experienced the miraculous sign of 6:1-15, they, too, "complain" about Jesus (v. 61). This was the same response of the Jews in verses 41-43, and the response of the Israelites in the wilderness (e.g., Exod. 15:24; 16:2, 7, 8). Scholars have often portrayed the disciples and the Jews as opposite characters in John's Gospel, with the disciples representing belief, and the Jews disbelief. Yet in this instance, John characterizes them with the same action, complaining.

Jesus identifies the problem as one of disbelief (v. 64). This was a problem for the Israelites as well (e.g., Num. 14:11; Deut. 9:23). Through the connection with the Israelites, John characterizes the disciples as group that is internally divided. Many of them turn away from following Jesus.

Even Jesus' closest disciples, the Twelve, exhibit similar division. Although the lectionary ends on a positive note with Peter's declaration of faith on behalf of the Twelve (vv. 68-69), the passage continues with an explicit reminder that the Twelve includes Judas (vv. 70-71; cf. v. 64). Thus, even among the Twelve, belief and unbelief exist side by side.

Many interpreters read the division among the disciples as one that separates "insiders" from "outsiders," those who believe from those who disbelieve. The language of verses 60 and 64, "many of his disciples" and "some of you," can be read to support this idea. Some of the disciples believe and stay with Jesus; those who turn away were not true believers to begin with. The problem with this approach for preaching is that many listeners do not experience themselves in such stark terms. They do not perfectly believe and follow Jesus, but neither do they completely disbelieve.

Another way to understand these verses is to read "the disciples" as a corporate or group character, one that by nature is divided about Jesus. In this sense, the disciples, even Jesus' closest disciples, are at once believing and disbelieving.[4] John's disciples are not set apart by their firm belief in Jesus. Even the Twelve, those chosen by Jesus (v. 70), waver in their belief. John underscores that Jesus has known this all along (v. 64).

Reading the disciples as ambiguous may allow readers to see themselves reflected in this portrayal. Discipleship need not be seen as an all-or-nothing affair, in which one either fully believes or disbelieves. Instead, John portrays a broad middle range between believing and disbelieving. Readers may come to understand themselves as being like the disciples and the Israelites: offered the opportunity to feed on manna, they are unable to fully trust in God's love. Nevertheless, as with the Israelites, God continues to feed and sustain this grumbling group.

Notes
1. Mordechai Cogan, *1 Kings*, Anchor Bible 10 (New York: Doubleday, 2000), 284.
2. James Limburg, *Psalms*, Westminster Bible Companion (Louisville: Westminster John Knox, 2000), 111.
3. See the discussion by Peter S. Williamson, *Ephesians*, Catholic Commentary on Sacred Scripture (Grand Rapids: Baker Academic, 2009), 174.
4. See my discussion of the disciples in Susan E. Hylen, *Imperfect Believers: Ambiguous Characters in the Gospel of John* (Louisville: Westminster John Knox, 2009), chap. 4.

September 2, 2012
Lectionary 22 / Twenty-Second Sunday in Ordinary Time / Proper 17
Fourteenth Sunday after Pentecost

Revised Common Lectionary (RCL)

Deuteronomy 4:1-2, 6-9 or Song of
Solomon 2:8-13
Psalm 15 or Psalm 45:1-2, 6-9
James 1:17-27
Mark 7:1-8, 14-15, 21-23

Lectionary for Mass (LFM)

Deuteronomy 4:1-2, 6-8

Psalm 15:2-3a, 3b-4a, 4b-5
James 1:17-18, 21-22, 27
Mark 7:1-8, 14-15, 21-23

First Reading
Deuteronomy 4:1-2, 6-9 (RCL)
Deuteronomy 4:1-2, 6-8 (LFM)

The Israelites stand on the border of the promised land, at the end of their long journey in the wilderness (cf. Deut 4:44-49). Moses first recounts that journey and God's mercy and judgment. Then, beginning in chapter 5, he recalls the law. The verses in Deuteronomy 4 are a preface or rationale for the law. They are both a call to obedience and a theological statement on the purpose of the law.

The opening verses call Israel to heed God's commands so that they may live, enter into the land, and thrive there (4:1). Observance of the law brings such "life," a life different in quality from the wilderness period. Verses 3-5, which the lectionary selection leaves out, remind the listeners of a recent example in which those who were faithful to the Lord God lived, but those who worshiped the god of Peor died in a plague (Numbers 25). There is both a literal and metaphorical sense to the "life" God gives through the law. It brings the fruitful life embodied in the gift of the promised land, and it protects adherents from judgment and death. It also brings a kind of abundant spiritual "life" characterized by proximity and devotion to God.

The latter verses emphasize that following the law is its own reward. As Israel keeps the law, others will see their "wisdom and discernment" (v. 6). The rhetorical questions of verses 7-8 suggest that through obedience to the law, others will come to know the nearness of God to Israel (v. 7) and the righteousness of God's word (v. 8).

These verses are a useful counterweight to the common Christian assumptions that the law is a negative aspect of Judaism, involving adherence to rules rather than meaningful devotion to God. By contrast, as Patrick Miller argues, "the righteous commandments and the keeping of them is the way that God is somehow known and found in the midst of the community."[1] Deuteronomy suggests that observing the law is an essential, positive feature of the relationship between Israel and God. It is God's gift to Israel, through which people may draw near to God.

Song of Solomon 2:8-13 (RCL alt.)

For centuries, Christians and Jews alike have read the Song of Songs metaphorically, as an expression of the love between God and Israel. The lectionary verses focus on the woman's perspective, as she imagines her lover coming, calling her to come to him. The devotion of the two parties is palpable in the yearning of each, the terms of endearment used, and the anticipation of their reunion.

Central to the poem's imagery is an idyllic spring setting. Robert Jenson argues that the setting is "an underlying motif of the Song's general construal of reality: whenever in the Song the lovers step outdoors or imagine themselves there, they enter an Eden . . . where even rainy weather appears only as something just past that brought the flowers."[2] The language encourages readers to use sight, smell, and hearing to evoke the beauty of the scene. It is a sensual poem.

Evoking the hearer's imagination is central to the task of preaching the Song. It should not be turned into an object lesson. Invite listeners to envision themselves as the female speaker, imagining her divine lover calling her to him. The woman may represent an individual, Israel/the church, or both. Encourage hearers to imagine themselves as one both seeking and sought by God.

Psalmody
Psalm 15 (RCL)
Psalm 15:2-3a, 3b-4a, 4b-5 (LCM)

The psalm's question (v. 1), asking who may draw near to God's presence, is answered by a series of prescribed actions. Those who speak and act with integrity, and do not seek their interests at the expense of others, may dwell on God's holy hill. The behaviors encouraged here are familiar from other parts of Scripture. Those who act in these ways enter into the security of living according to God's word: they shall never be moved (v. 5).

The psalm gives examples of behavior fitting for those who seek God's presence. In verse 2 the psalmist uses three basic verbs that suggest the wide-reaching implications of righteous behavior, which affects one's walking, doing, and speaking. A negative formulation follows: how one should *not* walk, act, or speak. The verb translated "slander" in verse 3a is related to the word *foot* (Heb.: *ragal*), and thus may be seen as a parallel of "walk" in verse 2.[3] Verses 4-5 characterize the righteous as those who respond to others without seeking their own gain. This attitude applies to situations of honor and social status (v. 4) as well as to financial gain (v. 5).

Psalm 45:1-2, 6-9 (RCL alt.)

The psalm was originally a royal wedding song. Both the king (vv. 2-9) and queen (vv. 10-15) are described in extravagant terms. The king is idealized: he is a mighty warrior (vv. 3-5), blessed (v. 2), and just (vv. 6b-7a). He is anointed by God (Heb.: *meshach*, v. 7b).

The description of the king as God's anointed has led both Jewish and Christian interpreters to read this psalm in a messianic light. Also, as with the Song of Songs, readers have seen the wedding imagery as a metaphor for the "marriage" between God and God's people.[4] The New Testament author of Hebrews understood verses 6-7 in reference to Christ (Heb. 1:8-9). Read in this way, the language of the psalm suggests the preparation of Christ for marriage to the church.

Second Reading
James 1:17-27 (RCL)
James 1:17-18, 21b-22, 27 (LFM)

The letter of James emphasizes the believer's need to act upon faith. The passage begins with a statement of the theological necessity of faith. God is the giver of every good gift (v. 17). This God gave birth to humans by a true word (v. 18). The imagery evokes the language of Genesis 1 and Proverbs 8:22-31, in which God's word or wisdom is active in creation. At the same time, this "true word" also evokes the gospel message and the law.

God's giving birth had a purpose: "that we would become a kind of first fruits" (v. 18). The imagery of fruitfulness is seen elsewhere in the New Testament (e.g., Matt. 3:8; Luke 6:43; Rom. 7:4). The metaphor suggests the human production of good deeds. God's creation by the word is intended to bear the fruit of human righteousness.

James elaborates on the good deeds in verses 19-21. Being "quick to listen, slow to speak, [and] slow to anger" (v. 19) are conventional virtues of the time, reflecting a life of religious understanding and self-control. The ability to cultivate these virtues is related to reception of "the implanted word" (v. 21). The phrasing suggests that God's word is both innate to the believer (or "implanted," as in the creation language of v. 18) and also something to be "received." God's word is the cause of human creation and is something the believer must receive again and again, in becoming a "doer of the word" (v. 22).

Verses 23-25 use the mirror as a metaphor, in ways that were conventional at the time.[5] The mirror was an image of self-contemplation, as seen in verse 23. Verse 25 reflects a slightly different idea, that the mirror is a model for right behavior. One looks at exemplary behavior as at a mirror, so that one's own behavior may come to reflect the example. For James, it is "the perfect law, the law of liberty" (v. 25) that provides such an example. James understands the law as one of God's perfect gifts (v. 17). Gazing into the law and acting on it leads to the happy or blessed life (v. 25).

Verses 26-27 anticipate the author's primary concerns with regard to keeping God's word. First, control of speech is important because it displays inner virtues like self-control. Second, the care of orphans and widows and distance from the values of the world are themes that recur in the letter. These are essential to James's understanding of true faith, a faith that is seen in the believer's actions.

Gospel
Mark 7:1-8, 14-15, 21-23 (RCL, LFM)

Christian tradition prepares us to read this passage in Mark as an example of Jesus' rejecting Jewish law in favor of a more spiritual devotion to God. However, this is a poor interpretation of this passage of Mark. The Pharisees' practice of washing hands is from "tradition" (vv. 3, 5), not the law. Part of the Pharisees' devotion was keeping the "oral law," which were traditions they believed God had given to Moses on Sinai but that were not written down. The Pharisees and scribes ask why the disciples do not keep these traditions. Jesus rejects such traditions, not the law.

Jesus' response identifies the washing of hands as a "human tradition": "You abandon the commandment of God and hold to human tradition" (v. 8). He accuses the Pharisees and scribes of neglecting the commandments of God in favor of such human teachings. Jesus' words underscore the importance of keeping God's law. God's word is more important than devotional practices with a human source.

The paragraph left out in the lectionary selection reinforces this idea by way of example. Jesus says that his critics neglect the law ("Honor your father and mother," v. 10) when they give money as an offering that would otherwise be used to support their parents (vv. 11-12). Jesus argues that their observation of the tradition interferes with their attention to God's law, which should be the more important concern.

Jesus' list of vices (vv. 21-22) is a traditional element of many ancient wisdom teachings (in the New Testament, see, e.g., Gal. 5:19-21; 2 Tim. 3:2-5). The list includes many behaviors that are forbidden by the law. For example, the Ten Commandments prohibit theft, murder, and adultery (vv. 21-22; cf. Exod. 20:13-15). Although Jesus does not mention the Old Testament Scripture directly, early Jewish or Jewish Christian readers of the text would likely have recognized Jesus' teachings as being in harmony with their understanding of the law. Thus Jesus should not be interpreted as offering an alternative set of standards to replace obedience to the law.

Jesus uses the catalog of vices to underline his point that such behaviors render one unfit to stand in God's presence. His message reflects a thread that runs through the teachings of the Old Testament, calling Israel to share God's concern for the poor and oppressed. Psalm 15, above, is one example of this concern (cf. Mic. 6:6-8; Isaiah 58). This critique is not meant as a complete rejection of the religion of Israel, but is a call to action. The psalmist reminds the hearer to turn toward acts of justice and mercy that are in accordance with God's will. When these foundational acts are not present, other devotional practices are seen as meaningless. Jesus' critique of the Pharisees echoes this Old Testament concern.

Because Christian interpretation of the New Testament has often understood Jesus as rejecting Judaism, many will find it difficult to read these verses as affirming Jewish law. It may help to remember that the Pharisees were only one branch of Judaism. First-century Jews had rich and diverse beliefs and practices. Moreover, Jewish people argued over the best spiritual practices, and the best ways to understand God. Thus Jesus' interaction with the Pharisees should not be taken as criticism of all of Judaism. Instead, Jesus enters into an ongoing debate about Jewish practice. He argues that the Pharisees are "hypocrites" (v. 6) because their practices lead them to neglect the law.

The view that Jesus rejects the law yields a familiar theological payoff: legalistic approaches to religion are not fruitful. Instead, one must be inwardly devoted to God. The preacher who turns away from reliance on negative stereotypes of Judaism must search for new ways to apply the passage to modern life. Like the lectionary texts from Deuteronomy and James, Mark may also be encouraging hearers to show their devotion to God through actions that are in harmony with the law. Human habits and traditions often sidetrack even those who intend to devote themselves to the service of God.

The challenge of reorienting the message of this text is compounded by the difficulty of finding contemporary practices that mirror the Pharisees' concern about washing hands. This difficulty stems from a cultural gap between contemporary readers and the text, because modern Christians do not have a parallel sense of "purity" and "defilement." The notion of God's holiness was important to many ancient religious traditions. Purification was required to enter into the presence of God. It was a way of marking the difference between human existence and divine holiness. The Pharisaic practice of hand washing was a way of making ritual purification a part of everyday life. Jesus' teaching about "what defiles" (v. 15) also speaks to the question of the believer's purity. Modern notions of purity are largely gauged on ethical and not ritual action. We have no difficulty accepting that one's actions are more important than anything that enters the body from outside. Because of this it may be difficult to hear the critique Jesus offers in a way that speaks to the modern reader.

Nevertheless, the preacher may find parallels in the actions the Pharisees take to ensure that others will practice the traditions the Pharisees deem important. Jesus criticizes the Pharisees for "honoring God with their lips" (cf. v. 6) as they question the disciples' piety. Their worship is only skin-deep, because the Pharisees' real concern is their own human teachings. In this sense, the passage may bring to mind an array of traditions or doctrines that are valued by a particular congregation.

When practices of worship or personal piety become all-important, they may deflect attention from behavior that is more important for a life lived in devotion to God. The passage may provide an opportunity to ask whether the expectations demanded of others are matched by the integrity of one's own life.

Notes

1. Patrick D. Miller, *Deuteronomy*, Interpretation: A Bible Commentary for Preaching and Teaching (Louisville: John Knox, 1990), 57.
2. Robert W. Jenson, *Song of Songs*, Interpretation: A Bible Commentary for Preaching and Teaching (Louisville: John Knox, 2005), 34.
3. Patrick D. Miller, *Interpreting the Psalms* (Philadelphia: Fortress Press, 1986), 44–45.
4. For a discussion, see James Luther Mays, *Psalms*, Interpretation: A Bible Commentary for Preaching and Teaching (Louisville: John Knox, 1994), 182.
5. See Luke Timothy Johnson, *Brother of Jesus, Friend of God: Studies in the Letter of James* (Grand Rapids: Eerdmans, 2004), 168–81.

September 9, 2012
Lectionary 23 / Twenty-Third Sunday in Ordinary Time / Proper 18
Fifteenth Sunday after Pentecost

Revised Common Lectionary (RCL)	**Lectionary for Mass (LFM)**
Isaiah 35:4-7a or Proverbs 22:1-2, 8-9, 22-23	Isaiah 35:4-7a
Psalm 146 or Psalm 125	Psalm 146:7, 8-9a, 9b-10
James 2:1-10, (11-13), 14-17	James 2:1-5
Mark 7:24-37	Mark 7:31-37

First Reading
Isaiah 35:4-7a (RCL, LFM)

The author envisions the return from exile as a journey on a highway (35:8) where the abundance of God's goodness is all around. Those who are anxious or fearful are encouraged to know that the vengeance of God comes (v. 4). The previous passage has narrated the negative consequences of God's recompense, but in the current passage the hearers experience God's coming in positive ways. God brings healing: the blind see, the deaf hear, the lame leap, and the speechless sing for joy (vv. 5-6).

Like the miracle stories of the wilderness period (Exod. 17:1-7; Num. 20:2-13), God's presence is made known in an abundance that transforms the desert into a spring of water (vv. 6-7). Along with the people of verses 5-6, creation itself is renewed by God's presence. The desert is transformed into a habitable and welcoming place. The prophet promises safety (cf. vv. 8-9), health, and provisions for the "ransomed of the LORD" (v. 10).

Proverbs 22:1-2, 8-9, 22-23 (RCL alt.)

The selected verses fit together thematically because they address the relative importance of wealth and the treatment of the poor. However, the last two verses belong structurally to a different section of Proverbs, the "Words of the Wise" (22:17—24:22).

Verse 1 emphasizes the importance of a good reputation above the pursuit of riches. Wealth is viewed positively in Proverbs, but a good reputation is even more important. The writer's assumption is that one's reputation is a reflection of wise behavior (11:16; 13:15). A similar teaching is found in Sirach 41:13: "The days of a good life are numbered, but a good name lasts forever."

Verse 2 underscores a similarity between rich and poor: they share one Creator. Elsewhere in Proverbs, a similar rationale is used to advocate kindness toward the poor (14:31; 17:5; 19:17; cf. 29:13). The shared relationship to God should remind the rich of their common humanity.

Although verse 7 recognizes the power of the rich over the poor, verses 8-9 are an exhortation not to misuse this power. Verse 8 articulates a notion of retribution that is common to Proverbs (see, e.g., 3:9-10; 14:32; 16:5; 21:7; 24:20). Those who do evil will suffer. The "rod of anger" (v. 8b) is not a specific kind of tool, but suggests an implement used by the powerful to oppress others. Such action will ultimately fail to bring good things to the one who "sows injustice" (v. 8a). Likewise, verse 9 exhorts the reader to generosity to the poor (cf. 11:24-25; 19:6; Pss. 37:21; 112:5; Sir. 35:12; 40:14).

Verse 22 shifts to a direct exhortation to the reader: "Do not rob the poor . . . or crush the afflicted at the gate." The "gate" of the town was the location of the local court. Thus the command prevents the rich from seeking an unjust judgment against the poor. Two reasons are given: first, the fact that the poor are poor (v. 22a) is reason enough. They do not have anything to spare. Second, God "pleads the plea" of the poor (NRSV: "pleads their cause") and will "despoil of life those who despoil them." The Hebrew verbs suggest a direct parallel between the unjust actions against the poor and God's defense of them.

Psalmody
Psalm 146 (RCL)
Psalm 146:7, 8-9a, 9b-10 (LFM)

This hymn of praise contrasts human capabilities with God's ability. The hearer is reminded not to trust earthly rulers (NRSV: "princes," v. 3), who cannot save (or "help"). Both their plans and their presence are fleeting (v. 4).

By contrast, the God who created all things keeps faith forever (v. 6) and reigns forever (v. 10). The faithfulness of God has been seen in God's care for those society disregards—the oppressed and the prisoner (v. 7), the sick (v. 8), strangers, orphans, and widows (v. 9; cf. Pss. 113:7; 147:6). Because God is eternal and loving, the one who seeks help from God rather than humans will be "happy" (or "blessed," v. 5).

Psalm 125 (RCL alt.)

Trust in God is a common theme of the Psalms (e.g., Pss. 37:3, 5; 56:3, 4, 11). In Psalm 125, the psalmist develops two metaphors expressing the security of the one who trusts in God. First, that person is like Mount Zion (v. 1). Mount Zion was the place where God's presence dwelt (e.g., Pss. 9:11; 46:4-5; 50:2; 76:2; 84:7), and a place God loved (Pss. 78:68; 87:1-2). The power of God's presence and God's love for Zion establishes it as a place of security. Those who trust in God share in the security of God's presence.

In the second metaphor, the one who trusts is like Jerusalem, and God is the mountains surrounding the city. The image evokes the nearness of God, and being surrounded on every side. As Jerusalem's mountains provided a natural defense against enemies, so also God protects the one who trusts God.

The psalm promises protection for those who trust, but also requires their effort. The "scepter of wickedness" (v. 3a) is probably an image of domination by foreign powers. It is a threat because it might lead even the righteous to acts of injustice (v. 3b). The righteous are not immune from such action, but resist as a result of God's protection. Furthermore, verse 5 suggests the possibility that the upright might "turn aside to their own crooked ways" and thus be left to associate with evildoers. The "peace" for which the psalmist prays (v. 5b) thus results from the combined action of God and those who trust in God.

Second Reading
James 2:1-10, (11-13), 14-17 (RCL)
James 2:1-5 (LFM)

The previous injunction to be "doers of the word" (1:22, 25) is carried forward in a specific example. The author begins by describing a scene that takes place within the Christian assembly (2:1-4). The seating offered to the rich and poor (v. 3) reflects judgment that is clouded by partiality for the rich. Leviticus 19:15 prohibits such partiality: "You shall not render an unjust judgment; you shall not be partial to the poor or defer to the great; with justice you shall judge your neighbor." Christians who are "doers of the word" do not give preferential treatment on the basis of wealth.

The author has already identified the heart of "religion that is pure and undefiled" (1:27), which involves care for orphans and widows. That same value system undergirds the example, as is seen in verse 5. God has chosen the poor to be "heirs of the kingdom" (cf. Luke 6:20), and this knowledge shapes faithful Christian action.

In the logic of the world, preferential treatment of the rich makes sense because of the benefits the rich can supply in turn. The letter reminds the reader not only of God's preference for the poor but also of the negative potential of the rich to oppress, prosecute, and blaspheme (vv. 6-7). Partiality to the rich is no small matter, but is evidence of a greater transgression against the law (vv. 9-10) and its guiding tenet, love of neighbor (v. 8).

The passage concludes with a restatement on the unity of faith and action. This concept was familiar in many philosophical traditions of the time: one's beliefs should correspond to one's actions. The accusation of hypocrisy was leveled at those who could not display such integrity. The example of verses 15-16 shows the hollowness of words that are not supported by deeds.

The question "What good is it?" (vv. 14, 16) has both practical and spiritual implications. On the one hand, empty words make no difference for the brother or sister who lacks daily food (v. 15). But the context of 2:14-18 suggests that the "good" in view is the shaping of the believer's character through the acting out of faith.

Gospel
Mark 7:24-37 (RCL)
Mark 7:31-37 (LFM)

Both healing miracles (vv. 24-30 and 31-37) echo Mark's tendency to describe the ministry of Jesus as a triumph over demons and a release from slavery. In the story of the Syrophoenician woman, the healing of her daughter is repeatedly described as the departure of the demon (vv. 26, 29, 30). In previous chapters, Jesus casts out demons and speaks with them (1:21-28, 32; 3:7-12; 5:1-20). The demons recognize Jesus, something few characters in Mark's Gospel do. Jesus' words describing the one who can bind the strong man and plunder his house (3:22-27) articulate one way Mark understands Jesus' ministry. He is the one with power to bind Satan and plunder his house, actions the reader sees acted out in the exorcism stories.

Likewise, the healing of the man who is deaf and cannot speak is described as a release from bondage. Following Jesus' actions and words in verses 33-34, the man's "ears were opened, [and] his tongue was released" (v. 35): literally, his hearing was unlocked, and the chain of his tongue was released. Mark's word choice echoes his description of the purpose of Jesus' ministry: "to give his life a ransom for many" (10:45). A "ransom" is a payment to release a slave from bondage. Mark's phrasing suggests a view of humankind being in bondage to sin or Satan, and Jesus' death as payment for the slaves' release. Yet Jesus does not simply pay Satan the ransom, for he does not remain dead. Thus he also "plunders his house" (3:27), releasing the slaves while at the same time vanquishing sin and death. Healing miracles like 7:31-37 act out this release in miniature. The kingdom of heaven has drawn near in Jesus (1:15), and thus the plundering of Satan's house has already begun in the release of those who are bound by demons and disease.

Such release comes even to the Gentiles, because in these passages Jesus travels among them. Jesus goes to the region of Tyre willingly, yet is initially reluctant to be known (7:24) or to heal a Gentile child (v. 27). This story has been controversial because Jesus does not act as kindly as readers expect, and he seems to reproduce the prejudices of his age, against Gentiles, women, and children. Interpreters often try to cover up Jesus' rudeness, either by claiming he is merely testing the woman, or by suggesting a kinder nuance to the slur "dogs" (v. 27). Neither explanation is especially convincing. Jesus' abrupt behavior here fits with other elements of Mark's portrait of Jesus, such as his cryptic speech (4:12) and his exasperation with the disciples

(8:17-21). Mark's Jesus is not always the warm and fuzzy Jesus that modern readers expect. Yet there may be value in hearing the message Mark sends through a more unpredictable and less approachable Jesus.

Jesus' reluctance to heal the Syrophoenician woman's daughter sets up the theological message of the story: Jesus' mission is to Israel, but others nonetheless benefit because of the abundance of the provision. It is interesting that this insight comes from the woman and not from Jesus. Her attitude is one that is unique in the Gospel, recognizing that she has no right to demand anything from Jesus, but that in the abundance of God's gift, she need request only crumbs from the table. She *We are all beggars.* proves herself to be a wise woman, responding to Jesus' words much as Jesus himself will respond to the challenges of others (see Mark 11:27-33; 12:13-17, 18-27, 28-34). Through her words, she merits her child's healing. Although the specific content of the story makes the woman's situation unique, her initial approach to Jesus and her theological acumen could be said to display the same kind of faith that results in healing elsewhere in Mark (e.g., 2:5; 6:34; 10:52).

This passage presents an interesting conundrum for interpreters interested in Jesus' interaction with and attitude toward women. His words seem to reflect common prejudices that deemed women and girls less important than men and boys. The male supplicant in the following story (vv. 31-37) does not negotiate his healing. At the same time, the wisdom of the passage—indeed, the theological rationale for this tour into Gentile territory (7:24—8:21)—comes from the mouth of a woman. She appears to understand Jesus' mission better than he, and he may learn something from their conversation.

Mark 7:31-37 is a healing story similar to other passages of Mark. The man cannot speak, so is brought by others who beg on his behalf (v. 32; cf. 2:3). The healing takes place away from the crowds (v. 33; cf. 5:40). Jesus heals through actions (v. 32; cf. 8:23, 25) and words (v. 34; cf. 5:41).

The miracle has a powerful effect on those who witness it. They "proclaimed" (or "preached"; *kērussō*, v. 36) the good news of the man's release. Just as John the Baptist and Jesus have proclaimed good news (cf. 1:4, 7, 14, 38), so these Gentiles also proclaim what they have experienced. In doing so they join other witnesses of Jesus' miracles (1:45; 5:20) and the disciples (3:14; 6:12).

The people's response of proclamation is understandable, yet Jesus' own response in verse 36, attempting to silence them, has always intrigued readers of Mark. The requests for secrecy are odd for three reasons. First, they seem to contradict Jesus' own intention to proclaim the gospel (1:38). Second, it is odd that the words of this powerful healer and authoritative teacher are largely ineffective (cf. 1:37, 45; 3:7-8; 7:36). Third, Jesus is inconsistent on this point, insisting in one case that the healed should go and tell others (5:19). For academically trained readers, verse 36 will likely evoke William Wrede's notion of the "messianic secret,"[1] the idea that Mark tried to explain people's rejection of the Messiah through Jesus' repeated demands for secrecy (e.g., 1:34, 44; 3:12; 5:43; 8:26, 30).

Jesus' secrecy and its futility may be part of Mark's attempt to communicate that divine power is present in Jesus. Jesus' power to heal is not entirely under his control. For example, his power to heal overflows without his effort for the woman who touches the fringe of his cloak (5:30). His power is so great that the demons recognize him immediately and beg for mercy (5:7, 10; cf. 1:24). Jesus' power flows in ways that are not entirely predictable. So also, the result, people's desire to tell of God's mercy, is irrepressible. Even Jesus' words cannot contain it.

Note

1. William Wrede, *The Messianic Secret* (Cambridge: J. Clark, 1971). Originally published in German: *Das Messiasgeheimnis: zugleich ein Beitrag zum Verständnis des Markesevangeliums* (Göttingen: Vandenhoeck & Ruprecht, 1901).

September 16, 2012
Lectionary 24 / Twenty-Fourth Sunday in Ordinary Time / Proper 19
Sixteenth Sunday after Pentecost

Revised Common Lectionary (RCL)
Isaiah 50:4-9a or Proverbs 1:20-33
Psalm 116:1-9 or Wisdom of Solomon
  7:26—8:1 or Psalm 19
James 3:1-12
Mark 8:27-38

Lectionary for Mass (LFM)
Isaiah 50:4-9a
Psalm 116:1-2, 3-4, 5-6, 8-9

James 2:14-18
Mark 8:27-35

First Reading
Isaiah 50:4-9a (RCL, LFM)

Many commentators identify this as the third of Isaiah's four "servant songs" (cf. 42:1-4; 49:1-6; 52:13—53:12). In these passages, Israel's mission comes to be identified with an individual person, the servant of God. The passages reflect the experiences of Israel's prophets, who spoke God's word to the people, yet were ridiculed and derided. Beginning early in the Christian tradition, the passages were also read in reference to Jesus.

In this passage the servant identifies himself as one who listens to and learns from God. The prophet "listens as those who are taught" (vv. 4-5), suggesting his openness to learning. This learning equips the prophet to teach others (v. 4). The servant is characterized as an obedient disciple (v. 5).

Bearing God's message has resulted in insult, however, as God's people do not receive the messenger. The servant submits to this disgrace (vv. 6-7). He knows that God will defend him in a legal case brought against him by these adversaries (vv. 8-9). The Lord GOD (*Adonai YHWH*, vv. 4, 5, 7, 9) helps the servant, who will not be put to shame. The servant's job is to encourage belief in God, even when the people turn away.

Proverbs 1:20-33 (RCL alt.)

In Proverbs 1:8-19, the father begins instructing his son by telling him to avoid "sinners" who will seek to entice him (v. 10). Competing for attention is Wisdom, whose voice is heard in 1:20-33 (cf. 8:1-36; 9:4-6). Wisdom is depicted as standing in a public place and calling out to all (vv. 20-21). The reader is also called to listen and is warned of the consequences of ignoring Wisdom's call.

"Fools" are those who refuse to listen to Wisdom's call (vv. 22-25). They "hate knowledge" (v. 29). They are portrayed as people who willfully reject the counsel of Wisdom.

The consequence of ignoring God's wisdom is that Wisdom will not be present in disaster (cf. 13:2). Repetition underscores the threat of disaster: calamity, dread, distress, anguish (vv. 26-27). In such a time of need, those who have rejected wisdom reap the fruit of that choice, for they lack the wisdom they need. Conversely, those who cultivate a life according to God's word will draw on the depths of that wisdom when they need it most.

Psalmody
Psalm 116:1-9 (RCL)
Psalm 116:1-2, 3-4, 5-6, 8-9 (LFM)

This is an individual psalm of praise for God's deliverance. The psalmist's situation of distress is described in general terms. He was "brought low" (v. 6) and "encompassed" by death (v. 3). Death appears with Sheol as something that invades human life, "laying hold" of people (v. 3). God delivers people from the power of this hold.

The psalmist called out in prayer to God (v. 1). God is described as responding to prayer (v. 1) and as gracious, righteous, and merciful (v. 5). God protects and saves the simple (v. 6) and delivers from death, tears, and stumbling (v. 8). The experience of God's deliverance leads to the psalmist's understanding of the nature of God.

The psalmist's response is love (v. 1). The song of praise emerges from a recognition and adoration of God's power and mercy. This love is carried out in the life of the singer, who now "walks before the LORD" (v. 9; cf. vv. 12-19). The speaker's experience of salvation has led to the recognition of God's presence in everyday life, and to a desire to live in response to God's mercy.

Wisdom of Solomon 7:26—8:1 (RCL alt.)

Chapters 7–10 of the Wisdom of Solomon describe the identity and wonder of divine Wisdom. The book is written in the name of Solomon, though by a later author addressing Jews in the Roman period. In this passage, Wisdom is described in ways that reflect older traditions of Scripture (e.g., Prov. 8:22-31) and that are echoed by later Christian understandings of Jesus (e.g., John 1:1-18; Col. 1:15; Heb. 1:3).

Similar to the mirror imagery in James (see the second reading for the Fourteenth Sunday after Pentecost, above), Wisdom is a mirror of God because she is a moral example for humans to follow. As Luke Timothy Johnson writes, "The point of this encomium of Wisdom is her ability to teach Solomon not only about the shape of reality (7:17-22) but above all how to live (8:8-18). The importance of Sophia's reflecting the working of God and his goodness, therefore, is that by gazing into that mirror, right knowledge might be gained, superior to that granted by 'nature.'"[1] By looking into Wisdom, one may see the goodness of God and come to reflect that goodness in one's own behavior.

The one who does this is transformed. Wisdom makes people into friends of God and prophets (7:27). Her reflection of God's light is superior even to the sun and stars, and it dispels evil (7:29-30).

Psalm 19 (RCL alt.)

The psalmist meditates on the goodness and glory of God, as seen in the wonders of creation and the instruction of God's word. The heavens point to the expansiveness of God. They speak of God's handiwork (v. 1) because they are all encompassing. Thus their voice goes out to the whole earth (v. 4), and the sun runs its circuit from one end to the other (v. 6). The inescapability of the sun's heat speaks of the presence and glory of God.

The teachings of God likewise declare God's nature. The variations in verses 7-9 suggest that every aspect of God's law and each individual precept embody the beauty and holiness of God. The qualities listed in verses 7-9 belong to God's nature, and the psalmist encounters them more deeply through reflection on God's word. Because the law shares in these divine virtues, the teachings are precious and desirable (v. 10).

The closing verse is a prayer that the psalmist's words speak rightly of God and glorify God. The wording of the verse reflects the approach of the psalm as a whole, and situates the psalmist as one element of God's creation, one who also "speaks" like the heavens and the firmament (v. 1). The Hebrew phrase in verse 14 translated "the meditation of my heart" is literally "the talking of my heart." Although the heart does not literally speak (cf. v. 3), the psalmist hopes that the product of his heart would display the wonder of God, just as the heavens and the law do. Although the final verse is often used as a prayer for illumination, in the context of the psalm, it situates the psalmist alongside these other testimonies to God's greatness. It is a prayer that the psalmist's own life might also testify to the glory of the Creator.

Second Reading
James 3:1-12 (RCL)

James's concern with human speech (cf. 1:19, 26) comes to the fore in this passage. The author highlights the role of the teacher as an example of the potential problems with speech. Teachers may often encounter the temptation to use speech in negative ways. Nevertheless, all people make such mistakes. In the author's mind, no one will be "perfect" (v. 2) with regard to speech. Nevertheless, the importance of the issue for James conveys that the believer's continued attention to speech is essential.

The passage is laden with metaphors that evoke the power and problem of human speech. In verses 2b-5a the tongue exerts control over the whole body. The person who is "perfect" is "powerful enough to bridle the whole body" (v. 2b; NRSV: "able to keep the whole body in check with a bridle"). The image suggests that control of the tongue leads to self-control of the body. As a horse is kept in check by a bridle, so the tongue guides the body as a whole. Speech is important for James because it relates to his overall theme of the continuity between faith and action. Those who speak empty words gain nothing (2:15-16). Those who control the tongue have the power to follow through with actions as well.

Although the tongue has this potential as bridle or rudder, it is also a "world of iniquity" (v. 6). It is untamable, "a restless evil, full of deadly poison" (v. 8). The primary problem is double-mindedness: the tongue can bless and curse (vv. 9-10). The examples of water and figs suggest that this capacity for double-mindedness is unnatural (vv. 11-12). Springs yield one kind of water, and trees yield one kind of fruit. Yet the tongue can speak both good and evil, and this, James says, "ought not to be so" (v. 10).

Such duplicity is inappropriate to the life of faith. Mixed speech is a mirror of the person. Just as salt water cannot yield fresh (v. 12), so the "pure and undefiled" (1:27) Christian displays integrity in their speech. James's message is that faith is visible in one's actions. Speech is one such action that should embody and be shaped by the believer's faith.

James 2:14-18 (LFM)

For commentary on this text, please see the second reading (RCL) for Proper 18, above.

Gospel
Mark 8:27-38 (RCL)
Mark 8:27-35 (LFM)

This familiar passage is often identified as the pivot point of Mark's Gospel. The previous chapters focused heavily on Jesus' healing miracles and other acts of power, and the later chapters focus on Jesus' teachings and his journey to the cross. The passage is crafted to prepare the reader to move toward the message of the latter half of the Gospel. It begins with the question from Jesus, "Who do people say that I am?" Thus the passage invites the reader to reflect upon the identity of Jesus.

The disciples begin by stating people's perceptions of Jesus: they think he is John the Baptist, Elijah, or one of the prophets (v. 28). These responses make sense, given what the people have seen and heard. Jesus proclaimed a gospel similar to John the Baptist's message (1:14-15; cf. 1:4). Jesus' cryptic teachings and his deeds of power recall Elijah and other Old Testament prophets. Thus the people appear to have a good initial understanding of who Jesus is. He displays the power of God and speaks God's word, just as other important leaders have done.

Yet Jesus' disciples show even greater understanding than the crowds. Peter represents the disciples as a whole when he steps forward with an answer that differs from the people. His answer to the same question shows that he has a different understanding of Jesus: he is the Messiah. Building on the understanding of the crowds, Peter has come a step closer to comprehension of Jesus' identity and mission.

Yet the disciples in Mark are always a mixed bag, and although Peter understands that Jesus is the Messiah, he shows limited understanding of what that means. When Jesus goes on to teach the disciples of his coming suffering, rejection, death, and resurrection, Peter begins to rebuke him (v. 32). Peter identifies Jesus as the Messiah, yet cannot comprehend how suffering and death fit into this picture, and tries to deter Jesus from enacting this part of his mission.

Jesus' decisive rebuke of Peter (v. 33) identifies Peter with Satan, whose temptation Jesus has already experienced (cf. 1:13). By rejecting Peter's approach, Jesus reaffirms that suffering, rejection, death, and resurrection are essential components of his identity as the Messiah. His acts of power have prepared people to understand that God's power is active in Jesus. Now the more difficult task begins of understanding that the Messiah's journey is not one of human glory, but is the road to the cross.

Following Jesus means following him on that road. In verse 34 the audience shifts, and Jesus begins to include the crowd with his disciples in his teachings. The call to be a follower of Jesus is not just for an elite group, those to whom Jesus reveals "the secret of the kingdom of God" (4:11). Instead, it is open to all: "If any want to become my followers, let them deny themselves and take up their cross and follow me" (v. 34). Being a follower of Jesus means following him to the cross.

One way to understand verses 34-38 is as a continuation of Jesus' teachings about his identity as the Messiah. Peter's rebuke seems to express his embarrassment about Jesus' prediction of his suffering and death. Jesus' words in verse 38 echo that response, exhorting the would-be follower not to be ashamed of this definition of his messianic purpose. The disciple who truly understands the teacher's words will display that wisdom in their own life, showing integrity in word and deed.

Followers must come to terms with the difficult purpose of Jesus' mission, so much so that his purpose is visible in their lives. In the context of Peter's rebuke, the words underscore that following Jesus involves accepting the disgrace of a crucified Messiah. He is not a savior according to the standards of political power and wealth. Jesus' life does not overthrow the Roman government, alleviate poverty, or immediately overturn the injustices of the world. Quite the contrary, he is killed by the Romans as a criminal, in a manner of death reserved for the poor and despised. Jesus' words call would-be followers to comprehend the claim that this one is nevertheless the Messiah.

Almost any negative effect can be given a religious validation if it is deemed "self-denial." A danger of preaching this passage is that it can be heard as a message to persist in rather than to resist various forms of injustice. Mark did expect Jesus' disciples to suffer as Jesus suffers (4:17; 13:9-13). Following Jesus may well bring difficulty and conflict with worldly standards. These verses are not a mandate to seek out abuse, however, but to follow Jesus. Mark also suggests that freedom is intrinsic to discipleship when he describes Jesus' death as a "ransom" from slavery (cf. 10:42-45). Disciples must exercise considerable judgment in discerning whether self-denial reflects accommodation to the "human things" that should be set aside, or "divine things" the disciple should pursue (v. 33).

Other passages of Mark add content to the meaning of self-denial and taking up one's cross, and may be useful for preaching in a contemporary context. Elsewhere in Mark, Jesus exhorts the disciples to behavior that suggests self-denial. They are to leave behind wealth and possessions (e.g., 6:7-9; 10:17-31) and to release their desire to be counted as the greatest or first (9:33-37; 10:35-45).[2] Disciples who understand that Jesus' identity includes suffering and death show this understanding through similar actions of self-denial.

Notes

1. Luke Timothy Johnson, *Brother of Jesus, Friend of God: Studies in the Letter of James* (Grand Rapids: Eerdmans, 2004), 176–77.
2. See Adela Yarbro Collins, *The Beginning of the Gospel: Probings of Mark in Context* (Minneapolis: Fortress Press, 1992), 66–68.

September 23, 2012
Lectionary 25 / Twenty-Fifth Sunday in Ordinary Time / Proper 20
Seventeenth Sunday after Pentecost

Revised Common Lectionary (RCL)	**Lectionary for Mass (LFM)**
Jeremiah 11:18-20 or Wisdom of Solomon 1:16—2:1, 12-22 or Proverbs 31:10-31	Wisdom of Solomon 2:12, 17-20
Psalm 54 or Psalm 1	Psalm 54:3-4, 5, 6-8
James 3:13—4:3, 7-8a	James 3:16—4:3
Mark 9:30-37	Mark 9:30-37

First Reading
Jeremiah 11:18-20 (RCL)

The prophets had a difficult task. They saw human life from God's perspective and communicated what they saw to others. The book of Jeremiah tells repeatedly of the prophet's rejection by the people. Scholars identify this passage as one of six laments attributed to Jeremiah (cf. 15:10-21; 17:14-18; 18:18-23; 20:7-13; 20:14-18). In each, the prophet mourns the rejection he experiences by those to whom God's message is addressed.

God initiates the prophet's message (v. 18). Yet the response of the people is to punish the messenger for the message (v. 19). Their attitude suggests that if they cut off the tree and its fruit, and even the remembrance of the prophet, the problem itself will disappear. Yet the prophet proclaims that God's justice ultimately prevails (v. 20). In the legal dispute (NRSV: "my cause"; Heb.: *riv*) against his opponents, God's righteous judgment will ultimately prevail.

Wisdom of Solomon 1:16—2:1, 12-22 (RCL alt.)
Wisdom of Solomon 2:12, 17-20 (LFM)

The Wisdom of Solomon opens with a contrast between the ungodly and the righteous. The selected verses present the perspective of the ungodly. They do not understand that God's intention for creation is not death, but life. Hades does not have dominion on earth, and righteousness is immortal (1:14-15). Instead, the ungodly believe that nothing exists after bodily life ends (2:1-5) and that, as a result of this situation, one's actions toward others do not matter (2:6-20). This fundamental mistake leads to all kinds of unjust behavior.'

The selected verses focus on the mistreatment of the righteous that results from the delusion of the unrighteous. The mere presence of the righteous is a reproof to the ungodly (2:12-16). The visible difference in the way the righteous live is a judgment against the unrighteous. Because they are aware of this judgment, they torment the righteous as a test. Their assumption is that, if what the righteous believe were true, God would rescue the righteous from their opponents (vv. 17-18). But their words are a deep misunderstanding of the mystery of God (v. 22). For God delivers the righteous to immortality (3:1-9).

For Christians, the plans of the ungodly to torment the righteous will bring to mind the suffering and death of Jesus. In their literary context, they are not a prediction about Jesus, but represent a pattern of behavior of the ungodly against those who follow in the path of Wisdom. Early Christians used ideas like this from Scripture to make sense of the suffering and death of Jesus. The treatment of Jesus fits the biblical pattern in which the ungodly mistreat the righteous. Yet God protects the righteous and rewards their faithfulness with life.

Proverbs 31:10-31 (RCL alt.)

Proverbs ends with this description of the virtuous woman. Many interpreters find these verses difficult to appropriate for modern times. The framing verses (vv. 10, 31) introduce the woman as something of value to her husband, a rare object to be acquired by men. And the woman described exhibits traditional virtues of caring for the household. She does not have a public presence in the city gate, the place of civic transactions. That is her husband's task (v. 23). She is devoted to her husband (v. 11). It can be difficult to think of a way to preach the passage that does not reinforce the harmful notion that a good woman looks only to the needs of others.

However, there is much in this passage to celebrate. The woman herself is the subject, not the object of verses 12-22, 24-27. Like many ancient women, the woman described here was not the political equal of men, yet she exercised considerable authority. She is praised for making decisions about what to buy (v. 16) and sell (vv. 14, 24). She oversees the production of clothing for the entire household (vv. 13, 19, 21, 22, 24; note that it is explicitly "her household" in vv. 15, 21, and 27). She cares for the needy (v. 20). This is not a picture of a woman who seeks only to please her children or to do her husband's bidding. Instead, she is a decision maker who controls household resources for the good of the household and community.

Instead of reading the passage as advice to men about finding a wife, the passage may instead be read as evidence that women, too, were considered able to cultivate a life guided by Wisdom. The virtues the woman exhibits are the same ones that are urged elsewhere in Proverbs. She "fears the LORD" (v. 30; cf., e.g., 1:7; 2:5; 14:2, 26-27).

Like others who cultivate wisdom, she prospers (cf. 2:21; 3:2, 10, 16, 18; 8:18, 21). Because her life reflects God's wisdom, other people honor her (cf. 3:4, 16, 18, 35; 4:8-9; 11:16) and call her "happy" (cf. 3:18; 8:32, 34). The woman is praised because her life shows the pursuit of wisdom. Indeed, she is a teacher of wisdom (31:26-27a; cf. 1:8; 6:20).

She is also a woman of strength. "A capable wife" (v. 10) might also be translated "a strong woman" (Heb.: *'eshet-chayil*). Her might (Heb.: *'oz*) is also described in verses 17 and 25. The Hebrew words used here often describe military strength (e.g., Num. 13:28; 1 Sam. 2:4; 2 Sam. 22:18) or wealth (e.g., Gen. 34:29; Isa. 30:6). As one who is shaped by the wisdom of God, she shares the warrior's strength and might.

Psalmody
Psalm 54 (RCL)
Psalm 54:3-4, 5, 6-8 (LFM)

Psalm 54 is a prayer for God's help in a time of trouble. It consists of a cry for help in the presence of enemies (vv. 1-3), a declaration of God's support and faithfulness (vv. 4-5), and a response of thanksgiving (vv. 6-7). The language of the psalm suggests the certainty of God's deliverance (vv. 4-5a, 7).

An early commentator on the psalm ascribed the song to David in a time when King Saul sought his life (Ps. 54:3; cf. 1 Sam. 23:15, 19-29). The superscription does not provide the historical background for the writing of the psalm, but creates a connection between the two texts that can help the interpreter flesh out the somewhat generic language of the psalm. David's hiding place is revealed to Saul (1 Sam. 23:19-20), who pursues him (v. 25). Saul is closing in on David (v. 26) when an attack by the Philistines diverts his attention away (v. 27). The story of David may add to the reader's understanding of the psalm. It describes the salvation God provides (escape from an enemy) and the way in which the salvation comes (a diversion).

Yet the psalm and the story of David do not fit neatly together. First, the enemies of Psalm 54 are literally "foreigners" (v. 3; Heb.: *zarim*; NRSV: "the insolent"), an odd description to apply to King Saul and his soldiers. When the texts are read together, it becomes clear that enemies may not literally be strangers, but familiar people with different values. They are people who "do not set God before them" (v. 3).

Another tension between the psalm and the superscription is that David's salvation does not come through Saul's immediate destruction. The reader might expect this from the language of the psalm (v. 7). Yet in David's story (1 Sam. 24:1-22; cf. 1 Samuel 26), he subsequently has an opportunity to kill Saul but spares his life, "for he is the LORD's anointed" (24:10). Thus the juxtaposition of the two texts may broaden the reader's understanding of the salvation (and destruction) God provides.

Psalm 1 (RCL alt.)

Psalm 1 contrasts those who live according to God's law with those who do not. God has created and ordered the world, and those who live according to that order are "happy." They are, by definition, set apart from the wicked. The three parallel phrases of verse 1 suggest the complete avoidance of the ways of those who are sinners: those who are happy do not walk, stand, or sit in the way of the wicked. Instead, they delight and meditate on the law of God.

Those who follow God's ways are secure, like a tree planted near a source of water (v. 3). Like the water, the word of God nourishes people and causes them to bear fruit, survive the dry seasons, and prosper. The wicked, in contrast, are insecure, like chaff blown about by the wind (v. 4). They bear no fruit and have no root or source of strength. Their "way" perishes, while the way of the righteous endures because it comes from and is known by God (v. 6).

Second Reading
James 3:13—4:3, 7-8a (RCL)
James 3:16—4:3 (LFM)

Preachers should consider 3:13—4:10 as a literary unit, from which verses have been selected for the lectionary reading. As a whole, the passage offers a strong indictment of the human propensity toward envy, and a call to repentance. Envy is a mind-set in opposition to God. The author identifies the desire for what others have as a source of great evil. As Luke Timothy Johnson points out, human envy represents a worldview in which "being depends on having, identity and worth derive from what is possessed. In such a view, to have less is to be less: less worthy, real, or important. To have more is to be more."[1] For the author, this perspective is equivalent to "enmity with God" (4:4).

Envy is associated with earthly wisdom (cf. 3:15), in contrast with "wisdom from above" (3:17). The contrast between earthly wisdom and wisdom from above reinforces the human choice between a life of envy and one of faithfulness to God's word. The one who is wise understands that those who ask God receive all that they need (4:2-3). The writer calls for a conversion in the hearer, to align one's will and actions with God's (4:7-10). As always for James, the life of faith is exhibited in one's behavior (cf. 2:14-26). Those who follow God's wisdom show their "good life" (3:13) and receive a "harvest of righteousness" (3:18). In the same light, the exhortation to "draw near to God" (4:8) does not simply reflect an internal change in the believer, but a change that manifests itself in a transformed life.

Gospel
Mark 9:30-37 (RCL, LFM)

Jesus announces his coming death and resurrection for the second time (cf. 8:31; 10:32-34). In this portion of the Gospel, Jesus teaches his followers about his purpose. The responses of the disciples in the story are in tension with Jesus' words. Through the tension, the reader learns something of the nature of discipleship.

The disciples do not understand what Jesus is telling them (v. 32). Mark's portrayal of the disciples suggests that some of their resistance is culpable. In prior passages, Jesus has questioned whether the disciples' hearts are hardened and has suggested that they should understand more than they do (8:17-21). He has rebuked Peter's attempt to suppress his first prediction of his death (8:33). Although it would be reasonable to assume that the disciples do not understand because this path toward suffering is unexpected, Mark has prepared the reader to see the disciples as people who are reluctant to understand Jesus' teachings.

Yet the disciples also show glimmers of understanding. In this case, they are afraid to ask Jesus to explain (v. 32). Fear and amazement are common responses to Jesus in Mark (cf. 4:41; 6:51; 10:32; 16:8). They suggest incomprehension in the face of such powerful miracles and authoritative teachings. As such, these responses also point toward the divine power and mystery that Jesus embodies. People who meet Jesus know that something about him is different, and this knowledge is expressed as fear. The question for the disciples is whether their fear can lead to faith.

The following verses reinforce the idea that the disciples misunderstand Jesus because they reject the posture of service implied by the crucifixion. On the road, they have argued about who among them is the greatest. The content of their conversation presents an attitude fundamentally at odds with Jesus' teaching about his death. The disciples want to be great according to human standards. Moving from fear to faith requires that they come to understand that Jesus does not accept glory on the world's terms. As disciples, they must come to model their behavior after the teacher's.

However, the disciples' fear again suggests some openness to change. They are afraid to tell Jesus what they were talking about (v. 34). Their silence may show that they understand enough about Jesus' mission to see how their desires are inappropriate. Yet Jesus pushes them toward actions that are shaped by a deeper understanding of who he is.

First, Jesus teaches them: "Whoever wants to be first must be last of all and servant of all" (v. 35). Instead of jockeying among themselves to be greatest (v. 34), Jesus teaches the disciples to seek a life of service. Slaves were numerous in the Roman world and were considered the lowest social class. Becoming "slave of all" represents the opposite of the disciples' attitude in their conversation. They must not seek greatness, but something quite different.

Jesus illustrates his teaching with an object lesson. Taking a child into their midst, Jesus enjoins the disciples to welcome such a child. Like slaves, children had low social status. There was nothing to be gained socially by welcoming children. Jesus exhorts the disciples to actions that require them to step away from seeking greatness and orient them toward those who have the least social and political power.

Jesus' words are not simply teachings about behavior, however. In the context of Jesus' teaching about his suffering and death (vv. 31-32), his words are also a remedy for the disciples' failure to understand his identity. Welcoming a child is an act that shows comprehension of Jesus' true mission. He is a powerful teacher and healer. Yet he is also despised and crucified. By acting contrary to the expectations of their society, disciples show their awareness of the full scope of Jesus' purpose.

In welcoming a child, the disciples prepare themselves not only to welcome Jesus but also to welcome God (v. 37). Jesus' words are a reminder that the shape of his own life reflects the identity of the one who sent him. Those who can understand how Jesus manifests divine power and yet does not use it for personal gain may begin to understand who God is.

Note

1. Luke Timothy Johnson, *The Letter of James*, Anchor Bible 37A (New York: Doubleday, 1995), 288.

September 30, 2012
Lectionary 26 / Twenty-Sixth Sunday in Ordinary Time / Proper 21
Eighteenth Sunday after Pentecost

Revised Common Lectionary (RCL)	**Lectionary for Mass (LFM)**
Numbers 11:4-6, 10-16, 24-29 or Esther 7:1-6, 9-10; 9:20-22	Numbers 11:25-29
Psalm 19:7-14 or Psalm 124	Psalm 19:8, 10, 12-13, 14
James 5:13-20	James 5:1-6
Mark 9:38-50	Mark 9:38-43, 45, 47-48

First Reading
Numbers 11:4-6, 10-16, 24-29 (RCL)
Numbers 11:25-29 (LFM)

God's gift of manna to sustain Israel in the wilderness (Exodus 16) is not enough for the people. They continue to complain, weeping for meat (Num. 11:4-6). This story continues the theme of Israel's complaining against God and Moses in the wilderness. They are dissatisfied with God's gifts and prefer the slavery of Egypt to following God's path.

God is angry with Israel, and Moses is displeased. Grammatically, it is not clear whether Moses is displeased because of Israel's behavior or because of God's anger. He recognizes the basic problem of the people's complaint (v. 13). But God is the main focus of Moses' words in verses 11-15. Moses accuses God of treating him badly (v. 11). His rhetorical questions are a pointed reminder that God is responsible for Israel's well-being. God, not Moses, is the mother of this people, and it is God's promise of land to Abraham that they have set out to fulfill (v. 12). Moses' words point a finger at God for asking too much of Moses' leadership.

Although the passage has much in common with other wilderness stories, the details of this story are difficult theologically. Both Moses and God appear angry, and this emotional state contradicts the expectations many readers have of both a loving God and an obedient and faithful leader like Moses. The anger of God and the almost sarcastic retort of God's servant, Moses, create a theological problem for the preacher.

Some commentators consider Moses' complaint a failure to trust in God.[1] This fits with the character of Moses, who is initially reluctant to lead God's people (see Exod. 3:11-13; 4:1, 10). However, this view fails to consider that Moses is also characterized as speaking directly to God, as one would to a friend (e.g., Exod. 33:11; Num. 12:6-8; Deut. 34:10). The frankness of this conversation suggests Moses' deep relationship with God, a relationship that can sustain even difficult words of accusation. Because of this, it may be better to understand Moses' words as a cry of desperation that, like a psalm of lament, voices a fear that God has abandoned the supplicant.[2]

If Moses' words are not a failure, this may suggest that Moses is right. The resulting picture of God is likewise unsatisfying: God appears angry and unforgiving. It may be best to read the story as one place the biblical witness captures the idea of God's deep relationship with humankind. Other portions of the biblical witness flesh out other elements of the character of God: God's long-suffering faithfulness to Israel, for example. The portrait of God in these verses captures particular aspects of God that are also important theologically. This is not an impassible deity, but one who seeks relationship with real people. As a result, God experiences anger at human failings and responds to human prayer. Moses' cry for help is an act of faithfulness that moves God to act (cf. Exod. 32:11-14; 33:12-17).

God responds by designating others to share the burden of leadership. Gathering seventy elders at the tent of meeting, God takes some of God's spirit from Moses and places it on these other leaders (vv. 24-25). Two of the seventy remained in the camp, but also prophesied. Their prophecy occasions an objection from Joshua. It is not clear whether the problem is that Eldad and Medad prophesy in the camp, or that they continue to do so after the others have ceased. What is clear is that Moses rejects Joshua's criticism: "Would that all the LORD's people were prophets!" Moses is not a leader who asks for help and then criticizes others for not doing things in the expected way. Instead, he appears ready to share the burden of leadership with others, and he recognizes the prophecy as a manifestation of God's spirit.

Esther 7:1-6, 9-10; 9:20-22 (RCL alt.)

These verses are the climax of Esther's story. Haman, a high-ranking official, plots to kill all of the Jews because Mordecai, Esther's uncle, refuses to bow down to him (Esth. 3:1-6). Esther invites her husband, King Ahasuerus, and Haman to a banquet. She wins the king's favor and he grants her wish—the salvation of her people.

The book of Esther's rich irony is seen in the mode of Haman's death. As he has tried to kill innocent people, so he is killed for a crime he did not commit. (He was not trying to kill Esther.) He receives the same punishment he intended for Mordecai. Similarly, in the previous chapter, Mordecai has been honored for his service to the king in a manner Haman devised for himself (6:1-11).

Esther risks her own life in two ways. First, she enters into the king's presence without being summoned (4:15—5:2). Second, she reveals that she is also a Jew, one of those Haman has destined for destruction. This is a part of her identity she previously kept a secret (cf. 2:10, 20). By siding with her people, Esther risks being seen as one of them. However, identifying herself as Jewish also allows Esther to frame the problem of the Jews' destruction as one of damage to King Ahasuerus.

Psalmody
Psalm 19:7-14 (RCL)
Psalm 19:8, 10, 12-13, 14 (LFM)

For a discussion of Psalm 19, see the psalmody for the Sixteenth Sunday after Pentecost, above.

Psalm 124 (RCL alt.)

This psalm reminds the hearer of Israel's reliance on God for salvation. Without God being "for us" (vv. 1, 2; NRSV: "on our side"), the enemy would have "swallowed us alive" (v. 3). The imagery suggests the threat of being consumed: swallowed alive (v. 3), covered by floodwaters (vv. 4-5), or eaten like a bird caught in a trap (vv. 6-7).

God's salvation is declared briefly: the trap is broken and we have escaped (v. 7). Although the verb is passive ("is broken"), the context of verses 1, 2, and 8 claims this as divine action. God has foiled the plans of the enemies and brought Israel to safety. The congregation singing this song now declares its reliance on the name of God, creator of heaven and earth. God alone delivers Israel to safety.

Second Reading
James 5:13-20 (RCL)

Throughout the letter, James has addressed many negative forms of speech: for instance, blessing God while cursing others (3:9-10); evil speech (4:11); boasting (4:16); and grumbling (5:9). Finally, in 5:13, the author advocates beneficial uses of speech. The one who suffers should pray; the one who rejoices should sing psalms.

The church should pray for a member who is sick. The gathering of the elders to pray over the sick person reestablishes social connections that illness threatens. The "sin" that is most relevant to these verses may be the alienation humans create in the face of illness. In verse 15 the sin of the sick person is in view, and the verse seems to corroborate an ancient view of sickness as a punishment for sin (cf. John 9:2). Yet verse 16 suggests a view in which sickness affects the "body" of the church, which needs healing. This healing is brought about by the mutual confession and forgiveness of the community. Similarly, James points to the power of church members to restore one another to faith by mutual correction (vv. 19-20).

In verses 17-18 Elijah serves as an example that "the prayer of the righteous is powerful and effective" (v. 16). Elijah is "righteous" because his ministry was aligned with the "righteous ones" oppressed by the wealthy of the world (cf. 5:6). He was a friend of God rather than the world (cf. 4:4). Yet James also describes Elijah as "a human being like us" (v. 17), emphasizing the similarity between the reader and the great prophet. James reaffirms the power of God to respond to the cries of the righteous (cf. 5:4).

James 5:1-6 (LFM)

James follows his teaching that "God opposes the proud" (4:6) with various examples of proud behavior (4:11-12, 13-17; 5:1-6). The lectionary verses are the most severe example of those who are "friends of the world and enemies of God" (cf. 4:4).

James describes the rich as those who have lived luxuriously at the expense of others (v. 5). They have defrauded laborers (v. 4). Their arrogance has even led to murder of "the righteous one" (v. 6)—wording that some interpreters read as a reference to Jesus, but which others understand simply as any innocent person wronged by the greed of the wealthy. Both interpretations are possible.

James's message is that God opposes the rich. The cries of the oppressed have reached God's ears (v. 4). The threat of the "miseries that are coming to you" (v. 1) echoes the language of the prophets who proclaimed God's judgment against the unfaithful. In the LXX, the same word translated "miseries" in the NRSV (5:1; Gk.: *talaipōria*) points to the coming "disaster" of God's judgment (e.g., Isa. 47:11; Jer. 4:20). The rich may have power to oppress others now, but they should not expect this to last.

This view of wealth is consistent throughout the letter. James wants the reader to understand that wealth is fleeting (1:9-11). The rich store up wealth for the last day, but it rots and rusts (5:2-3). Envy, the desire for what others have, leads to severe problems, like murder (4:2; cf. 5:6).

The passage is one of the Bible's most unrelenting critiques of wealth. James does not speak a word of hope to the wealthy. The following verse, "Be patient, therefore, beloved, until the coming of the Lord" (v. 7), is not a consolation for the rich but for those faithful who await their judgment. In wealthy congregations it will be difficult to hear James's message because it implicates everyone. James portrays all wealth as unjustly oppressing another and diverting the rich person's attention away from divine justice.

Gospel
Mark 9:38-50 (RCL)
Mark 9:38-43, 45, 47-48 (LFM)

John voices the disciples' discomfort with something they have experienced: one who is not following Jesus is nevertheless casting out demons in Jesus' name. The disciples' concern seems reasonable at first. They are suspicious that someone uses the power of Jesus' name but is not a true disciple.

Through the centuries, the church has required confirmation of acts of power in Jesus' name. It is not enough to cast out a demon, unless it is backed up by faith in God that manifests itself more broadly in acts of mercy and profession of faith. As a biblical example of this, Matthew cautions to "beware of false prophets, who come to you in sheep's clothing but inwardly are ravenous wolves. You will know them by their fruits" (Matt. 7:15-16). Likewise the author of 1 John warns, "Every spirit that confesses that Jesus Christ has come in the flesh is from God, and every spirit that does not confess Jesus is not from God" (1 John 4:2-3). The disciples' wariness regarding this stranger's charismatic gifts reflects common concerns.

Yet Mark also gives the reader reason to be wary of the disciples' motivations. The disciples have reasons for concern, but they also have something to protect. John says, "We tried to stop him, because he was not following us" (v. 39). His wording suggests that the disciples are less concerned about being followers of Jesus themselves, and more concerned about others following "us."

This concern is consistent with the disciples' behavior in Mark. Just prior to this passage, they have responded to Jesus' second prediction of his passion by arguing among themselves over who is the greatest (see Proper 20, above). Jesus answers, "Whoever wants to be first must be last of all and servant of all" (v. 35). The disciples' attempt to hinder the man casting out demons in Jesus' name is related to their desire to be the greatest. That man is not following after them. He should be stopped, so that the proper hierarchy can be restored.

Stepping back a little further in the context, the disciples' motives may even seem a little sinister. Earlier in this chapter, they have failed to cast out a demon from an epileptic child (9:14-29). Along comes someone else who is successfully casting out demons. The disciples may feel jealous of a power to which they aspire but cannot fully live into.

Jesus' own response to the disciples confirms that the one casting out demons may be less than genuine. He tells the disciples, "Do not stop him; for no one who does a deed of power in my name will be able soon afterward to speak evil of me" (v. 39). His words suggest that this person has been speaking evil of Jesus. Although the acts of power do not come from a place of pure intentions, the use of that divine power results in transformation. The one performing acts of power will no longer speak evil of Jesus.

The disciples' mistake is to try to exert control over the places or ways that God can act. Jesus' words assert that acts of power in Jesus' name exceed the disciples' control. Such acts manifest themselves in unlikely places, at the hands of unlikely people. In hindering the man casting out demons, the disciples show their certainty that God's power only shows itself among the good and the powerful.

This is the same mistake that the disciples have made in their misunderstanding of and resistance to the death of Jesus (8:32-35; 9:33-37; 10:35-37; see Propers 19 and 20, above). They want to be recognized and honored by others, and they want this for Jesus as well. Their response to the man casting out demons seems to reflect a similar desire that the power of God should be limited to established and respectable channels. Yet Jesus' response to the disciples suggests that God's power may be manifest strongly in people who are truly outside of what society deems righteous or acceptable.

There are dire consequences for those who try to stop the manifestation of the power of God. "It would be better for you if a great millstone were hung around your neck and you were thrown into the sea. If your hand causes you to stumble, cut it off; it is better for you to enter life maimed than to have two hands and to go to hell, to the unquenchable fire" (vv. 42-43). God's power in Mark is a mighty force, manifest in Jesus, but overflowing in surprising ways. Jesus' words are a powerful warning not to get in its way.

Notes

1. E.g., Richard N. Boyce, *Leviticus and Numbers*, Westminster Bible Companion (Louisville: Westminster John Knox, 2008), 149.
2. For a discussion, see Katharine Doob Sakenfeld, *Numbers*, International Theological Commentary (Grand Rapids: Eerdmans, 1995), 74–75.

Time after Pentecost / Ordinary Time
Lectionary 27 / Proper 22 through Christ the King / Reign of Christ
Tracy Hartman

Fall is finally upon us. At home and at school, many of us are breathing a sigh of relief as back-to-school excitement transitions into new school routines and households return to "normal" rhythms. In the life of the church, many of us have experienced the excitement of end-of-summer Sunday school promotions and the launch of new fall programs. In worship, however, we remain in the Time after Pentecost—Ordinary Time. While the colors begin to change outside our sanctuary windows, our vestments and paraments remain green, signifying the season of growth in discipleship for both individuals and the church as a corporate body. If we take a closer look, however, there are shifts and changes ahead for us in worship, too, as the call to discipleship becomes anything but ordinary! We also find two special days during this cycle: All Saints Day/Sunday (November 1/4) and Christ the King or Reign of Christ Sunday, which concludes the liturgical year.

On Ordinary Sundays, the Gospel readings continue through the Gospel of Mark. Preachers will find opportunities for prophetic preaching as the Gospel lections and the readings in the complementary Old Testament track challenge our presuppositions on the timeless topics of divorce, wealth, spiritual blindness, the desire for recognition and prominence, and self-sacrifice. As Jesus turns toward Jerusalem, we, like the disciples, learn that after the initial excitement wears off, we may have a difficult time following and remaining faithful when things get hard.

The second Old Testament track continues the semicontinuous emphasis on the Wisdom literature. This section of Ordinary Time opens with four Sundays focused on the book of Job. In a time when many popular televangelists and authors promote a prosperity gospel, these lections give preachers the opportunity to take a hard and honest look at suffering and our response as believers to what may appear to be insurmountable challenges in our daily lives.

Entering November, the semicontinuous Old Testament track moves into the book of Ruth for two Sundays. Read parabolically, Ruth provides a surprising prophetic word for those of us who consider ourselves to be "insiders." In this story, it is Naomi, the insider, who needs redeeming, and it is Ruth, the outsider, who is the agent of redemption. In the same way, Ruth encourages "outsiders" to be attentive to how God might be using them in unexpected ways.

This Old Testament track concludes with two great songs: Hannah's in 1 Samuel 1 and David's in 2 Samuel 2. These songs of praise, which focus on two unlikely heroes, frame one of the greatest periods of transition in Israel's history. The remarkable story of Hannah and the birth of Samuel can also help us hear and believe the remarkable story of the birth of Christ that we will begin to prepare for soon.

The epistle lessons for this season of the year come from the book of Hebrews. This letter, which was written for a discouraged and struggling congregation, has much to offer many of our churches today. As he builds his case, the writer will remind us over and over again of the ultimate sacrifice Christ made on our behalf and the eternal consequences of this great gift. Week after week, we will come to a deeper understanding of what it means for Christ to be our high priest as well as what it means for us to now live as priests in the world.

All Saints Day/Sunday is the first feast day in this cycle of lections. Many of us will pause from "ordinary" time to grieve and honor those we have lost in the last year and to reflect on and honor the multitude of saints that have come and gone before us. In our culture that obsesses over youth and sanitizes death, this important day can help us reframe our worldviews and gain a larger, healthier perspective.

The second special day in this cycle is the Reign of Christ/Christ the King Sunday. As the liturgical year ends, we must all decide if we believe that Christ is indeed the King and if we are willing to place our lives under his rule and reign. For those of us used to living in a democracy where ideally we are all equal, this will be a difficult concept to grasp. If we are serious about following Jesus, however, this commitment will require significant transitions and a new "normal" for many of us.

October 7, 2012
Lectionary 27 / Twenty-Seventh Sunday in Ordinary Time / Proper 22
Nineteenth Sunday after Pentecost

Revised Common Lectionary (RCL)
Genesis 2:18-24 or Job 1:1; 2:1-10
Psalm 8 or Psalm 26
Hebrews 1:1-4; 2:5-12
Mark 10:2-16

Lectionary for Mass (LFM)
Genesis 2:18-24
Psalm 128:1-2, 3, 4-5, 6
Hebrews 2:9-11
Mark 10:2-16 or 10:2-12

Today's texts tie together in interesting ways and provide the preacher with a variety of sermon themes. The passages in Genesis 2 and Mark 10 talk about the sanctity of human relationships, while Genesis 2, Psalm 8, and the Hebrews text lead to thoughts about humanity's role in the world. Alternately, Job and Psalm 26 speak of righteousness and faithfulness in the presence of trials and the challenge of true piety.

First Reading
Genesis 2:18-24 (RCL, LFM)

Although beloved by many, the creation stories present preachers with a number of challenges. For starters, many of our listeners have so embraced an evolutionary view of our cosmic origins that the idea of a creative and active God has lost its meaning for them. Then we must contend with long-standing interpretations that have condoned the despoiling of the environment and the subjugation of women to men.

Regardless of the direction our sermons from Genesis take, we are wise to remind our hearers that the creation accounts as a whole address the questions of *who* and *why*, not the questions of *how* and *when*. As a prescientific people, the Israelites did not focus on the factual answers to the questions of how and when God created. They were much more concerned with the theological questions of who created them and why.

In Genesis 2, the second creation account, we find a very active and hands-on God. God forms man from the dust and breathes the breath of life into him. God plants a garden, places man in it, and gives him basic instructions to guide his life.

However, in contrast to Genesis 1, all is not good. Today's text begins with the words, "It is *not good* that man should be alone; I will make him a helper as his partner." Terence Fretheim notes that God's presence alone does not suffice for the man. Once God identifies this problem within creation, God moves to makes changes to improve it. At this stage, God has also delegated the final word to the man. God brings all of the creative possibilities (the animals and then woman) to the man, who declares, "This at last is bone of my bones and flesh of my flesh."[1]

The Hebrew word for the helper God creates is *ezer*. Interestingly, this word occurs nineteen times in the Old Testament, and twelve of the references refer to God as the helper. When the word refers to a human helper, someone is in need of deliverance from a predicament or danger posed by a powerful individual or group. Marsha Wilfong argues that human loneliness is the predicament from which the man needs rescue. However, she notes that *ezer* is modified in Genesis 2:18 to mean that the woman is an equal helper, not a superior or more powerful one.[2]

Several scholars note that the nature of the relationship between the man and the woman in Genesis 2 is a model for relationships in the larger human community. The diversity among us should be complementary, not divisive, and we are to live in intimate equality and mutuality. God gives us freedom to make choices, both good and bad. Fretheim notes that this commits God to a permissive and flexible relationship with humanity that requires creative adjustments to the divine will for the world.[3]

Who is identified as subordinate or "other" in your faith community? What might it look like to honor those people as equals in the larger human community? What would we need to do to live in intimate mutuality? Many Christians hold fast to the idea that God never changes. How can we as preachers help them hear and respond to the idea of a flexible God who is willing to change and grow in response to the needs of the world?

Job 1:1; 2:1-10 (RCL alt.)

Job 1:1 tells us three things about Job: his name, where he is from, and his character. Job is described with two pairs of descriptors: blameless and upright, and one who feared God and turned away from evil.[4] Job is further described as a very wealthy man with ten children. As chapter 1 unfolds, God gives the satan permission to test Job's faithfulness by taking away all of his wealth and his children. Although such a heavenly contest sounds odd to our ears, it would not have seemed unusual to the original hearers of this story. It is likely that the story of Job originated not with Israel but with one of the other people-groups living among them. These people would have held a polytheistic view that could easily accommodate the image of competing gods. We should also remember that "the satan" in this story is not Satan or the devil of the New Testament. At this point in Israel's history, "the satan" refers to a particular being in the heavenly court whose sole function was to seek out and accuse persons disloyal to God.[5] Today's text begins the second round of Job's testing, and in this scene God gives the accuser permission to attack Job's health. As in the first test, Job remains faithful, refusing to sin or charge God with wrongdoing.

For generations, Israelites believed that if they were living in accordance with God's will they would be blessed, and if they were experiencing hardship or difficulties, they had displeased God. Carol Newsom points out that when God blesses us, we flourish, and this flourishing motivates us to good conduct. However, this mind-set can quickly deteriorate into a religion for barter where we agree to live righteously for God if God will bless us.[6] Job's wife, perhaps observing that God had not kept God's end of the bargain, encourages Job to curse God and die. Job responds, "Shall we receive the good at the hand of God and not receive the bad?"

Job wisely recognizes that bad things happen to good people, and his statement calls Israel's theology of suffering into question. He seems to understand that if we only associate God with the good things that happen in our lives, we feel forsaken when trouble occurs. The wisdom of Job's stance is that it allows him to recognize the presence of God in even the most desolate experiences.[7] Depending on our circumstances, today's text can give hope in the midst of suffering or challenge those who lean toward a prosperity gospel.

Psalmody
Psalm 8 (RCL)

Psalm 8, the first psalm of praise in the Psalter, declares God's sovereignty over the heavens and the earth and reminds humanity of their responsibility in caring for the earth that God has created. In this psalm we hear echoes of Genesis 2:18-24, where God gives Adam the responsibility of naming every living creature. In today's second reading from Hebrews 2, the words of the psalm are applied to Jesus. Although the lectionary does not pair this psalm with the Job text, J. Clinton McCann Jr. points out that Psalm 8 figures prominently in the book of Job as Job's suffering leads him to deny the royal status and vocation of humanity; then he comes full circle to reclaim it as he comes to understand that full humanity involves suffering as well as glory.[8]

Psalm 26 (RCL alt.)

Psalm 26 is a psalm of David, but it could easily be a psalm of Job. In this psalm it is commonly assumed that the psalmist has been falsely accused by his enemies and he is seeking justice from God. Throughout the psalm, the writer holds fast to his innocence and implores God to redeem him.

Psalm 128: 1-2, 3, 4-5, 6 (LFM)

This psalm is a psalm of ascent and blessing. It begins by reminding the reader that we are truly blessed or happy only when we order our lives around God as we reverence God and walk in God's ways. Then we will be in a position to offer thanks to God regardless of what material blessings might come our way. This psalm complements the creation account where humans are given both the blessing and responsibility of dominion over the earth.

Second Reading
Hebrews 1:1-4; 2:5-12 (RCL)
Hebrews 2:9-11 (LFM)

The book of Hebrews is likely an extended sermon written for a discouraged and disheartened congregation in need of a new vision and new hope. The RCL begins today's reading with Hebrews 1:1-4, where the writer sets the stage for the sustained argument that is to follow. God has spoken to us before through a variety of means, he begins, but now God has spoken to us by a Son. Something is new here, something is different. We should pay attention. The writer goes on to tell us that this Son, who is the reflection of God's glory and being, has made purification for our sins and now returned to reign with God on high.

In chapter 2, the writer of Hebrews quotes Psalm 8 and interprets it christologically, reflecting on Jesus' cosmic journey from majesty through shame and back again to exaltation.[9] The path we see here is similar to the one that Job travels as he is stripped of all he has, tested beyond measure, and then finally restored.

In these verses we also see a very human Jesus who stands in total solidarity with humans, suffering with us and calling us brothers and sisters. This passage, along with the texts from Job, reminds us that suffering and trials are an integral part of our daily existence.

Many of our parishioners are struggling—with relationships, with the poor economy, with discouragement and defeat. Hebrews can provide hope by reminding us of the mediating presence of the Son and can challenge us all to live in a posture of grace and humility in the midst of our difficulties.

Gospel
Mark 10:2-16 (RCL)
Mark 10:2-16 or 10:2-12 (LFM)

As I read this passage about Jesus' teaching on divorce, I immediately think of my brother and sister-in-law who are divorcing after twenty-eight years of marriage. My brother would very much like to find a soul mate with whom to share life fully as he moves forward. I think of several of my divorced clergy friends who are now experiencing wholeness in a second marriage. I think about the fact that nearly half of Christian marriages end in divorce. I wonder how we can preach this passage with integrity and not do more harm than good to those in our congregations who have already been deeply wounded.

Understanding the context of this passage can help us be faithful proclaimers. First, the original question to Jesus comes from the Pharisees as a test: "Is it lawful for a man to divorce his wife?" As usual, the Pharisees were trying to put Jesus in a no-win situation; no matter how he answered this question, he would offend someone. In Israelite society in Jesus' day, there were two groups with opposing views on divorce. The Shammai believed that a man could only divorce his wife for adultery or unfaithfulness. However, the Hillel gave men much more leeway. Based on the words in Deuteronomy 24:1, "Suppose a man enters into marriage with a woman, but she does not please him because he finds something objectionable about her, and so he writes her a certificate of divorce," the Hillel believed that a man could divorce his wife for almost any reason. If the woman could not return to her father's house, she found herself out on the street, begging or prostituting herself to survive. The history of the opposing sides and the Pharisees' question indicate that divorce was a reality in Jesus' day, just as it is in ours.

Not surprisingly, however, Jesus refuses to play the Pharisees' game and he answers their question with one of his own. "What did Moses command you?" They are quick to refer to Deuteronomy where Moses permits a man to divorce his wife. Jesus does not disagree that divorce is permissible, but he quickly points out that it is a concession made to life in a broken world. "Because of the hardness of your heart he wrote this commandment to you," Jesus replies. Then he shifts the discussion from divorce to marriage. Drawing on both Genesis 1 and 2, Jesus reminds the Pharisees that God created humanity to live in intimate equality and mutuality (see the commentary on Genesis 2, above). Instead of focusing on the negative, Jesus reminds them of both the beauty and permanence intended in the marriage relationship. It's as if Jesus were saying, "Yes, you can divorce your wife, but it doesn't mean you should. It may be lawful, but that doesn't mean it is right."

The conversation was over with the Pharisees, but the text tells us that the disciples had some lingering questions. Here Jesus' response is both liberating and convicting. His words are liberating to women who find themselves needing to divorce. In Roman culture, women could initiate divorce proceedings, but not in Hebrew culture. In this statement, Jesus was elevating the status of women in the marital relationship and granting them the same rights as men. (This would undoubtedly have infuriated the Pharisees had they heard it.)

The difficult words come in Jesus' matter-of-fact statement that whoever initiates a divorce and then remarries commits adultery against his or her former spouse. It seems that Jesus is reminding the disciples that although a legal union can be dissolved, we can never completely separate two who have been one. We can move forward, but as those who are in second marriages can attest, lingering issues will remain.

It is also important that we recognize that this text deals with a specific question in a specific place in time. The idea of mutually divorcing did not exist in Jesus' day. The passage should also never be used to keep an abused spouse (either male or female) in a harmful relationship (this type of "marriage" would be considered no marriage at all in God's original created order).

While remaining sensitive to those in our congregations who have experienced the pain of divorce, we do need to call ourselves to higher standards. While the tabloids are filled with news of Elizabeth Taylor's ninth marriage, Larry King's eighth divorce, and numerous infidelities by people we idolize, we need to remind our hearers of the seriousness of marriage. We also need to teach that with commitment and real *agape* love, most marriages can and should be successful.

Perhaps the final verses of today's lectionary passage can help us in this regard. In verses 13-16 Jesus welcomes the children into his arms and blesses them, reminding us all that whoever does not receive the kingdom of God as a little child will never enter it. In ancient Israel, children were truly the least of these, the ones most likely to be exploited and taken advantage of, the ones most in need of protection. Perhaps we will begin to live faithfully in our human relationships when we acknowledge that we need God's provision, protection, and blessing on them.

Notes

1. Terence Fretheim, "Genesis," in *The New Interpreter's Bible* (Nashville: Abingdon, 1994), 1:352.
2. Marsha Wilfong, "Genesis 2:18-24," *Interpretation* 42, no. 1 (January 1988): 59.
3. Fretheim, "Genesis," 1:356.
4. Carol Newsom notes that the presence of four adjectives is significant—that Noah only had two. "The Book of Job," in *The New Interpreter's Bible* (Nashville: Abingdon, 1996), 4:345.
5. Ibid., 4:347.
6. Ibid., 4:358.
7. Ibid., 4:360.
8. J. Clinton McCann Jr., "Psalms," in *The New Interpreter's Bible*, 4:713.
9. Thomas G. Long, *Hebrews*, Interpretation: A Bible Commentary for Teaching and Preaching (Louisville: John Knox, 1997), 34.

October 14, 2012
Lectionary 28 / Twenty-Eighth Sunday in Ordinary Time / Proper 23
Twentieth Sunday after Pentecost

Revised Common Lectionary (RCL)

Amos 5:6-7, 10-15 or Job 23:1-9, 16-17

Psalm 90:12-17 or 22:1-15

Hebrews 4:12-16

Mark 10:17-31

Lectionary for Mass (LFM)

Wisdom of Solomon 7:7-11

Psalm 90:12-13, 14-15, 16-17

Hebrews 4:12-13

Mark 10:17-30 or 10:17-27

Today's texts provide preachers with the opportunity to do some prophetic preaching—not a favorite for many of us! Why are some of us so hesitant to bring a much-needed prophetic word from the pulpit? In her book *Prophetic Preaching: A Pastoral Approach*, Nora Tubbs Tisdale names seven common reasons, ranging from a pastoral concern for our struggling parishioners who don't need more "bad" news from the pulpit to our fears of stirring up conflict, dividing our congregations, or being personally rejected or even fired for preaching prophetically.[1] However, Tisdale reminds us that while prophetic preaching might begin with the "bad" news of God's anger and judgment, it is ultimately hopeful as we call God's people to live into God's vision for the kingdom of God on earth. Furthermore, prophetic preaching is not primarily about addressing social or political issues; rather, it is about helping the people of God radically reorient their worldview and their consciousness so that they can see the world the way God sees it.[2] With this definition in mind, today's texts offer us a variety of ways to help our parishioners both envision and live into new realities.

First Reading
Amos 5:6-7, 10-15 (RCL)

The book of Amos is the earliest of the prophetic books and the first to bear the name of a prophet. It sets the prophetic tone for the rest of the canonical prophets.[3] Unfortunately, it is prophets like Amos who give prophetic preaching a negative image, for his message is almost exclusively one of mortal gloom and doom for Israel. Although he does champion the themes of justice and righteousness, his primary purpose is to warn Israel that they will be destroyed.

The form of speech used most prominently in Amos is the announcement of divine judgment combined with a reason for the judgment (usually Israel's sins).[4] One example of this form is found in today's text in 5:11. Prior to this announcement, we find two interesting units. The first is an exhortation (5:4-7), one of only four in the entire book. In this exhortation, the people are encouraged to seek God in order that they may live (or not be destroyed). Verses 8-9, which are eliminated from the lectionary reading for today, are fragments from an ancient hymn that remind the readers that God is sovereign over nature and may even use nature as a means of judgment.[5] In verses 10-12, the prophet appeals to the canonical law to remind Israel once again of their sins. Finally, in verses 14-15, the prophet exhorts the people to seek good and not evil so that they might live. There is no guarantee promised in this passage, just a thread of hope that God might indeed save a remnant of Israel.

Amos began his prophetic work near the end of a long and prosperous period in the Northern Kingdom of Israel. In a time when people equated prosperity with God's favor and blessing, Amos had the difficult task of bringing a harsh word. In less than a generation after Amos began preaching, the Northern Kingdom would fall to the Assyrians and the people would lose their land and their status as an independent nation. This reality would have been unimaginable to the people of Israel in Amos's day. Later, exilic and postexilic Jewish communities would seek to make sure that they lived justly and in dependence on God so that there would be no need for this level of prophetic preaching again.[6]

The differences between twenty-first-century America and eighth-century BCE Israel are numerous, and the words of Amos cannot be applied wholesale to our context. However, Amos still has relevance for us today. Despite facing some significant economic challenges in the last few years, the United States is still one of the wealthiest nations on earth. Like ancient Israel, we tend to rely on our own military strength and we perpetuate economic, political, and legal systems that favor the wealthy at the expense of the poor. Many of our actions, whether they be intentional or not, grieve God's heart as deeply now as they did then. As pastors, many of us will have to show our people how we participate in oppression before we can ask them to reorient their worldview and their consciousness and exhort them to work to bring about the kingdom of God on earth.

In congregations where people are committed to living simply and justly, it is easy for folks to become discouraged and wonder if their efforts are making a difference. For these worshipers, Amos offers a word of hope. Although both the kingdoms of Israel do fall, and the people of Judah spend time in exile, God does indeed restore a remnant through whom God's work continues.

Job 23:1-9, 16-17 (RCL alt.)

This chapter is Job's first speech in the third cycle of speeches. By now, Job's patience has waned; he is bitter and ready to be vindicated. In this chapter, Job's mood swings back and forth between confidence, defiance, and despair. Verses 1-7 are full of legal language as Job speaks of his desire to make his case before God. Maintaining his innocence, Job envisions arguing his points and reasoning with God the righteous judge who will acquit Job forever.

Job has a major problem, however: he cannot find God. In verses 8-9, I picture Job frantically moving forward and backward, to the left and to the right, searching in vain for God who is hiding from him. This is not a portrait of a confident or innocent man.

Verses 10-15 are eliminated from today's reading, but without them we lose the progression of Job's thoughts. In verses 10-12, Job appears to calm down. He regains confidence as he reasserts his innocence, but his bravado does not last. By verse 13 he acknowledges that God will act as God desires. By verse 15 Job is filled with terror and dread at the very thought of God's presence.

The lectionary picks back up in verses 16-17. Scholars offer two basic interpretations of verse 17. In the NRSV, Job seems to be in despair, wishing that he could simply vanish into the darkness. In the NIV, Job is seen as defiant, claiming, "Yet I am not silenced by the darkness, by the thick darkness that covers my face."[7]

Both Job and the rich young ruler in today's Gospel text want to *do* something. Job wants to argue his case and be cleared of the charges his friends have brought, and the rich young ruler wants to know what he must do to be saved. Interestingly, neither gets what he wants or hopes for. The prophetic word here is that God doesn't do life on our terms. The hopeful word is that if we will indeed trust in God, God will provide for us in ways that we cannot yet even imagine.

Wisdom of Solomon 7:7-11 (LFM)

The Wisdom of Solomon was written in the late first century BCE. The author chose to write under the persona of Solomon in hopes that the authority of the father of wisdom would stand behind his words. This book, a product of Hellenistic Judaism, is found in the Septuagint (the Greek Old Testament), but not in the official Jewish canon. The book was written to help the readers endure persecution and resist the pull of Hellenistic culture.[8]

Today's selection is part of Solomon's prayer for wisdom. After praying for and then receiving wisdom, Solomon recounts its value. He states that wisdom is to be preferred and valued over all else: the kingship, gold, silver, jewels, beauty, or even health. However, Solomon then discovers that all good things come along with wisdom, especially friendship with God (v. 14).

This passage serves as a nice antithesis to today's Gospel text, where the rich man finds himself unable to release his wealth to follow Jesus. This passage also complements Psalm 90, where today's reading begins, "Teach us to number our days that we may gain a wise heart."

Psalmody
Psalm 90:12-17 (RCL)
Psalm 90:12-13, 14-15, 16-17 (LFM)

Psalm 90, the only psalm attributed to Moses, begins the fourth book of the Psalter. Several scholars note the strategic placement of this psalm. Psalm 89 ends with the announcement of the rejection of the covenant with King David. The crisis described here is as acute as the crisis that Amos warns of in today's Old Testament lesson. Psalm 90 begins the response to this crisis by reminding Israel that God has always been their dwelling place. When Moses led the people, there was no promised land, no temple, and no monarchy. The theological gist of this psalm is that even without these commodities, relatedness to God is still possible if we will put our trust in God.[9] In the verses in today's reading, the psalmist calls on God to have compassion and restore the people to full relationship.

Psalm 22:1-15 (RCL alt.)

As with last week's psalm, Psalm 22 is a psalm of David, but it could easily be a psalm of Job. Here the psalmist, like Job, is lamenting God's absence. However, the psalmist has not lost faith. He still calls God "my God," and after each complaint, he voices an expression of trust that recalls a time when life was better. This psalm is best known because Jesus quotes it from the cross in Matthew and Mark.

Second Reading
Hebrews 4:12-16 (RCL)
Hebrews 4:12-13 (LFM)

Today's second reading captures the essence of prophetic preaching because it holds God's judgment and God's grace in tension. In verses 12-13 we are reminded that God still speaks and that the word of God calls us into account. No one is exempt from examination, and the test will not be an easy one, for the word penetrates deeply, into our very being, so that even our thoughts and the intentions of our hearts are known. For most of us, these will not be encouraging words.

But a word of hope follows the word of judgment. Verses 14-16 remind us that we have a high priest, Jesus, who is sympathetic to our plight, because he was tested just as we are. As a result, we can approach God, the throne of grace, with boldness. In return, we will receive mercy and grace to help in time of need. Tom Long asserts that this is a daring, audacious prayer; it is a bold prayer that is an expression of theological trust in who God is and in God's relationship to us.[10] This type of prayer is reminiscent of the lament psalms where the Israelites boldly call on God to be true to God's self and to be actively working on their behalf. We see examples of these prayers in both of today's psalms.

What are the struggles that your congregation is facing? As in Amos's day, are there things that people need to confess and give an account for? Or, like Job, are they suffering due to little fault of their own? Are they trying to figure out where God is in the midst of the chaos, or do they feel like God is absent? No matter where they find themselves, Hebrews reminds us that in Christ we have an advocate who will grant us grace and mercy to help us live as new people in the world.

Gospel
Mark 10:17-31 (RCL)
Mark 10:17-30 or 10:17-27 (LFM)

For the second week in a row, the lectionary has given us a difficult Gospel text, the story of the rich young ruler (in Mark he is only identified as wealthy). Today's lesson is divided into two parts: the first a conversation between Jesus and the wealthy man, and the second a conversation between Jesus and the disciples.

The conversation between the man and Jesus begins simply and sincerely. A man runs up, kneels before Jesus, and asks, "Good Teacher, what must I do to inherit eternal life?" Often scholars contrast this man's question about what he must *do* (behavior) with the preceding verses where Jesus teaches we must *be* like children to enter the kingdom of God. However, I am not sure that the man's question is a contrast. Usually when we inherit something, it is from our parents. Was this man's question his way of asking, "What do I have to do to become your child? What do I have to do to receive a share of this inheritance called eternal life?" And even when we know that an inheritance is a gift, we often "work" to be good sons and daughters so that we will remain in the good graces of the family benefactor. The man's question is quite reasonable.

As discussed last week, children were the most vulnerable people in society because they were totally dependent on others for protection and security. In asking the rich man to relinquish his wealth, Jesus is asking him to give up the things that allowed him to be secure and self-dependent. Jesus is telling the man that in order to be saved he must be willing to become as a child, totally dependent on God to meet his needs. Mark tells us that the man was shocked and went away grieving, for he had many possessions.

In the second half of today's lesson, Jesus turns his attention to the disciples, commenting on how difficult it will be for the wealthy to enter the kingdom. The disciples are perplexed, for in the ancient patronage system of their day, the wealthy were celebrated as communal benefactors. Since it was their gifts that supported the synagogues and temple sacrifices, people assumed that the wealthy had a special relationship to God and were more likely to be saved. In this context, Jesus' words were shocking.[11] However, he quickly adds that what is impossible for humans is more than possible with God.

Peter then reminds Jesus that they had all left everything to follow. Jesus replies that they would receive a hundredfold in this age (including persecution, a cost of following) and eternal life in the next.

Today this passage is most often interpreted symbolically. Attachment to wealth was this man's particular problem. As contemporary believers, we must each determine what keeps us from following God and be willing to leave it behind to follow. For most of our congregations wealth is indeed the problem. Even those of us who consider ourselves to be middle class live at a far higher standard than most of the world, and we knowingly and unknowingly participate in the oppression of the poor that Amos preached about. Although this is difficult prophetic preaching, most of us will also admit that the wealth we have sought so diligently has not brought the happiness we expected. The good news is that if we are wise enough to leave it and follow, we will be fulfilled in ways we do not yet understand.

Notes

1. Leonora Tubbs Tisdale, *Prophetic Preaching: A Pastoral Approach* (Louisville: Westminster John Knox, 2010), 11–20.
2. Ibid., 7.
3. Jefferson H. McCrory Jr., "The Book of Amos," in *The Discipleship Study Bible* (Louisville: Westminster John Knox, 2008), 1250.
4. Donald E. Gowan, "The Book of Amos," in *The New Interpreter's Bible* (Nashville: Abingdon, 1996), 7:343.
5. Ibid., 7:345.
6. Ibid., 7:397.
7. Carol A. Newsom, "The Book of Job," in *The New Interpreter's Bible* (Nashville: Abingdon, 1996), 4:509.
8. Gary Light, "The Book of Wisdom of Solomon," in *The Discipleship Study Bible*, 1382.
9. J. Clinton McCann Jr., "Psalms," in *The New Interpreter's Bible*, 4:1040.
10. Thomas G. Long, *Hebrews*, Interpretation: A Bible Commentary for Teaching and Preaching (Louisville: John Knox, 1997), 63–64.
11. Pheme Perkins, "The Gospel of Mark," in *The New Interpreter's Bible* (Nashville: Abingdon Press, 1995), 8:650.

October 21, 2012
Lectionary 29 / Twenty-Ninth Sunday in Ordinary Time / Proper 24
Twenty-First Sunday after Pentecost

Revised Common Lectionary (RCL)
Isaiah 53:4-12 or Job 38:1-7 (34-41)
Psalm 91:9-16 or 104:1-9, 24, 35c
Hebrews 5:1-10
Mark 10:35-45

Lectionary for Mass (LFM)
Isaiah 53:10-11
Psalm 33:4-5, 18-19, 20 + 22
Hebrews 4:14-16
Mark 10:35-45 or 10:42-45

First Reading
Isaiah 53:4-12 (RCL)
Isaiah 53:10-11 (LFM)

Today's Old Testament reading is part of the fourth servant song found in what is commonly known as Second Isaiah or Deutero-Isaiah. This section of Isaiah, which presupposes a Babylonian exile, was most likely written between 597 and 539 BCE. Second Isaiah is characterized by long, lyrical promise oracles and an emphasis on the beauty and justice of the new age that will follow the years of the Babylonian exile.[1]

Many scholars believe that Moses was the original servant in the Old Testament. By the time this text was written, the servant is assumed to be a metaphor for the community of Israel. In First Isaiah, the people are anticipating a new king who will once again teach them how to be God's people. This idealized king personified Israel as the true people of God. It is likely that in Second Isaiah, the servant represents the community of Israel in exile with overtones of the Coming One who would represent the true people of God. What was important for Isaiah was not the specific identity of the servant or the new king, but the new work that God was doing among the people.[2]

Preachers who wish to work with this text in its original context can begin prophetically by examining how their congregations are like Israel. In what ways have they gone astray from who God is calling them to be? In what ways do they feel they might be in exile? What might be required for a new age of beauty and justice to dawn? The good news is that we, like Israel, can be restored to full relationship with God and we can be agents of God's grace and justice in the larger world. For those using the Revised Common Lectionary, the promise of God's presence in the midst of current trials in Psalm 91 serves as a nice complement to this text. Those following the Lectionary for Mass will find similar resonance with Psalm 33, which claims God's reign when our circumstances, such as exile, speak otherwise.

In addition to speaking to the people of Isaiah's day, the servant songs have been used since the early days of the church to help Christians understand who Jesus was and the nature of his ministry. Handel's *Messiah* quotes seventeen texts from Isaiah, including parts of today's lection. The fourth servant song is quoted at least nine times in the New Testament, making it one of the most familiar Old Testament texts. Today's text is often cited by those who hold a substitutionary theory of atonement. In this theory, Christ vicariously bore our sins, once and for all. Now, as the resurrected Christ, he has become our high priest, mediating on our behalf (see the commentary on the Hebrews passage, below). This text is also linked to Jesus' statement in Mark 10:45 that he will give his life as a ransom for many, although Jesus may not have been referring to a substitutionary atonement (see the Gospel commentary on Mark, below).

The image of Jesus as a sacrificial lamb being slain for the sins of the world is problematic for many and it is just one of several theories of atonement.[3] Those who hold to other theories focus on the parts of this passage that emphasize Jesus' willingness to lay down his life and the example of justice and liberation he set for us all.

Job 38:1-7, (34-41) (RCL alt.)

In last week's lection, Job spoke of his desire to make his case before God. In today's passage, he gets his audience with God, but it is certainly not what he is expecting. Throughout the book, Job's "friends" are confident that God is punishing Job for some sin he has committed. Job, who continues to maintain his innocence, laments God's absence and the character of a God who would punish a righteous man. Instead of vindicating Job and answering Job's questions, God is the one who does the asking, posing more than sixty rhetorical questions to Job in the divine speeches.[4] It is as if Job is the one on trial as God says, "I will question you and you shall declare to me."

Scholars have long debated the meaning of the divine speeches in Job. Viewed in conjunction with today's Gospel lesson, it is appropriate to focus on the misunderstanding that Job and the disciples both had about who God is and what their role was in the larger scope of the universe or the kingdom of God. God questions Job about the creation of the universe and later about the creatures that inhabit it. (The images are similar to those found in Psalm 104, the RCL alternate for today.) This universe is a complex one, filled with mystery, surprise, and wonder; it is one in which God does not reward or punish in a mechanical or expected way. God does not address Job's complaints overtly, and the implication is that Job and his friends have been asking the wrong questions and working from the wrong assumptions.[5]

Especially when we are suffering, our worlds can become very small and tightly focused; this is self-protective instinct and human nature. However, it is an easy step from there to the attitude that it is all about me (or us). In what ways do we put God in a box, or how do we expect God to respond to our needs or desires? In our preaching contexts, how can we help our congregants frame their suffering and their expectations of God in appropriate ways?

Psalmody
Psalm 91:9-16 (RCL)

Psalm 91 is a psalm of confidence and trust. Some scholars believe that the rare use of the words "dwelling place" in both Psalm 90 (see last week's lection, above) and Psalm 91 link them together as responses to the crisis lamented in Psalm 89. Further linkage is seen because two petitions listed in 90:13-17 are answered in 91:16.[6]

It would be easy for readers of this psalm to gain a false sense of security, for the poem is full of the language of protection and deliverance. However, this psalm is not a mystical guarantee against trials and suffering or a formula to avoid harm. Satan tried to convince Jesus of this false guarantee when he quoted verses 11-12 and tempted Jesus to jump from the pinnacle of the temple. Fortunately, Jesus, and later the disciples who were also subjected to great suffering, understood that this psalm is a reminder of God's love and presence in the midst of trials and tribulations.

Psalm 104:1-9, 24, 35c (RCL alt.)

This psalm is a beautiful poem of praise to God who is both creator and provider. As noted above, many of the images in these verses are similar to the ones in the divine speeches in Job. The psalmist describes a God of great power and majesty who is to be revered and respected, not trifled with.

As we become increasingly aware of our need and responsibility to protect the world that God created, many scholars are developing works on green theology.

J. Clinton McCann Jr. reminds us that much of today's environmental effort focuses on how we can maintain our lifestyles without depleting our resources and trashing the environment. Such efforts, which are motivated by fear, are doomed to fail. Drawing on this psalm, McCann asserts that successful environmental work must be grounded in praising God and motivated by a desire to live under God's sovereignty and rule.[7]

Psalm 33:4-5, 18-19, 20 + 22 (LFM)

Scholars suggest that Psalm 33 is a response to Psalm 32, a psalm of forgiveness. Those who are forgiven in turn rejoice and praise the goodness and the greatness of God. Today's portion begins in verses 4-5, which focus on the love, faithfulness, righteousness, and justice of God. These verses correlate well with Isaiah 53:11 where the servant is called the righteous one who will make many righteous. As with many of the psalms, this one is eschatological, as it claims God's reign in the midst of persons and circumstances that deny it.[8]

Second Reading
Hebrews 5:1-10 (RCL)
Hebrews 4:14-16 (LFM)

Today's second reading picks up where last week's lection left off. In fact, many interpreters believe that 4:14—5:10 functions as one unit. Verses 14-16 remind us that we have a high priest, Jesus, who is sympathetic to our plight, because he was tested just as we are. As a result, we can approach God, the throne of grace, with boldness. (See the second reading for Proper 24, above, for additional commentary on 4:14-16.) Tom Long calls 5:1-10 a theological version of the "right man for the job speech."[9] The author begins in verses 1-4 by listing the qualities of a high priest: he must be one of the people and he must be appointed or called by God. The priest is to deal gently with the ignorant and wayward. Here, gently does not mean sympathetically; rather, it means that the priest must moderate or control his emotions and practice restraint toward them.[10]

In verses 5-10 the writer lists Jesus' qualifications to be the Great High Priest. The words about Jesus' suffering make it clear that he was indeed one of us. The writer is also clear that Jesus was appointed by God for this priestly role. But Jesus' priesthood is unique because Jesus is more than a human representative appointed by God; he is part of the Godhead. His humanity and divinity make him the ideal one to mediate before God on our behalf.

In verse 7 we are reminded that Jesus had an active intercessory prayer life during his earthly ministry. Jesus was honest in his prayers, lamenting his own approaching death and asking that the cup might pass from him. Instead of yielding to the temptation to call the angels to rescue him, he willing gave himself for us, becoming the source, not just the avenue, of our eternal salvation. Tom Long reminds us that suffering, limitations, and weaknesses do not equal sin; these are part of the human condition. For Jesus, experiencing these frailties led to a deeper reverence for God rather than rebellion.[11] The contrast between Job's and Jesus' response to suffering is strking.

Prophetically, a sermon based on this passage could begin by naming both how the community is experiencing suffering or limitations and how they are responding to it. Are the problems leading to rebellion or to a deeper dependence on God in the midst of the suffering? Pastorally, the good news is that we do not face such trials alone. We serve a risen Savior who understands us and who mediates for us.

Gospel
Mark 10:35-45 (RCL)
Mark 10:35-45 or 10:42-45 (LFM)

Today's Gospel lesson can be divided into two distinct sections: Jesus' conversation with James and John (vv. 35-40) and Jesus' lesson to the disciples (vv. 41-45). Taken together, they bring a countercultural challenge about the nature of both discipleship and leadership.

Like the rest of the disciples, it is easy for us to stand in judgment of James and John for their seemingly brazen and selfish request to be given places of honor when Jesus comes into his glory, but we really shouldn't be so surprised. How many of us work on an election campaign because we support the candidate, but we also hope for a position in the new regime? How many of us gladly do volunteer work or ministry but appreciate the recognition or further opportunities it brings us? The disciples shouldn't have been surprised either. John Hutchinson describes the culture of Jesus' day as one based on kinship, patronage, and honor. In this context it would have been an appropriate and common practice for James and John to use their kinship connections with Jesus to approach him as their benefactor and to request preferential treatment.[12]

What would have been surprising in this scene is Jesus' response. Honor was linked with power in the New Testament world. To hear Jesus talk about spiritual authority and leadership coming through suffering and sacrifice went against the cultural norms. When Jesus says one must become a slave, he uses the word *doulos*, indicating a move from a position of highest honor to that of the lowest slave. Being humbled by someone else in that culture was common, but willingly humbling yourself was unheard of.[13]

Lamar Williamson Jr. notes that Jesus had recently used a child as an example of following in total trust and dependence, but here the disciples make a childish request, "Teacher, we want you to do for us whatever we ask of you."[14] Like a wise parent, Jesus does not grant their request until they have articulated it. It appears that the disciples still believe that Jesus will establish an earthly kingdom; they still do not understand that the journey to Jerusalem will end in his death. It is interesting to note that Jesus does not criticize James and John (perhaps because their request was not as inappropriate as it appears to us). Instead, he tells them that they have no idea what they are asking. Indeed, in just a few days thieves will be crucified on Jesus' right and left.

In the first century, the cup and baptism (or water) could be symbols of joy and salvation or woe and suffering. When Jesus asks the disciples if they can drink the cup or be baptized, he is likely thinking the latter while the disciples' answer perhaps assumes the more positive interpretation. Even if Jesus had wanted to grant the disciples' request, they are surprised to learn that he does not have the power and authority to do so.

Not surprisingly, the other disciples are angry at James and John. Jesus calls them all together and totally redefines what it means to be a leader. Leadership means servanthood, and even voluntary slavery. In this context, when Jesus said that he was giving his life as a ransom for many, it likely meant that he was purchasing a slave or a prisoner in order to grant him or her freedom and redemption. Dawn Ottoni Wilhelm notes that this use of the word *ransom* suggests that humanity is held captive by powers from which we need deliverance, and that Jesus' death provides the means for our freedom and redemption.[15]

It is easy for us to believe that we have the heart of a servant. A friend once remarked that the true test comes in how we respond when someone treats us like a servant. It is easy to give and serve when we expect to be rewarded, but this ultimately is self-serving. James Thompson notes, "Self-sacrifice for a disciple of Jesus Christ must be in the service of something higher than the self. The promise of the gospel is that in the sacrifice of self for others, not only will a higher and better self emerge, but the reign of God will continue to unfold."[16] As preachers we must remember that Jesus' words, and these interpretations of them, were directed to insiders who wanted increased status and power, not to those already marginalized.

Notes

1. W. Sibley Towner, "The Book of Isaiah," in *The Discipleship Study Bible* (Louisville: Westminster John Knox, 2008), 930–31.
2. Dennis Bratcher, "The Servant of the Lord, Verse Commentary on Isaiah 52:13—53:12," http://www.crivoice.org/isa53.html, accessed May 4, 2011.
3. For example, homileticians who stand in the line of critical communicative reason are rethinking the idea of substitutionary atonement through the testimony of victims of violence. See John S. McClure's *Otherwise Preaching: A Postmodern Ethic for Homiletics* (St. Louis: Chalice, 2001).
4. Mark A. Throntveit, "Exegetical Perspective," in *Feasting on the Word*, Year B (Louisville: Westminster John Knox, 2009), 4:175.
5. John Holbert, "Job," in *The Discipleship Study Bible*, 726.
6. J. Clinton McCann Jr., "Psalms," in *The New Interpreter's Bible* (Nashville: Abingdon, 1996), 4:1047.
7. Ibid., 4:1100.
8. Ibid., 4:811.
9. Thomas G. Long, *Hebrews*, Interpretation: A Bible Commentary for Teaching and Preaching (Louisville: John Knox, 1997), 66.
10. Fred B. Craddock, "The Letter to the Hebrews," in *The New Interpreter's Bible* (Nashville: Abingdon, 1998), 12:60.
11. Long, *Hebrews*, 68.
12. John C. Hutchinson, "Servanthood: Jesus' Countercultural Call to Christian Leaders," *Bibliotheca Sacra* 166 (January–March 2009): 60–62.
13. Ibid., 63, 67.
14. Lamar Williamson Jr., *Mark*, Interpretation: A Bible Commentary for Teaching and Preaching (Louisville: John Knox, 1983), 192.
15. Dawn Ottoni Wilhelm, *Preaching the Gospel of Mark* (Louisville: Westminster John Knox, 2008), 185.
16. James Thompson, "Theological Perspective," in *Feasting on the Word*, Year B, 4:192.

October 28, 2012
Lectionary 30* / Thirtieth Sunday in Ordinary Time / Proper 25
Twenty-Second Sunday after Pentecost

Revised Common Lectionary (RCL)	Lectionary for Mass (LFM)
Jeremiah 31:7-9 or Job 42:1-6, (10-17)	Jeremiah 31:7-9
Psalm 126 or 34:1-8, (19-22)	Psalm 126:1-2a, 2b-3, 4-5, 6
Hebrews 7:23-28	Hebrews 5:1-6
Mark 10:46-52	Mark 10:46-52

For several weeks the lectionary texts have had a prophetic edge. This week we see a shift to a tone of restoration and celebration. In Jeremiah, the exiles are restored to Jerusalem. In Job, Job's wealth and family are restored. In Mark, blind Bartimaeus's sight is restored. In Hebrews, Jesus is lauded as the High Priest who intercedes for us once and for all. The words of the text are a welcome relief. But, lest we get too comfortable, there are unsettling lessons to be learned here as well.

First Reading
Jeremiah 31:7-9 (RCL, LFM)

Scholars have long recognized that chapters 30 and 31 of Jeremiah are one unit that describes the restoration of Israel in great detail. It is important to note that the restoration includes both the Northern and Southern Kingdoms. In chapter 30 God reminds the people that they have suffered in exile because of their disobedience and that their wounds and grief are deep. However, God also assures the people that they are loved with an everlasting love and that God's faithfulness to them has continued. Early in chapter 31, God promises to rebuild Israel and assures them that there will once again be dancing and fruitful vineyards. Today's reading, which begins just after these promises, is a divine announcement addressed to the Northern Kingdom.

*Lutheran and some other Protestant traditions may celebrate this Sunday as Reformation Sunday. For commentary on the Reformation texts, see *New Proclamation Commentary on Feasts, Holy Days, and Other Celebrations*, ed. David B. Lott (Minneapolis: Fortress Press, 2007).

The passage begins with God calling the people to exuberant praise. In verse 7 they are called to sing aloud with gladness, to raise shouts, to proclaim, and to give praise; it is a rowdy celebration. Beginning in verse 8a, God tells them why they are to rejoice—God is going to gather a great company of people from the farthest parts of the earth. In verse 8b the company is described in detail: it will include the most vulnerable members of society, those who are often pushed to the margins, the blind and the lame, and pregnant and laboring women. Everyone, even the "outsiders," will be restored.

In the second half of verse 9, readers will note language that echoes Psalm 23. Once again God will allow them to walk by brooks of water and on a straight path where they will no longer stumble. Patrick Miller notes that although Israel remained connected with God while they were in exile in Babylon, salvation in this passage is associated with a specific place and the possibilities of life there. The people are coming home at last.[1]

The prophetic word in this text is that in the fullest extent, this restoration is still to come. Chapter 30 begins with the exhortation from God to write in a book all the words that God has spoken. The days are surely coming when the restoration will be complete, but it seems that they are far enough off that Israel will need a written reminder of God's promise in the meantime.[2]

Has your congregation felt like it has been in exile? What happened that led to this experience? Do they need to hear God's promise that the day is coming when they will be restored? What might restoration look like? What are their still waters and straight paths? Who are the most vulnerable in the community whom God expects to be included? How can you encourage your faith community to be faithful until the days of great praise and rejoicing return?

Job 42:1-6, (10-17) (RCL alt.)

In last week's lection we heard a small portion of the divine speeches to Job. This week, in verses 1-6, we have Job's second reply to God (the first is in 40:3-5). These verses provide a challenge to translators and subsequently to preachers because they can be translated and interpreted in a variety of ways. Carol Newsom suggests that the ambiguity is intentional, requiring readers to wrestle with the meaning of the divine speeches and how they might resolve the conflict between Job and God.[3]

In verses 2 and 3 Job quotes slight variations of 38:2-3 (part of the divine speech read last week) back to God, confirming that he has heard God's words to him. It is the meaning of his response to God that is uncertain. Some scholars suggest that verse 6 is correct as translated, that Job despises himself when he realizes the error of his ways and that he repents in dust and ashes.

However, this verse can also be translated, "I repent of dust and ashes," meaning that Job has changed his mind and rejected his lamentation and fury on the ash heap, for he now sees that God is not his adversary. Rather, he now understands that human beings are not at enmity with God, but that they live in a creation where chaos is restrained but never fully eliminated.[4]

In effect, Job's eyes have been opened and he "sees" God and his own situation in a whole new way. When Job was looking at his situation from a legal perspective, all he could see was the injustice of his situation. Although faulty, this view of reality was more secure and more comfortable than accepting the reality that tragedy strikes randomly (and that there is nothing we can do to prevent it or protect ourselves from it). Newsom suggests that the divine speeches insist that the presence of the chaotic be acknowledged as part of the design of creation without justifying such chaos. However, the good news is that God supports and sustains creation in the midst of the chaos.[5]

Preachers will do well to ask what theologies or paradigms their congregations hold onto that help them deny the reality of the fallen and chaotic world in which we live. How can you as a leader help your people trust in a God who sustains and supports in a world that is beyond God's complete control?

The second half of today's alternate reading recounts the restoration of Job. Job's friends and family come to comfort him and to share a meal with him, and God gives Job twice as much as he had before. Job's world and perspective have also been transformed. Breaking culture and custom, Job's daughters are named in these verses (not his sons) and they are given an inheritance along with their brothers. Job lives to see four generations of descendants before he dies "old and full of days." God has won the divine wager with the satan, Job has passed the cosmic test, and, after forty-two long chapters, readers have a happy ending.

Or do they? When I teach the book of Job at the collegiate level, it is not unusual for female students who are mothers to be incensed at the conclusion of this book. In particular, they are disturbed by the implication that the children Job lost in the divine contest can simply be replaced with new ones. Any pastor worth his or her salt knows that you don't comfort grieving parents with the platitude that it is okay, they can have another child. They don't want a new child; they want the one they had.

Unfortunately, the book of Job leaves us more questions than answers. Good preachers will honor this reality and carefully avoid offering their hearers platitudes that ring hollow. Perhaps the most important lesson that Job has to teach us is that in every faith community, well-meaning and faithful people hold a variety of opinions about the nature of God and about the presence of good and evil in the world. We will be wise to listen to one another, to affirm one another where possible, and to allow our own misperceptions of God to be corrected as we wrestle with God together. Kathleen O'Connor notes that Job presses us to hold our theologies humbly and to remember that new times require renewed and reformed theological expressions for a God who transcends all speech.[6]

Psalmody
Psalm 126 (RCL)
Psalm 126:1-2a, 2b-3, 4-5, 6 (LFM)

This psalm, the seventh song of ascents, voices the praises of the exiles who are restored to their homeland in today's passage from Jeremiah. Although written for this context, it has application in any situation where thanksgiving for deliverance is appropriate. Verses 1-3 are translated in the past tense with a tone of praise and thanksgiving, while verses 4-6 are a petition for restoration. J. Clinton McCann Jr. suggests that this apparent tension in the psalm reflects the lived tension of the Babylonian exiles. Although they did return to Jerusalem to rebuild, the full vision of restoration in Isaiah 40–55 did not materialize and a disillusioned people found themselves in need of further restoration.[7] Paired with the Jeremiah text, this psalm can help us live into the already but not yet that is our reality in the world today.

Psalm 34:1-8, (19-22) (RCL alt.)

This psalm is an acrostic poem that functions both as a liturgical prayer and as a teaching tool to help readers cope with the challenges they face. The psalm is full of praise and thanksgiving for God's deliverance from trouble and with the promise of further rescue and restoration. It would be easy to associate this psalm with prosperity theology, but this would be a misuse of this piece. The psalmist acknowledges in verse 19 that "many are the afflictions of the righteous." Rescue from such afflictions may occur later rather than sooner.

It is important to note that "this poor soul" in verse 6 may refer to the most vulnerable in society. Lisa Driver suggests that true worshipers are called to be the angels or messengers referred to in verse 7, relieving and protecting any poor soul.[8]

In addition to pairing well with the restoration texts in today's lections, this psalm is also commonly used for communion services. The words "Taste and see that the LORD is good" have long been used as an invitation to the table.

Second Reading
Hebrews 7:23-28 (RCL)

In Hebrews 7:1—10:18, which functions as a unit, the author's goal is to help first-century Jews understand how Jesus, who was not of the Levitical priestly line, can be their new and ultimate high priest. The author begins to build his case by referring readers to the priestly order of Melchizedek, arguing that in Melchizedek there is historical precedence for a priest who is outside the Levitical line. In the same way, Jesus can become a high priest, because God has sworn it to be so (vv. 21-22).

Beginning in verse 23, the start of today's lection, the author shows us how and why Jesus is superior to every earthly priest. First, the resurrected Jesus is superior because, unlike Levitical priests, he will never die or need to be replaced. Since he will hold the position of high priest forever, Jesus will be able to intercede for us for all time. Jesus is also superior because he is sinless and does not first have to atone for his own sins.

This passage also calls for great celebration and rejoicing. We have an advocate who is always there, mediating for us and restoring us to God! We can say, like the Israelites in Psalm 126, "The LORD has done great things for us, and we rejoiced." A pastoral sermon can help congregants rejoice in and live into a relationship with this perfect High Priest. How might our lives be different if we availed ourselves more of Christ's priestly work on our behalf?

Despite the celebratory note, this text also has a prophetic edge. This is the author's first introduction of the idea that Christ offered or sacrificed himself for us; the concept awaits further development later in the book. David Cunningham notes that we laud sacrifice but that it is easily abused. Although Christ's sacrifice is praiseworthy and good, it is sometimes used to underwrite abuse and oppression. Ideally, Christ's work eliminates the need for others to be forced into offering sacrifices that are really just a form of submission to more powerful interests.[9] How might our congregations use the language of sacrifice to perpetuate oppression? How might God be calling us to view Christ's sacrifice as a means to end this cycle?

Hebrews 5:1-6 (LFM)

For commentary on this text, please see the second reading for Proper 24, above.

Gospel
Mark 10:46-52 (RCL, LFM)

In today's Gospel lesson, it is the blind beggar Bartimaeus who receives restoration. In response to his persistent cries, Jesus calls Bartimaeus to him and asks, "What do you want me to do for you?" In last week's lection, James and John responded to this same question out of blind ambition, asking for power and prestige. But Bartimaeus's request, made from physical blindness, is only for Jesus to allow him to see again. In response, Jesus proclaims that Bartimaeus's faith has made him well. Immediately, Bartimaeus follows Jesus on the way, making this text as much a call story as a healing one.

It appeared at first that this final healing in the book of Mark might not occur at all. When Bartimaeus first began to call out to Jesus, the crowd sternly ordered him to be quiet. This sounds cruel, but don't we do the same today? When a celebrity is scheduled to appear in any major urban area, the police often conduct a sweep to remove the homeless and the beggars before the esteemed guest arrives. Fortunately, Bartimaeus was not discouraged by the crowd; he refused to be defined and confined by the crowds that were protecting Jesus. He would not be silenced or swept away. When Jesus stopped and called him forward, the members of the crowd suddenly changed their tune, urging Bartimaeus to get up. As the scene unfolded, they witnessed and rejoiced in the blind man's restoration.

It is noteworthy that Bartimaeus called Jesus "Son of David." Although this was a familiar designation for the messianic king of Israel, Bartimaeus was the only one besides Peter to correctly identify Jesus as the Christ.[10] Although Bartimaeus "saw" more than many of the "insiders" did, it appears that he expected Jesus to establish an earthly kingdom. There was no indication that he knew what he would face in Jerusalem as a new follower of Christ.

This passage offers many sermon options. It is appropriate to ask ourselves as "spiritual insiders" how we marginalize or sweep away the "outsiders" among us. Who do we define as outsiders? How can we reconnect with this vital group and once again become witnesses to the work that Christ is about in the world around us?

It is also appropriate to ask others where our blind spots are. What are we not able to see? Once we have learned how we experience blindness, are we willing to be like Bartimaeus, persistent in our quest for healing and willing to throw aside our most prized positions in order to follow Jesus, wherever that may take us?

Notes

1. Patrick D. Miller, "Jeremiah," in *The New Interpreter's Bible* (Nashville: Abingdon, 2001), 6:815.
2. John M. Bracke, "Jeremiah," in *The Discipleship Study Bible* (Louisville: Westminster John Knox, 2008), 1079.
3. See Carol A. Newsom, "Job," in *The New Interpreter's Bible* (Nashville: Abingdon, 1996), 4:627. See 4:629 for a discussion of the interpretive options.
4. Ibid., 4:629.
5. Ibid., 4:630.
6. Kathleen M. O'Connor, "Theological Perspective, Job 42:1-6, 10-17," *Feasting on the Word*, Year B (Louisville: Westminster John Knox, 2009), 4:196.
7. J. Clinton McCann Jr., "Psalms," in *The New Interpreter's Bible*, 4:1195.
8. Lisa D. M. Driver, "Theological Perspective, Psalm 34:1-8, (19-22)," *Feasting on the Word*, Year B, 4:202.
9. David S. Cunningham, "Theological Perspective, Hebrews 7:23-28," *Feasting on the Word*, Year B, 4:208.
10. Dawn Ottoni Wilhelm, *Preaching the Gospel of Mark* (Louisville: Westminster John Knox, 2008), 188.

November 1 or 4, 2012
All Saints Day/Sunday

Revised Common Lectionary (RCL)

Isaiah 25:6-9 or Wisdom of Solomon
  3:1-9

Psalm 24

Revelation 21:1-6a

John 11:32-44

Lectionary for Mass (LFM)

Revelation 7:2-4, 9-14

Psalm 24:1-2, 3-4, 5-6

1 John 3:1-3

Matthew 5:1-12a

In the Christian Church in the West, All Saints Day commemorates the saints, the martyrs, and all the faithful deceased. In the Roman Catholic Church, All Saints Day honors all those who have attained the beatific vision in heaven. The next day, All Souls Day, commemorates the departed faithful who have not yet been purified and reached heaven. Catholics celebrate All Saints Day and All Souls Day in the fundamental belief that there is a prayerful spiritual communion between those in the state of grace who have died and those who are living.[1]

Protestants generally regard all true Christian believers as saints. When they observe All Saints Day, all Christians both past and present are remembered. In some congregations, a special emphasis is placed on members who have died within the last year. Often a candle is lit by the acolyte as each person's name is called out by the clergy. Prayers and responsive readings offer the whole community of faith the opportunity to participate in this special service.

In addition to offering a special service of worship, All Saints Day offers congregants a unique opportunity to continue their grief work for those who have died. Wise pastors will remind the faith community that God, who is the object and recipient of our corporate worship, grieves with us in our losses and provides hope for a future that is yet to come.

First Reading
Isaiah 25:6-9 (RCL)

Isaiah 25 is largely a chapter of praise for deliverance from oppression. Verses 1-5 contain a song of praise and thanksgiving addressed to God. Verses 6-9 (today's lection) describe the salvation of the people and a celebratory banquet that is yet to come.

The banquet meal described in verse 6 evokes memories of the Sinai event in Exodus 24:9-11 and Solomon's dedication of the first temple in 1 Kings 8:62-66. These images recur in Matthew 8:11; 22:1-4; and Revelation 19:9, passages that describe the kingdom of heaven.[2] In verses 7-8a readers are assured that the Lord will swallow up death forever. As postresurrection readers, it is easy for us to interpret this passage in light of the promise of eternal life. However, Jews of this period held no such idea of an afterlife. Some interpreters believe that these verses refer to the end of Israel's exile. Others believe it refers to a new age beyond current history where death will be no more. Interpreted this way, this passage is without parallel in the Old Testament.[3]

Verse 8 continues with the promise that the Lord will wipe away the tears from all faces. Both here and in verse 6, these promises are for all people, not just a select group. Verse 9 records the response of the people to God's provision and deliverance: gladness and rejoicing. The stress is on the end of mourning and the celebration of life.

While this passage is celebratory, it does not deny the present reality of death and the tears and mourning it brings. Verse 9 begins, "It will be said *on that* day," and twice the people talk about waiting for God whose hand *will* rest on this mountain. Like Isaiah, preachers who use this text to offer a word of hope must begin by acknowledging the shroud of death and the resulting tears that often cover us in times of grief and loss.

Wisdom of Solomon 3:1-9 (RCL alt.)

These verses are commonly known as the reward or the destiny of the righteous. In this passage, the wisdom writer shifts from the Old Testament idea of eternal life (which meant being remembered by your descendants) toward the New Testament idea of eternal life in heaven.[4] The writer assures us that death is not a disaster but rather that the souls of the righteous are at peace in the hand of God.

Although this passage is the alternate reading for the Revised Common Lectionary, the theology here is more consistent with Catholic theology of purgatory, for the peaceful destiny with God comes after discipline and testing. Two metaphors that are used to describe this process both share the image of fire. The first, the purification of gold, stresses transformation and purification. The second, a burnt offering, signals God's acceptance of and union with the just.[5] After this testing and discipline, however, the faithful abide with God in love because God's grace and mercy are upon those who are holy.

Pastors can use this passage to remind the community of faith that death is not the end that it appears to be. Rather, it is a transition to a state of wholeness and completeness that continues forever under the watchful eye of a loving and merciful God.

Revelation 7:2-4, 9-14 (LFM)

The book of Revelation is a pastoral letter sent to seven churches in Asia Minor, part of the Roman Empire in the first century. The purpose of the letter was twofold: to encourage those experiencing oppression and to encourage all the churches to resist the temptation to accommodate the empire.[6]

The vision in chapter 7 gives the churches hope for their future by identifying the source of their strength; they have been sealed by God. In verses 2-4, 144,000 (a figurative number of the twelve tribes multiplied by twelve apostles, which represents all the people of God) are sealed. This sealing indicates that they are loyal to God, not to the nation or empire. In verses 9-14, the inclusive nature of the multitudes is explicit: they come from all tribes and peoples and languages. Together they stand in white robes waving palm branches and offering praise to God and to the Lamb. In the midst of this beautiful scene of heavenly celebration is the sobering reminder that those who arrived here came via the great ordeal.

Consistent with other passages in Scripture, this text does not deny the reality of the human condition even as it celebrates the wonder and beauty of what is to come for those who live with God forever. As we help our congregants envision eschatological hope, we must also begin with the acknowledgment of the pain of loss.

Psalmody
Psalm 24 (RCL)
Psalm 24:1-2, 3-4, 5-6 (LFM)

This psalm may have originally celebrated the entry of the ark of the covenant into Zion, but it also previews the ascension of the risen Christ to heaven. Michael Morgan divides the psalm into three segments. The first, verses 1-2, is a celebration of God's past work (founding the world and claiming it as God's own). The second segment, verses 3-6, focuses on the present. These verses list qualifications for ascending the hill of the Lord. The final four verses deal with the future and the expectation of the coming king of glory.[7]

Second Reading
Revelation 21:1-6a (RCL)

This passage is one of the most beloved in Scripture because of the words of consolation and comfort it offers to people in any age who have been subjected to evil, pain, and sorrow in their current realities. The passage begins with John's vision of the new heaven and the new earth. The first earth is gone and the sea, which symbolized chaos in the ancient Near East, is no more. Contrary to popular belief, this is not a vision of heaven, for God and the New Jerusalem descend to the new earth.

After John saw the vision, he heard a voice from the throne proclaiming that God would now dwell among the people, God's people. The picture of God here is intimate and compassionate. As in the Isaiah passage discussed above, God wipes away every tear, eliminates mourning and crying and pain, and even death itself. Then the voice reports, "It is done!"

Between the wars raging on several fronts, the predominance of cancer and AIDS, the poor economy, and the unusually large number of natural disasters that have wreaked havoc around the world, everyone has been touched by tragedy in one form or another. For most of us, our deepest longing is to hear someone say, "It is done, it's over. No more suffering, no more tears, no more death, no more mourning." It is difficult to even imagine the relief and joy that would accompany those words. Until they come true in their fullest sense, we are called to remain diligent in doing what we can to contribute to the peaceable kingdom and the current reign of God on earth.

I John 3:1-3 (LFM)

Today's text is 3:1-3, but scholars widely hold 2:28—3:3 to be the larger unit. This passage balances the reality of what is with the anticipation of what is to come, a theme that runs through many of the All Saints Day texts. For our current situations, there is good news and bad news. The good news is that we are indeed children of God. The bad news is that the world does not recognize us or know us because they also do not know God. As "strangers" we can expect to be rejected and treated as other. Implied in this description is some measure of grief and hardship along the way. In the midst of the present challenges we can have great hope, for the best is yet to come. When Christ is revealed, we are promised that we will be like him. Until then, we are challenged to purify ourselves and to live righteous lives.

Particularly in North America where Christianity was so deeply inculturated for many years, Christians are not used to being treated as "other." Our brothers and sisters in less hospitable areas of the world are much more familiar with this experience of being the "other." In an increasingly post-Christian and postmodern society, however, we will continue to experience increased marginalization both individually and as a corporate body. As we pause today to honor the saints and martyrs who have gone on before us, we can encourage our congregants to live lives worthy of our calling, just as our spiritual ancestors have.

Gospel
John 11:32-44 (RCL)

In this Gospel text, we continue to see the theme of our present reality contrasted with our future hope. We join the story of the raising of Lazarus well past the halfway point in the narrative. As readers, we are privy to the larger picture that Mary and Martha do not yet see. We know that Jesus intentionally delayed his coming so that Lazarus would die before he got there. We also know that Jesus plans to raise him from the dead so that God will be glorified and others may come to believe.

Mary and Martha are like so many of us. In the midst of the reality of their grief and loss, they are still able to acknowledge and hope for the resurrection of their brother Lazarus on the last day. They are also in such an intimate relationship with Jesus that they are free to lament the fact that if Jesus had arrived sooner, he could have healed Lazarus and prevented his death.

Jesus' reaction to the sisters has challenged commentators for centuries. Although often translated "deeply moved" or "greatly disturbed," the emotion is clearly translated in other parts of the New Testament as "angry" or "indignant."[8] So what or who is Jesus angry with? We don't know for sure. Some have suggested that he was angry at death—either his own impending death or the power that death had over Lazarus. However, since Jesus intentionally delayed his coming until after Lazarus had died so that he could raise him from the dead, this explanation is unlikely.

Others, such as Rudolf Bultmann, suggest that Jesus was angry at the unbelief of either Mary and Martha or the Jews who had gathered. Since they did not know that Jesus planned to raise Lazarus, it seems unlikely that this is the case.

Gail O'Day suggests that Jesus was angry that the raising of Lazarus had become a public affair. Perhaps like the foot washing with the disciples, Jesus wanted this to be an intimate moment between his closest friends and disciples. The presence of a large crowd of mourners turned this resurrection into a very public event.[9]

Today's lection ends with Lazarus being unbound and set free to reclaim his life. But we do the story an injustice if we stop here. The remainder of chapter 11 informs the reader that many believed, which accomplished Jesus' original purpose of glorifying God. But the reader also learns that this event added serious fuel to the Pharisees' fire, and they began to plan in earnest to put Jesus to death. As a result, Jesus went into seclusion in the wilderness.

Even in Jesus' life we see the reality of present circumstances contrasted with the hope of what will be. Even Jesus experienced being rejected as "other" and suffered the very human experiences of grief and death before he experienced resurrection glory. As such, Jesus understands our own suffering and grief and our need for a hope of things to come. These are powerful truths to offer on All Saints Day.

Matthew 5:1-12a (LFM)

Mention "the Beatitudes," and most people will think exclusively of Jesus and the Sermon on the Mount (and maybe the Sermon on the Plain in Luke). As a literary form, however, beatitudes have deep roots in the Wisdom and prophetic literature in the Hebrew Bible. All beatitudes follow the same basic three-part form. First, there is the declaration that someone is blessed or happy. In secular culture this word means "privileged" or "fortunate." In the religious sense the word means "blessed," as opposed to "cursed." The second part is composed of an adjective or brief clause describing the behavior or attitude that brings about the blessing. Finally, the beatitude ends with a promise of what the blessed will receive. It is important to note that the Beatitudes are given to the community of faith, not to individual believers.

Originally the Hebrew people assumed that God blessed those who were leading righteous lives and withheld blessing from those who had violated the law. The books of Job and Ecclesiastes called this theology into question, however, as Israel realized that not only were the good not always rewarded, but that bad things happened to good people. In the Beatitudes, the blessing does not occur now, but in the glorious rewards of the future.[10]

Liberation theologians warn that the delay in obtaining the blessing can lead to passivity here on earth. However, as John Meier notes, God's future impinges on our present and molds it, energizing, galvanizing, and empowering us to reflect God's saving action in our own action.[11] On All Saints Day as we worship and remember those who have gone before, may their example and this text challenge us to be about the work of bringing about the kingdom of God on earth.

Notes

1. For Gail Ramshaw's commentary on the All Souls Day texts, see *New Proclamation Commentary on Feasts, Holy Days, and Other Celebrations*, ed. David B. Lott (Minneapolis: Fortress Press, 2007), 214–19.
2. W. Sibley Towner, "Isaiah," in *The Discipleship Study Bible* (Louisville: Westminster John Knox, 2008), 963.
3. Gene Tucker, "Isaiah," in *The New Interpreter's Bible* (Nashville: Abingdon, 2001), 6:217.
4. Gary Light, "Wisdom of Solomon," in *The Discipleship Study Bible*, 1386.
5. Michael Kolarcik, "Wisdom of Solomon," in *The New Interpreter's Bible* (Nashville: Abingdon, 1997), 5:469.
6. Gail O'Day, "The Book of Revelation," in *The Discipleship Study Bible*, 2097.
7. Michael Morgan, "Pastoral Perspective, Psalm 24," *Feasting on the Word, Year B* (Louisville: Westminster John Knox, 2009), 4:224.
8. Gail O'Day, "John," in *The New Interpreter's Bible* (Nashville: Abingdon, 1995), 9:690.
9. Ibid.
10. Allison Trites, "The Blessings and Warnings of the Kingdom," *Review and Expositor* 89, no. 2 (Spring 1992): 179–96, 184.
11. John P. Meier, "Matthew 5:3-14," *Interpretation* 44, no. 3 (July 1990): 281–85, here 283–84.

November 4, 2012
Lectionary 31 / Thirty-First Sunday in Ordinary Time / Proper 26
Twenty-Third Sunday after Pentecost

This week, both the Old Testament reading and the Gospel deal with the greatest commandments, loving God and loving neighbor. The alternate Old Testament reading, the psalms, and the Hebrews passage all give us differing views about what it means to love God and others with our whole beings, even in the midst of difficult times.

First Reading
Deuteronomy 6:1-9 (RCL)
Deuteronomy 6:2-6 (LFM)

In this text, Israel stands ready to cross the Jordan and take possession of the promised land. This should be a time of great celebration and rejoicing, but Moses appears more anxious than celebratory. Moses is not worried about the Israelites' safety or physical provision; he is concerned about them spiritually. He knows that the people have a short memory, and how dangerous this tendency is. In the previous chapters, the people received the commandments and they were reminded of the history of God's provision for them throughout their history. Once again, Moses urges the people not only to keep the commandments, but to perpetuate them by passing them down to each successive generation. His desire is that the people will prosper and multiply as they are obedient to God.

Verse 4 begins what is known as the *Shema*, the Great Commandment. After affirming that God is God alone, Moses proclaims to them, "You shall love the LORD your God with all your heart, and with all your soul, and with all your might." For the Hebrews, "heart" conveyed what we associate with the mind; it was the center of the will, volition, and decision making.[1] To love God with all of one's heart, soul, and strength was a command to love God with one's whole being; nothing was excluded. Ronald Clements observes that the command to love God becomes a central aspect of the entire biblical tradition, shaping both the Jewish and Christian traditions.[2]

How could Israel accomplish this great command? They could live into it by keeping the law in front of them constantly. Moses told the people to recite the law to their children both at home and when they were away, before they went to bed and first thing when they arose, by carrying a copy with them and displaying it prominently in their homes. This is serious business.

All of these instructions sound like overkill, but God understands human nature. In our lives, we all tend to turn to God for help when things are difficult. When we are wandering in our personal or corporate wilderness and must depend on God's provision for our very survival, we tend to pay closer attention to the things that are important to God. After all, we wouldn't want to bite the hand that feeds us. But what happens when we enter the land that flows with milk and honey, when we gain a sense of security (however illusory that may be) and think we can take care of ourselves? Those commandments can quickly fade from our conscious minds. No matter where we find ourselves, personally or corporately, Moses' words provide a timely reminder to keep the main thing the main thing.

Ruth 1:1-18 (RCL alt.)

The book of Ruth provides readers with a beautiful example of what it means to obey the second great commandment, to love one's neighbor as oneself. This story functions parabolically, for the hero (Ruth) is a foreigner. Surprisingly, it is the Israelite insiders who find themselves in need of Ruth's extraordinary loyalty and rescue.

The story begins when Elimelech, Naomi, Mahlon, and Chilion must leave Bethlehem (the land of bread) because there is no bread. Their journey takes them to Moab, a very unlikely destination. The Moabites began as a result of incest between Lot and his daughter (Gen. 19:30-38). In Numbers 25:1-3, when Israel was encamped at Moab, the men consorted with Moabite women, which led to religious apostasy. By the time Deuteronomy was written, Moabites were forbidden from entering the assembly of the Lord, and Israel was not to promote a Moabite's welfare or prosperity. Elimelech and Naomi's decision to leave Bethlehem and go to *live* in Moab, while radical and foolish, revealed the depth of their desperation.[3]

Instead of life and health, the family experienced the death of Elimelech, their breadwinner. Naomi's life was sustained through the marriages of her sons to Ruth and Orpah, Moabite women. However, ten years later all three women found themselves widowed and thus disadvantaged. Phyllis Trible notes that at this point, Naomi was stripped of her identity. She was moved from wife to widow, from mother to not mother. The security provided by a husband and children was no longer hers; the definition of worth in that culture no longer applied to her. The blessings of old age (given through progeny) were no more.[4] At this point, Naomi could not point with any confidence to YHWH's blessing on her life. She accused YHWH of having turned against her, leading her to a bitter end (and a new name: "Mara" or "bitter"). She decided to return to her home in Bethlehem and she encouraged her daughters-in-law likewise to return to their mothers' homes. Not only were they an additional liability for Naomi, it was irrational for the young women to remain with someone God had apparently forsaken.[5] It was in this context that Ruth made her confession of faith and commitment: "Do not press me to leave you or to turn back from following you! Where you go, I will go; where you lodge, I will lodge; your people shall be my people and your God my God." Katherine Sakenfeld observes that for Ruth, the commitment to accept Naomi's people as her own was made in the face of possible, even probable, rejection by that people. Ruth was risking much in committing herself to Naomi's people and Naomi's God.[6]

Naomi was not pleased with Ruth's unwillingness to submit to her wishes and return to her mother's home. When Naomi saw that Ruth was determined to go with her, Naomi said no more to her (v. 18). It appears that these two women began their journey to Bethlehem in silence and at a point of disagreement. It is easy to chide Naomi for her response to Ruth's loyalty and commitment. In addition to being a liability, however, Ruth's presence was likely a constant reminder of all that Naomi had lost.

When we are in the midst of deep grief, it can be very difficult to see or feel the extraordinary love and care that God provides through those who surround us. All's well that ends well in this beautiful book, but we do it a disservice if we ignore the tragedy and deep pain that begins this narrative. Although possible, it is unlikely that those who are deeply grieving will be able to hear the exhortation to see, acknowledge, and respond to those who are providing extraordinary care around them. However, this story can offer strong affirmation and encouragement to the ones who are providing that care. Their faithfulness to loving their neighbor as themselves may not go unnoticed in the end.

Psalmody
Psalm 119:1-8 (RCL)

Psalm 119, the longest in Scripture, is an acrostic poem with twenty-two sections, one for each letter of the Hebrew alphabet. In today's reading, the first section of the psalm, the writer begins with two beatitudes that declare that those who keep the law and seek after God with their whole hearts will be happy or blessed. The psalmist then expresses in a beautiful prayer to God his own desire to keep the law and remain faithful. It is clear that keeping the law and seeking God wholeheartedly involve both knowing and doing, and that the psalmist is deeply committed to both.

Psalm 146 (RCL alt.)

Echoing the *Shema*, this psalm begins "Praise the LORD, O my soul," indicating that the author's whole being is engaged in praise to God. The psalmist is also quick to note that praise is a lifelong habit. The writer then reminds us that we are not to put our trust in princes, who are mortal and temporal, but to keep our trust in God.

Verse 5 is a beatitude, the last one in the Psalms. Verses 6-10 describe the attributes and actions of God. God, the creator of all, is active on behalf of humanity. Notice those who are listed specifically: the oppressed, the hungry, the prisoners, the blind, the bowed down, the strangers, the orphans, and the widows. To love God with our whole being and to love our neighbor as self means to be active on behalf of all of these brothers and sisters.

Psalm 18:2-3a, 3b-4, 47 + 51 (LFM)

This selection begins with verse 2, but verse 1, "I love you, O LORD, my strength," sets the psalm in the context of today's theme. This psalm echoes King David's words in 2 Samuel 22, so this psalm has long been attributed to David. However, the cosmic and universal nature of the imagery suggests that this psalm also has an eschatological orientation.[7] In verses 1-6 the king calls out to God from his distress. After a dramatic theophany and rescue, the psalm ends with words of praise from the king for God's deliverance. J. Clinton McCann notes that if we decide to trust in the righteous, steadfastly loving God rather than the forces of evil in the world, then we are in for a fight just like the king in this psalm and just like Jesus. He notes, however, that our fight involves waging peace.[8]

Second Reading
Hebrews 9:11-14 (RCL)

In order to understand today's verses, one must have a basic understanding of the nature and purpose of sacrifice in the ancient Near East. The Hebrews had two purposes for sacrifice: to atone for their sin and to offer firstfruits back to God as an acknowledgment that they were only stewards of all that belonged to God. Chapter 9 of Hebrews contrasts this earthly sacrificial system with Christ's superior sacrifice.

The chapter begins (vv. 1-8) by describing the earthly tent or tabernacle and the process by which the priest entered (time and time again) to offer sacrifices for the sins of the people. The writer of Hebrews is clear in verses 9-10 that this system cannot perfect the conscience of the worshiper and that it is only temporal, "until the time comes to set things right" (v. 10).

Today's lection begins with the description of Christ who, as the High Priest, enters the greater and perfect tent (or Holy of Holies) once and for all to obtain eternal redemption with his own blood. This perfect sacrifice, the author insists, will purify our conscience from dead works to worship the living God.

Scholars generally agree that Christ's sacrificial gift of himself eliminated the need for priestly sacrifices in the tent or temple and freed believers to worship anywhere and anytime. Tom Long says that now, whenever the Christian community gathers for worship, it follows its Great High Priest into "the greater and perfect tent," into a sanctuary that will not decay, to join in a fellowship that will not perish, and to sing hymns of praise that will not cease to a God whose mercy is everlasting.[9]

Regardless of how one feels about blood-atonement theology, in today's text in Hebrews, Christ fully models for us what it means to love God and love others with all of one's being. As we follow Christ, we are called to do the same in a world that is still waiting to see the full manifestation of the kingdom of God on earth.

Hebrews 7:23-28 (LFM)

For commentary on this text, please see the second reading for Proper 25, above.

Gospel
Mark 12:28-34 (RCL)
Mark 12:28b-34 (LFM)

Like many of Jesus' other teaching opportunities, this one begins with a question. Unlike all of the other questions posed to Jesus in the latter part of Mark's Gospel, this question is not an attempt to test or trap Jesus. It appears the scribe, who has joined the group already engaged in a theological debate with Jesus, is genuinely interested in Jesus' answer. In response to the question about which commandment is the first, Jesus quotes Deuteronomy 6:4-5, the *Shema* discussed above. In the other Synoptic Gospels, Jesus' quote begins with verse 5, but here he begins with verse 4, "Hear, O Israel, the Lord our God, the Lord is one." He also alters the commandment slightly, adding "with all your mind." Some scholars believe this addition may have reflected the current Hellenistic influence.[10]

Jesus could have ended here—he has answered the scribe's question—but he is not yet finished. He wants the crowd to know what the second command is: "You shall love your neighbor as yourself." Dawn Ottoni Wilhelm notes that for Jesus, religion is a matter of divine and human relationships; it is a matter of both personal devotion and public consequence.[11]

Although this conversation is part of a prolonged theological debate, there is no debating Jesus' answer to the scribe's question. The scribe immediately agrees with Jesus, first that God is one and second about the primacy of these commandments. It is interesting to note that the declaration that these commandments are more important than all burnt offerings and sacrifices was made *by* a scribe, *in* the temple. Just as Jesus does not dismiss the Torah, the scribe does not condemn sacrifice, but much like the prophets Amos and Micah, he subordinates this form of worship to love.[12] The story ends with the note that after that, no one dared ask Jesus any more questions. A. K. M. Adam quips that Jesus "won" this round, in Jerusalem (the scribes' and Pharisees' "home turf") and in a debate about the law (their area of expertise).[13]

As noted above, Jesus' command to love both God and neighbor makes what could be a very abstract concept very concrete. In Luke 10 the lawyer asks Jesus, "Who is my neighbor?" In response, Jesus tells the story of the Good Samaritan, a tale of extraordinary hospitality and care. It is noteworthy that in this story, and in the story of Ruth (see the first reading, above), it is the outsider, the foreigner, and even the enemy of Israel that is the one who models this level of love and care. In both stories it is the "insider" in the story who needs rescued and loved.

What does it mean for us as twenty-first-century Christians to keep the greatest commandments ever before us? What might happen if we got serious about meditating on them day and night, at home and at work, and teaching them to successive generations? Who are the "others" in our midst who might teach us what it really means to love God and to love one another wholeheartedly and sacrificially? What would happen if we gave primacy to issues of justice and righteousness over our sacred rituals? What if . . .

Notes

1. Nancy Bowen, "Deuteronomy," in *The Discipleship Study Bible* (Louisville: Westminster John Knox, 2008), 251.
2. Ronald E. Clements, "The Book of Deuteronomy," in *The New Interpreter's Bible* (Nashville: Abingdon, 1998), 2:343.
3. Frank Anthony Spina, *The Faith of the Outsider: Exclusion and Inclusion in the Biblical Story* (Grand Rapids: Eerdmans, 2005), 120–21.
4. Phyllis Trible, *God and the Rhetoric of Sexuality*, Overtures to Biblical Theology (Philadelphia: Fortress Press, 1978), 167–68.
5. Spina, *Faith of the Outsider*, 124.
6. Katharine Doob Sakenfeld, *Ruth*, Interpretation: A Bible Commentary for Teaching and Preaching (Louisville: John Knox, 1999), 31.
7. J. Clinton McCann, "Psalms," in *The New Interpreter's Bible* (Nashville: Abingdon, 1996), 4:747.
8. Ibid., 4:749.
9. Thomas G. Long, *Hebrews*, Interpretation: A Bible Commentary for Teaching and Preaching (Louisville: John Knox, 1997), 97.
10. Dawn Ottoni Wilhelm, *Preaching the Gospel of Mark* (Louisville: Westminster John Knox, 2008), 213.
11. Ibid.
12. Lamar Williamson, *Mark*, Interpretation: A Bible Commentary for Teaching and Preaching (Louisville: John Knox, 1983), 229.
13. A. K. M. Adam, "Exegetical Perspective, Mark 12:28-34," in *Feasting on The Word, Year B* (Louisville: Westminster John Knox, 2009), 4:263.

November 11, 2012
Lectionary 32 / Thirty-Second Sunday in Ordinary Time / Proper 27
Twenty-Fourth Sunday after Pentecost

The texts for this week remind us that women play a key role, not only in Scripture, but in teaching us today what it means to be agents of God's grace and God's will in the world. The three women featured in today's texts, the widow of Zarephath, Ruth, and the widow in the temple, would have been considered the most vulnerable and needy of their day. Yet we see each revealing or carrying out God's plan in very surprising ways.

First Reading
1 Kings 17:8-16 (RCL)
1 Kings 17:10-16 (LFM)

By this point in the book of 1 Kings, things are really heating up. At the end of chapter 16, we learn that Ahab did evil in the sight of the Lord more than all who were before him. Ahab angered God by erecting an altar and a sacred pole to Baal and worshiping him. Baal was a Canaanite god that was responsible for the fertility of the land. When Elijah declared in chapter 17 that there would be no dew or rain except by God's word, he was issuing a direct challenge to Baal. The risk of the challenge was serious enough that God sent Elijah into hiding by the Wadi Cherith, where he was fed by ravens until even this wadi dried up.

At this point, today's reading begins as God sends Elijah to Zarephath, the very heart of Baal's territory. Zarephath was a Phoenician commercial capital known for exporting a variety of goods such as wine, grain, and oil. When Elijah arrives, however, the city is in dire straits because of the drought.[1] At the town gate, Elijah sees a widow gathering firewood, and he asks her first for a drink and then for some bread to eat. Widows were generally known to be the most vulnerable members of society, and often the most impoverished. Such is true for this woman, for she tells Elijah that she is gathering wood to cook one final meal for herself and her son before they succumb to starvation and death. Elijah assures her that her oil and meal will not run out until the day that the Lord (as opposed to her Baal) sends rain. The widow does as Elijah commands, and her provisions sustain her as promised.

Some scholars and preachers praise the widow for using the last of her meager resources to feed Elijah, but why wouldn't she? The decision seems like a no-brainer. If you are going to die soon anyway, why not take a risk that this guy might be for real and that you really might experience a miracle? She has nothing to lose.

The far more interesting story here lies in God's choice of a destitute, foreign, Baal-worshiping widow as the channel of life and sustenance, even salvation, for Elijah. I suspect that is not where Elijah would have looked for help, and it's not where we look today either. Whom do we identify as religiously, ethnically, socioeconomically, and even gendered others today? How would we respond to the news whom they are the ones that God has ordained to meet our most basic needs and sustain us?

Perhaps your congregation is composed of those folks who are often labeled as "other" by many in society. This story of the widow of Zarephath can bring a powerful word of hope about whom God chooses to use as agents of grace and sustenance.

Ruth 3:1-5; 4:13-17 (RCL alt.)

By the time we get to today's readings in Ruth, Naomi and Ruth have made it back to Bethlehem in time for the barley harvest. Naomi's return causes quite a stir, but no one even inquires about Ruth, and Naomi does not acknowledge her presence. Naomi goes so far as to say that she went away full, but the Lord has brought her back empty. At this point, Ruth, who has sacrificed everything for Naomi, is an invisible other. When she is mentioned in 1:22; 2:2; and 3:5, it is always as "Ruth the Moabite." The continuation of this defining label suggests that the Israelite insiders view her with ongoing suspicion.

Ruth, however, refuses to allow others' definitions to limit her. She takes the initiative to go to the fields to glean food. Not only does Naomi not go with Ruth (perhaps she is still overwhelmed with her own grief), she does not even instruct Ruth on how to stay safe among the harvesters who often took advantage of poor, single (not to mention foreign) women in the fields. Fortunately, Ruth meets Boaz, a wealthy kinsman who has heard of Ruth's care for Naomi. He takes her under his wing, feeding her a noon meal, offering her protection, and providing her with plenty of grain to glean.

Although Boaz is generous, gleaning was a short-term solution to a long-term problem. As chapter 3 opens, Naomi initiates a daring plan for their future that Ruth must implement. Scholars debate what actually happens when Ruth dresses up and goes to the threshing floor where she lies down with Boaz. Both Ruth's actions and the words the narrator uses to describe those actions are rich with sexual innuendo, but the extent of their actions that night is unclear. Even if no sexual activity occurred, Naomi has clearly asked Ruth to go beyond the acceptable boundaries of female behavior and to act out the stereotype of the foreign woman who leads on Israelite men.[2]

It is interesting to note that although Naomi instructs Ruth to let Boaz tell her what to do once she has made her presence known on the threshing floor, it is Ruth who tells Boaz what to do. Phyllis Trible observes, "A foreign woman calls an Israelite man to responsibility. Boaz reacts to Ruth, he doesn't initiate. Ruth is portrayed throughout as a defier of customs, a maker of decisions, and a worker of salvation."[3] Eunny Lee writes, "Ruth's proposal is indicative of women everywhere who must overcome socially constructed obstacles in order to secure a future for themselves."[4]

The next morning, Boaz sends Ruth home before daybreak in order to protect her reputation. Before she leaves, Boaz loads her down with grain. Ruth, who arrived at the threshing floor empty, goes back to Naomi full of both grain and the promise of long-term security. In the meantime, Boaz meets with the men in the marketplace to work out the details of Ruth's, and Naomi's, redemption.

Chapter 4 tells us that after Boaz and Ruth were married, the Lord made Ruth conceive and she bore a son. The women of Bethlehem clearly identify the child, whom they name Obed, as Naomi's redeemer. Obed's arrival restores to Naomi the security and blessing of old age that were stripped from her in Moab. Once again she is full. Naomi owes her restoration to a Moabite woman. As the townswomen remind Naomi, "[It is] your daughter-in-law who loves you, who is more to you than seven sons, who has borne [Obed]." In a society where sons were valued above all else and where seven was the number of completion, to identify Ruth as being more than seven sons was an expression of ultimate worth and value.

In reading Ruth as a parable, we all must ask ourselves how we are in need of redemption. Then we are reminded to look for God's grace coming through unlikely people and places. Finally, this book calls us to challenge the stereotype of God condoning submissive and obedient women. For Ruth, the hero and redeemer of this story, disobeys her mother-in-law on more than one occasion and initiates a daring plan that secures not only the women's future but the future of Israel (as David's great-grandmother) and the world (as an ancestor of Jesus).

Psalmody
Psalm 146 (RCL)
Psalm 146:7, 8-9a, 9b-10 (LFM)

Last week the verses of this psalm that resonated with the *Shema* leapt out at us. This week the verses that talk about whom we are to trust are the first to jump off the page. All of the women in today's passages make conscious, intentional choices about whom they will trust and whom they will follow. The widow in 1 Kings invests the last of her resources in Elijah; Ruth leaves her home and family (and presumably her gods) to become a part of the redemption of Israel. The widow in the temple perhaps understands better than any insider the true nature of Jesus' mission as he turns toward his final days in Jerusalem.

The next verse that jumps out at us today is verse 9, "God upholds the orphan and the widow." God does indeed uphold the widows in today's texts, not only as those who are in need of the care of the community, but as models of grace, provision, and true discipleship. (For additional comment, see the RCL alternative psalmody for Proper 26, above.)

Psalm 127 (RCL alt.)

Psalm 127, the eighth psalm of ascents, is attributed to Solomon. On a Sunday when three of the other readings deal with widows (one of whom lost two sons to death), a psalm about the blessings of home and the heritage of a houseful of sons seems odd, if not downright cruel. However, J. Clinton McCann suggests that since Solomon spent twice as much time building his own house as he did the temple (God's house), perhaps we should read this poem ironically.[5] If we choose to read the psalm more literally, the first two verses challenge us to trust in the Lord and not be anxious, for God will indeed give us rest.

Second Reading
Hebrews 9:24-28 (RCL, LFM)

In today's reading from Hebrews, the author repeats and summarizes material we heard just last week (see the second reading for Proper 26, above, for fuller exegesis). We are reminded of the superiority of Christ and of his work: Christ entered the heavenly sanctuary, not an earthly one; Christ did not have to make atonement for himself, only for us; and the gift of his life was permanent, offered once and for all.

After this recap, the preacher/teacher of Hebrews turns his attention to a new topic, the second coming of Christ. The parables of the foolish bridesmaids and the separation of the sheep and the goats, along with the descriptions of the judgments and the eternal lake of fire in Revelation, have left many anxious about meeting Christ either through death or through his return. After all of the descriptions of death and sacrifice, however, the book of Hebrews gives us good news. When Christ comes, he will not deal with sin (remember, he has already done that once and for all). Rather, he will come to save those who are eagerly waiting for him! The old adage "It is appointed for humans to die once and then the judgment" has been replaced with "It is appointed by God that Jesus died once for all, and then comes the saving mercy."[6]

Gospel
Mark 12:38-44 (RCL)
Mark 12:38-44 or 12:41-44 (LFM)

Many churches have their annual stewardship campaigns in November, and this story of the widow giving her all to the church has been a favored text for years. Unfortunately, Jesus wasn't interested in tithing that day in the temple; there is much more going on here. Today's lection begins with Jesus denouncing the scribes who enjoy all the privileges of wealth. They dress well, they command respect in public, and they have seats of honor in church and at community events, all while devouring widows' houses. They will receive great condemnation for their false piety, Jesus says.

Then Mark tells us that Jesus sat down across from the treasury and watched the crowd putting money into the treasury. (How would we like our offering scrutinized by Jesus?) Not only does he know how much folks are contributing, he calls the disciples over to discuss it with them. It looks like it's going to be a message about giving, but it's not. We expect Jesus to laud the woman who gave everything and condemn those who gave only out of their abundance, but he doesn't. He merely makes an observation about who gives what. There is no commentary.

Many scholars assert that instead of being laudable, the widow's gift was foolish. In today's Old Testament reading, Elijah asked the widow to use the last of her oil and flour to bake a cake for him, promising her that her flour and oil would sustain them until the drought ended. But the widow offering her two last coins in the temple was offered no such promise; there was no assurance that she would be provided for. Ideally, she should have had this assurance of provision. Sometimes when a husband died, his property was entrusted to the temple. Instead of being good stewards on behalf of the widows, however, some of the scribes were selling these widows' homes for a profit and using the money to fund their lavish lifestyles. The whole system had become perverted, and everyone, even the widows, knew it was going on. If this widow did indeed know that her last two coins would be used to help the leaders live lives of wealth and comfort, if she knew that the temple was corrupt, why would she give anything at all, much less everything?

This story of the widow is the last scene in Jesus' public ministry. From this point forward, Jesus teaches only the disciples. He tells them that the corrupt temple will be torn down and that as his followers they will be persecuted. Then the Gospel moves quickly into the events of the Last Supper, Jesus' persecution, and his death. From here, we see Jesus on his way to giving his whole life, everything he had, for something that was corrupt and condemned—all of humanity.[7]

How long would it be before the disciples understood what Jesus was trying to tell them that day seated at the treasury? The disciples understood, just as Jesus and the widow did, that synagogues (or churches) and the people who lead them often go terribly awry. Perhaps they also understood that Jesus and the widow would have both been justified in turning their backs and walking away. We feel that way ourselves sometimes, don't we? But there was much they still did not understand: How long would it be before they realized that the widow's gift of all she had was an example of what Jesus was about to do, give everything he had to redeem a world gone terribly awry? How long would it be before the disciples realized that following Jesus would mean that they, too, were being asked to give their all as well? How long will it be before we, too, understand?

Notes

1. Choon-Leong Seow, "I & II Kings," *The New Interpreters Bible* (Nashville: Abingdon, 1999), 3:128.
2. Anna May Say Pa, "Reading Ruth 3:1-5 from an Asian Woman's Perspective," in *Engaging the Bible in a Gendered World*, ed. Linda Day and Carolyn Pressler (Louisville: Westminster John Knox, 2006), 55.
3. Phyllis Trible, *God and the Rhetoric of Sexuality*, Overtures to Biblical Theology (Philadelphia: Fortress Press, 1978), 184.
4. Eunny P. Lee, "Ruth the Moabite: Identity, Kinship, and Otherness," in Day and Pressler, *Engaging the Bible in a Gendered World*, 97.
5. J. Clinton McCann, "Psalms," in *The Discipleship Study Bible* (Louisville: Westminster John Knox, 2008), 850.
6. Thomas G. Long, *Hebrews*, Interpretation: A Bible Commentary for Teaching and Preaching (Louisville: Westminster John Knox, 1997), 101.
7. Peter Perry, "Homiletical Perspective, Mark 12:38-44," in *Feasting on the Word, Year B* (Louisville: Westminster John Knox, 2009), 4:287.

November 18, 2012
Lectionary 33 / Thirty-Third Sunday in Ordinary Time / Proper 28
Twenty-Fifth Sunday after Pentecost

Revised Common Lectionary (RCL)	**Lectionary for Mass (LFM)**
Daniel 12:1-3 or 1 Samuel 1:4-20	Daniel 12:1-3
Psalm 16 or 1 Samuel 2:1-10	Psalm 16:5 + 8, 9-10, 11
Hebrews 10:11-14, (15-18), 19-25	Hebrews 10:11-14, 18
Mark 13:1-8	Mark 13:24-32

The texts for this week focus on times of great change and challenge in the life of the people of God. In 1 Samuel, Israel is about to enter a period of profound transition in governance that will affect every aspect of their lives from this point forward. Daniel, Mark, and part of the Hebrews passage apocalyptically warn believers never to become complacent, for earth-changing events are occurring and will continue to occur until Christ returns as the ultimate victor. The Psalms and Hebrews passages provide encouragement and advice for living in these difficult but exciting times.

First Reading
Daniel 12:1-3 (RCL, LFM)

Today's lection is part of Daniel's vision for the future that fills chapters 10–12. Chapter 10 recounts an angelic battle with the powers on earth, while chapter 11 describes persecutions among the Jews. In chapter 12 the angels and nations are at war. Michael, who is described as the great prince and the protector of God's people, is the hero in verses 1-3. He was believed to be a patron angel of Israel who battled the Persian and Greek forces in chapter 10. In a time of great distress and persecution, he is a comforting presence to the people of Israel.[1]

Verse 2 reads, "Many of those who sleep in the dust of the earth shall awake, some to everlasting life, and some to shame and everlasting contempt." This is the first clear and explicit reference to resurrection with a resulting reward or punishment in the Old Testament. Several scholars assert that the book of Daniel was included in the canon because of the importance of this verse for developing Jewish thought. It is interesting to note that not all will rise, and those who do will be judged and divided, although the criterion for judgment is not explained here.

Light and images of light are the main symbol of righteousness in the book of Daniel.[2] In verse 3 the wise and those who lead many to righteousness are affirmed and described as shining stars forever and ever.

The book of Daniel claims to be from the time of the Babylonian exile; however, some scholars assert that it was written much later, perhaps even in the Hellenistic period, around the time of the Maccabean revolt (167 BCE).[3] Either date argues for a work that encourages readers to stand firm in the midst of oppression and exile, knowing that a better day is coming.

1 Samuel 1:4-20 (RCL alt.)

As the book of 1 Samuel opens, the people of Israel are on the threshold of one of the most significant changes in their corporate history. The book of Judges ended with the observation, "In those days there was no king in Israel; all the people did what was right in their own eyes" (21:25). Early in 1 Samuel we learn that the sons of Eli the priest, the spiritual leader of the people, are corrupt. The country is rife with moral issues and there is no clear leader to guide them. The internal leadership problem is exacerbated by the fact that the Philistine army is threatening invasion. It is a tense and anxious time.

In the midst of all of this turmoil and uncertainty, the book of 1 Samuel begins not with national concerns, but with a family drama of barrenness, provocation, desperate initiative, and miraculous intervention. Hannah, the first wife of Elkanah, is barren. In the ancient Near East, a woman's worth was tied to her ability to conceive and bear children, and barrenness was viewed as punishment from God. Elkanah's second wife, Peninnah (whose name means "fertile" and who had borne him children), provoked and taunted Hannah, constantly reminding her of what she lacked.

One year when the family was in Shiloh for their annual sacrifice, Hannah reached the breaking point. Scripture tells us that she rose up and presented herself to the Lord. Hannah's time in the temple is a model of genuine and intimate prayer, for she holds nothing back from God. Weeping bitterly, she pours out her soul to God, asking for a son and vowing to return him to God if God grants her request. Marcia Mount Stoop asserts that Hannah's prayer signals that she is aware of a divine concern for those who are of questionable cultural worth. As such, she becomes an icon of one who knows herself and sees herself as known and loved by God.[4] It is interesting to note that Eli the priest serves mostly as a bystander in this narrative. Hannah does not seek his assistance in offering her prayer to God, and Eli believes that she is drunk. When she assures him that she is not drunk but "pouring herself out to God," he offers her a brief blessing without even inquiring about the nature of her request to

God. Whether as a result of her intimate time with God or Eli's clumsy blessing, when Hannah returns from the temple, she is no longer sad. She is changed before she even conceives or becomes aware of God's answer to her prayer. But God does answer and soon Hannah conceives and bears a son whom she names Samuel.

When a barren woman conceived a child, the event was considered a miracle. People believed that a child born in this way was destined to be important in history. Such was the case with Samuel. It will not be long until readers learn that Samuel will become the next great prophet in Israel and the spiritual leader of the people. In this role, he will anoint the first two kings of Israel and be the voice of the Lord for many years to come.

This narrative offers several rich options for preaching. First, the historical books in the Old Testament were written as interpreted *religious* history to show the people how God had been with them at various stages of their corporate journey. Note how prominent God's actions are in the birth of Samuel. God closed Hannah's womb, Hannah prayed and offered a vow to God, the Lord remembered Hannah and opened her womb, and then Hannah gave the child back to God. These chapters introduce Samuel as an agent of God's sovereign initiative and establish God as the one who determines Israel's future.[5] In our own settings, we can point to times of less than stellar moral living where a strong leader was needed to move the people forward. Are we able to see God at work in these very challenging times?

In this case, as in the case of the birth of Jesus that we will begin preparing for in just two short weeks, God is at work in unusual ways and through unlikely people. God's choice to bear Samuel is a distraught, barren, and taunted woman named Hannah. How can she help prepare us to hear the good news of a Savior born to an unmarried teenager who claims to still be a virgin?

Finally, some scholars note that this story functions as a parable for Israel's political situation. Robert Polzin notes that Israel's anxiety over not having a king is reflected in Hannah's anxiety over not having a son. Hannah is taunted by Peninnah while Israel is taunted by the Philistines. Hannah's persistence in asking for a son parallels Israel's persistent request for a king.[6] God hears and answers Hannah's prayer and God, against better judgment, allows Israel to have a king. As we will see soon enough, a human king in Israel solves some problems but creates many others. As God's spokesperson, Samuel is called to the difficult job of addressing many of these issues.

Today we rarely attribute fertility and childbearing to the hand of God, but on a corporate level we often look for God's presence, action, and blessing as we seek to make sense of difficult times. First Samuel reminds us that although God is at work, God will not prevent us from exercising our free will, even when we make dubious decisions. In the national arena as well as in our local congregations, we often choose our leaders and our actions assuming that they reflect the will of God. Later we are surprised when God speaks through an unlikely candidate to call us to account.

Psalmody
Psalm 16 (RCL)
Psalm 16:5 + 8, 9-10, 11 (LFM)

This psalm is a psalm of confidence and trust in God attributed to David. In the opening verses, David asks for refuge and protection, acknowledging that he is nothing apart from God. After intentionally choosing to follow God alone, David vows to keep the Lord ever before him. The knowledge that God is at his right hand allows David to rest physically and to rejoice in and worship God. As king, David made some serious mistakes that cost him dearly and at times alienated him from God. At other times, however, David was truly a king who sought after God's own heart. In this psalm, we see his conscious decision to trust and rest in God in the midst of an unnamed but challenging situation.

1 Samuel 2:1-10 (RCL alt.)

Preachers using the 1 Samuel reading have the option of using Hannah's song as the psalm for the day. Think back to a time when you were carrying what felt like the weight of the world on your shoulders. Suddenly that weight is lifted in such a miraculous way that you can't help but burst into a song of pure joy. Such is the case with Hannah as she rejoices in the birth of her son.

In addition to celebrating the birth of a child, this song also celebrates the birth of a new Israel. As such, some scholars assert that Hannah's song stands as the theological center of 1 Samuel 1:1—4:1. In this piece, which has roots in Psalm 113 and other public hymnody of the day, Hannah connects the fulfillment of her personal prayer to God's promise for the whole community. She proclaims the inclusive reign of God, the coming king, and the reordering of the social hierarchy. As Kate Connors notes, this was remarkable for a woman in her day.[7]

Second Reading
Hebrews 10:11-14, (15-18), 19-25 (RCL)
Hebrews 10:11-14, 18 (LFM)

Again this week, the author repeats and summarizes material we have heard before as he concludes the exposition that makes up the central section of Hebrews (7:1—10:18). Once again we are reminded that Christ offered himself once and for all. Now that his work is done, Christ is seated at the right hand of God, waiting for the full effect of his work to come to fruition. In verses 15-18, optional in today's reading, the Spirit quotes Jeremiah 31, reminding us of the new internal covenant and reassuring us that God remembers our sin no more.

Elizabeth Forney notes how Christ's single sacrifice radically altered the thinking and behavior of the Hebrew people. No longer ordering their life around the sacrificial system, the Israelites likely felt a shift in their very identity.[8] What are they to do now? How are they to live? The author makes this turn in verses 19-25, spelling out the implications of life with a new high priest, Jesus. First, we are to approach God with a true heart and in full assurance of faith. The work of Christ has torn the veil that separated humanity from God, and we now have full access to the heavenly holy of holies—both to worship and to petition God.

Second, we are to hold fast with confidence to the end. As noted in verse 13, Christ's work is finished, but the fullness of that has not yet come. We are called to live faithfully while we wait.

Finally, we are to encourage one another to gather as a community, to love one another and to be about the work of the kingdom. Back in Proper 22 we noted that the author, of Hebrews is writing to a discouraged congregation. Here he is reminding them that in Christ they have the resources they need to do what they are called to do, if they will come together to worship and to encourage each other.

Gospel
Mark 13:1-8 (RCL)

This passage, often called the little apocalypse, is Jesus' longest speech and farewell address in the Gospel of Mark. Verses 1-2 are considered transitional. Jesus and the disciples are leaving the temple. In response to a disciple's comment about the awesome building, Jesus replies that it will all be torn down. He is marking the end of his Jerusalem ministry and disqualifying the temple as a focal point for the kingdom of God.[9]

Verse 3 finds Jesus and the disciples on the Mount of Olives opposite (or in opposition to) the temple. The disciples ask the same questions that people do today in response to apocalyptic writings: When will this happen and what will be the signs? Instead of answering their questions, Jesus gives them warnings about false messiahs, wars, and natural disasters. Today's lection concludes with the statement that this is but the beginning of birth pangs. Although it is a painful process, a birth is a joyous event to be celebrated. Things will get worse before they get better, but something new and wonderful will emerge from this time. (See below, at the end of the LFM Gospel, about preaching these texts.)

Mark 13:24-32 (LFM)

Verse 24 begins the second part of this apocalyptic section. Verses 24-27, which all come from the Old Testament, describe the coming of the Son of Man. Here the darkened sun and moon highlight the unparalleled brilliance of the Christ who comes in power and glory to gather the elect. There is no terror or judgment here, only good news! In verses 28-32 Jesus uses the fig tree as an object lesson to be watchful for the return of the Son, although he acknowledges that even he does not know when these things will occur.

Preaching apocalyptic texts is always a challenge. On one hand, the recent increase in the number of natural disasters is fueling the talk about the end time.

On the other hand, a steady stream of rapture predictors, such as Harold Camping in 2011, has left most folks skeptical at best about the possibility of Christ's return. As tempting as it may be, we cannot ignore these texts. Setting the Markan text in its historical context is informative. Mark was likely written during or near the siege of Jerusalem in 66–70 CE. For the disciples listening to Jesus teach, these events were all in the future. A generation later, however, the author of the Gospel may have felt he was living in the midst of the apocalypse. As with Daniel, these texts can encourage contemporary readers to stand firm in the midst of the current reality, knowing that a better day is coming.

Notes

1. Daniel L. Smith-Christopher, "Daniel," *The New Interpreter's Bible* (Nashville: Abingdon, 1996), 7:148.
2. Ibid.
3. Stephen Breck Reid, "The Book of Daniel," in *The Discipleship Study Bible* (Louisville: Westminster John Knox, 2008), 1199.
4. Marcia Mount Shoop, "Theological Perspective, 1 Samuel 1:4-20," in *Feasting on the Word, Year B* (Louisville: Westminster John Knox, 2009), 4:294.
5. Bruce Birch, "I and II Samuel," *The New Interpreter's Bible* (Nashville: Abingdon, 1998), 2:970.
6. Ibid., 2:973, 976.
7. Kate Connors, "Pastoral Perspective, 1 Samuel 2:1-10," in *Feasting on the Word, Year B*, 4:300.
8. Elizabeth Forney, "Pastoral Perspective, Hebrews 10:11-25," in ibid., 4:302.
9. Lamar Williamson, *Mark*, Interpretation: A Bible Commentary for Teaching and Preaching (Louisville: John Knox, 1983), 236.

November 25, 2012
Christ the King or Reign of Christ Sunday
Lectionary 34 / Last Sunday in Ordinary Time / Proper 29 / Twenty-Sixth Sunday after Pentecost

Revised Common Lectionary (RCL)
Daniel 7:9-10, 13-14 or 2 Samuel 23:1-7
Psalm 93 or 132:1-12, (13-18)
Revelation 1:4b-8
John 18:33-37

Lectionary for Mass (LFM)
Daniel 7:13-14
Psalm 93:1a, 1b-2, 5
Revelation 1:5-8
John 18:33b-37

Today is the last Sunday of the liturgical year and Christ the King Sunday. Today's passages all focus on issues of just and righteous kingship and our response as believers to Christ the King.

First Reading
Daniel 7:9-10, 13-14 (RCL)
Daniel 7:13-14 (LFM)

Three shifts occur in Daniel 7, which is considered to be the heart of the book. First, the dreams we see now are Daniel's, not the king's. Second, chapter 7 is written in Aramaic, perhaps so only insiders could read it. Third, the book makes a theological and ideological turn in a dramatic, darker direction. The hope for a change in the empires expressed in chapters 1–6 is abandoned and the empires are revealed as beasts that rose out of chaos and evil.[1]

In verse 9, the beginning of today's lection, the scene shifts to a throne room where Daniel watches thrones being put into place. The One who is enthroned is described as ancient, pure, and fiery with tens of thousands of servants. The books, which may be a heavenly record of human deeds, are opened and the court sits in judgment. After this (in vv. 11-12), beasts, which represent empires, are dethroned. Then Daniel sees one like a son of man (but not a human) presented to the Ancient One. This being is given everlasting dominion, kingship, and glory.

Later, New Testament writers would draw on this imagery of the son of man and use it to describe Jesus. In this context, this passage describing an everlasting king is appropriate for Christ the King Sunday. However, faithful interpreters must also consider to whom this image referred in the time of Daniel. The most likely candidates are the angel Michael, who battles for Israel in chapter 10, and the angel Gabriel. In both contexts, Daniel's and ours, the implication is that a day will come when evil earthly rulers are defeated and one approved by God will rule and reign.

Preachers who serve in democratic contexts like the United States are challenged to help their congregations imagine and look forward to living under the rule of a king. Many Americans are enamored with British royalty, as evidenced by the obsession with Prince William and Kate Middleton's wedding and their subsequent visit to Canada and the United States in July 2011. However, we view royals more as stars to be tracked and emulated than as sovereign powers to whom we are willing to subject ourselves. As individuals living in a democracy, I suspect most of us would flinch at the idea of kneeling in humility before any ruler, earthly or heavenly.

In countries and cultures where a monarchy is the norm (including ancient Israel), people were often very happy to have a king or queen who ruled justly and offered protection and security. Anyone who flies commercially today faces a similar choice. We must be willing to sacrifice some of our rights and privileges in order to be safer and more secure. How might we help our congregations apply this principle to our entire lives and place ourselves under the leadership of Christ the King?

2 Samuel 23:1-7 (RCL alt.)

Originally the books of 1 and 2 Samuel were one book that opened with Hannah's song and closed with David's. Themes such as justice and just rule appear in both songs that frame this narrative history of Israel's transition from tribes led by judges to a unified nation under the leadership of a king. David's song is presented as an oracle, which is usually a prophetic utterance. From this point forward, David can be seen as both a king and a prophetic figure.

A human king in Israel was a compromise between God and the people who struggled to trust a heavenly king whom they (and other threatening nations) could not see. As noted in Proper 28, above, when Israel chose to become a monarchy with a human ruler (instead of a theocracy ruled by God), they experienced both blessings and problems. While God remained faithful to the everlasting covenant that was forged with David, the earthly king violated the covenant and pursued his own interests on more than one occasion. This song of David reflects the tension between the ideal of the covenant and the reality of David's reign.[2]

The song opens with an introduction of the oracle giver (David) and an acknowledgment of God as the source of the oracle. Verses 3-4 contain the oracle from God. This oracle is interrupted in verse 5 by an aside from David, then the song concludes with an antithesis to verses 3b-4.

Marcia Mount Shoop asserts that the tragic subtext of this song is an acknowledgment of how difficult it is for human beings to handle the sacred responsibility of public leadership.[3] For those preaching in 2012, two weeks ago, the citizens of the United States elected (or reelected) our national leader. The road to the presidential office is now littered with those whose careers and aspirations were destroyed by the revelation of a lapse in moral judgment that disqualified them from public service. As David learned, the temptations that come with power and authority (even in the church) are enormous. In the twenty-first century we still live with the tension of a political ideal and the reality of the humanity of our leaders. May we commit to pray for those who have been elected that they will pursue the type of just leadership that only Christ the King can fully embody and model.

Psalmody
Psalm 93 (RCL)
Psalm 93:1a, 1b-2, 5 (LFM)

Psalms 93 and 95–99 are known as enthronement psalms that assert God's sovereignty. This particular song may have been written in response to the crisis of the exile, yet it has more general eschatological overtones. After asserting that the Lord is indeed king, the psalmist mentions floods three times. Water is often a symbol for chaos in the Old Testament, and the repetition here signifies the magnitude of the crisis. However, the psalmist asserts that the Lord on high is more majestic than the mighty waters. Used liturgically, this psalm helped Israel to affirm their trust in God's rule and reign, even when circumstances seemed to deny it.[4]

Psalm 132:1-12, (13-18) (RCL alt.)

Psalm 132 is the thirteenth song of ascents that talks of God's dwelling in Zion. This psalm recalls poetically the events of 2 Samuel 6 and 7, where David brings the ark of the covenant to Jerusalem. It also echoes Psalm 89, which addresses the reality of the failed Davidic covenant and the exile of Israel. In its original context, the psalm was used to express hope for the postexilic generation. Later, the references to David were heard messianically for they concretely symbolize hope for the future of God's people.[5] Of particular note for Christ the King Sunday is verse 1, which can also be translated "extreme self-denial," the defining characteristic of Jesus.[6]

Second Reading
Revelation 1:4b-8 (RCL)
Revelation 1:5-8 (LFM)

Teaching and preaching from Revelation must be done with great care and with significant education about the historical context that gave birth to this cryptic book. Since this is the only time verses from Revelation appear in the lectionary until New Year's Day, preachers would be wise to weave the relevant pieces of this second reading into the content of a sermon that focuses on another of today's texts on the kingship of Christ.

That being said, there are nuggets to mine from this passage. Revelation is first and foremost a pastoral letter that was written to be read aloud in worship; in fact, both those who read and those who hear are promised a blessing from this book that originally dealt with both the oppression and pull of the Roman Empire. After identifying this letter as a revelation of Jesus Christ to John, the author begins with the customary salutation offering grace and peace to the recipients from the God who is and who was and who is to come. The order of these descriptors is significant. The God "who is" comes first, indicating that God reigns now, in the midst of the current difficult circumstances. The author offers a word of hope and encouragement from the very beginning!

Next Jesus is identified as the faithful witness, the firstborn of the dead and the ruler of the earthly kings. Through his earthly ministry and the offering of himself, Jesus created us into a kingdom and made us priests to serve God. Then John encourages us to look, to be alert, for Christ is coming with the clouds. All will see him, even those who persecuted him. Today's passage ends with the Lord's declaration, "I am the Alpha and the Omega" (the beginning and the end), and the one "who is and was and is to come, the Almighty."

New Testament scholar Gail O'Day asserts that the purpose of the book of Revelation is to help the churches of Asia Minor see the Roman Empire for the evil that it is.[7] The Israelites were known to participate in cultic worship related to the empire, asserting that it did not violate their covenant with God. God disagreed and wanted to call the people back to pure worship. Numerous scholars note how easily we, as individuals and as churches, get caught up in worshiping the idols of consumerism and entitlement and how often we look to earthly powers for the answers to our questions. The consequences for these actions are as serious today as they were in John's day.

Gospel
John 18:33-37 (RCL)
John 18:33b-37 (LFM)

On first reading, this seems like a very odd passage to read in celebration of Christ the King Sunday. After reading about psalms of praise and apocalyptic passages about the King who will return in glory, why turn our attention to the human Christ who is on trial for treason?

To begin to answer this question, today's five verses must be set in their larger context in the Gospel of John. This pericope is part of Jesus' trial before Pilate that is reported in 18:28—19:16a. In this larger unit, Pilate moves from Jesus to the Jews and back again in seven different scenes. Jesus' identity as king will dominate John's narrative from here through the crucifixion.[8]

In John, Pilate is portrayed as a mean-spirited ruler who has a real disdain for the Jews. He has no vested interest in this case; in fact, in verse 31 he encourages the

Jewish leaders to judge this case on their own. Jesus' accusers are seeking the death penalty, however, and only Rome had the power of execution. When today's lection begins, Pilate has just summoned Jesus into his headquarters to begin interrogating him.

Pilate gets right to the point with no preliminaries: "Are you the King of the Jews?" This is Pilate's primary concern since Rome insisted that all citizens acknowledge Caesar as king. For charges of treason, the governor could bring the full weight of Rome to bear on the accused. Even in this tense and highly charged environment, Jesus takes control of the conversation and follows his habit of answering a question with a question. Jesus wants to know if Pilate is asking this question of his own accord or if someone else put him up to it. Basically, Jesus is challenging Pilate's authority, implying that Pilate cannot act on his own, but only react to the wishes of others.

In response we can almost see Pilate sneer as he responds, "I am not a Jew, am I? It is your own people who have brought you to me. What have you done?" Jesus does not deny the title of king; he merely replies that his kingdom is not of this world. This reference does not imply location but origin; that is, his kingdom is from God.[9] To support this claim, Jesus points out that if his were an earthly kingdom, his followers would be fighting to keep him from being handed over to the Jews. This is an interesting development since many of Jesus' followers were looking for and expecting an earthly king who would free them from the oppression of Rome. It appears that even this early his followers have fled.

Pilate tries again, "So you are a king?" Again, Jesus does not give a direct answer. "You say that I am a king," he responds. He then elaborates that the purpose of his birth and earthly life was to testify to the truth. Truth has been a major theme throughout the Gospel of John and the author returns to this theme one last time here. On trial, Jesus is testifying to the truth. Pilate's final question is "What is truth?"

In verse 39 Pilate returns to the Jews and proclaims that he finds no case against Jesus. He seems to think that Jesus is no threat to Rome. On a surface level, this is true, but as Robert Bryant points out, the kingdom of God is profoundly subversive to any authority that demands allegiance over loyalty to God.[10] When Christianity became the official religion of the Roman Empire, it lost this subversive edge. The same is true in the United States, where Christianity was deeply inculturated for many generations. Our brothers and sisters in Africa, South America, and Asia who work in the areas of liberation, feminist, and postcolonial theologies have a much deeper understanding of how the good news of the gospel speaks a subversive, prophetic, and liberating word to the powers that be. In contexts where we support and/or participate in the status quo, these words are threatening and generate resistance. As pastors and preachers, how can we help our congregants be open to the challenges the gospel needs to bring us?

Even today's text is subversive if we read it carefully. Gail O'Day asserts that at the deepest level, Jesus is not the one on trial after all. Pilate and the religious leaders think that the moment of judgment on Jesus has arrived and that his "kingship" will end as soon as he is put to death. However, they do not realize that like a good shepherd-king, Jesus has made the choice to lay down his life for his flock. They also do not realize that soon Jesus will overcome death and ascend to his eternal throne where he will rule forever. The reality, O'Day observes, is that all those who turn their backs on Jesus are the ones on trial.[11] Instead of accepting God's gifts of love and restoration, they have chosen to alienate themselves from God and God's Son who embodied those gifts for us. It is easy for us to criticize Pilate and the Jewish leaders, but Jesus' closest followers were gone by that point, too. If we had been part of the proceedings that day, I suspect we would have been convicted as well.

Notes

1. Bruce C. Birch, "I and II Samuel," in *The New Interpreter's Bible* (Nashville: Abingdon, 1996), 2:100.
2. Frank Yamada, "Exegetical Perspective, II Samuel 23:1-7," in *Feasting on the Word, Year B* (Louisville: Westminster John Knox, 2009), 4:315.
3. Marcia Mount Shoop, "Theological Perspective, II Samuel 23:1-7," in ibid., 4:316.
4. J. Clinton McCann Jr., "Psalms," in *The New Interpreter's Bible* (Nashville: Abingdon, 1996), 4:1053–54.
5. Ibid., 4:1211.
6. Carol M. Bechtel, "Exegetical Perspective, Psalm 132," in *Feasting on the Word, Year B*, 4:323.
7. Gail O'Day, "Revelation," in *The Discipleship Study Bible* (Louisville: Westminster John Knox, 2008), 2097.
8. Robert Bryant, "Exegetical Perspective, John 18:33-37," in *Feasting on the Word, Year B*, 4:333.
9. Gail O'Day, "John," in *The New Interpreter's Bible* (Nashville: Abingdon, 1995), 9:817.
10. Bryant, "Exegetical Perspective, John 18:33-37," 4:336.
11. O'Day, "John," 9:827.

November 22, 2012 (USA) /
October 8, 2012 (Canada)
Thanksgiving Day
Ira Brent Driggers

Revised Common Lectionary (RCL)	Lectionary for Mass (LFM)
Joel 2:21-27	Deuteronomy 8:17-18 or 1 Kings 8:55-61
Psalm 126	Psalm 113:1-2, 3-4, 5-6, 7-8 or 138:1-2a, 2bc-3, 4-5
1 Timothy 2:1-7	Colossians 3:12-17 or 1 Timothy 6:6-11, 17-19
Matthew 6:25-33	Mark 5:18-20 or Luke 12:15-21 or Luke 17:11-19

The ecclesial celebration of a national holiday such as Thanksgiving can prove awkward for Christian preachers, given that the gospel is inherently transnational, indeed *catholic*. Of course, it is perfectly fitting to offer thanksgiving to God for a particular country's "blessings" and to petition God for national guidance, protection, and so forth. The constant danger (perhaps especially in the United States) is to assume a place of privilege for that country, to assume that those "blessings" imply divine favor, as if the nation constituted a coherent community that had earned those blessings—as if the nation (rather than the "one holy, catholic, and apostolic church") was the fundamental locus of communion with God. Stated simply, it is through the body of Christ, not the body politic, that God brings salvation and sends us out for the building of the kingdom.

Note to those preaching from the Lectionary for the Mass: I have chosen to comment on only four of the possible nine readings for Thanksgiving, primarily in an effort to bring greater substance (saying more about less, rather than saying less about more).

First Reading
Joel 2:21-27 (RCL)

The oracles of Joel are notoriously difficult to date and contextualize historically. Their themes range from judgment, to lament, to assurance. This week's reading fosters rejoicing among the people of Judah. Given that Joel's first series of oracles anticipated the nation's destruction (e.g., 1:1-12), the present verses suggest that God's mercy is always the final word. Subsequent verses continue this assurance by promising the pouring out of God's spirit among all people as part of Judah's restoration. Thus God will prove faithful to Judah, making it whole (*shalem*; NRSV: "repay," 2:25) after the allotted time of punishment.

Because military conquest typically harms both humans and nature, Joel describes the "making whole" of Judah in holistic terms. Neither soil nor animals need fear, for God will protect and provide (vv. 21-23). Likewise, the "children of Zion" will rejoice, not only in the safeguarding of land and beast, but in plenteous rains (v. 23) and bountiful harvest (v. 24). The healing of Judah means the elimination of material want. The people will eat and be satisfied (v. 26), and in this way they will know that God is with them (v. 27). Jesus speaks of this same divine provision in the Gospel reading from Matthew, while also clarifying that it is not a license for decadence and hoarding. If the threshing floors are full of grain (v. 24), then all should be satisfied.

Deuteronomy 8:17-18 (LFM)

Deuteronomy is Moses' final speech to the Israelites before they enter the promised land without him. He has just promised them an abundance of wealth: houses, herds, silver and gold (8:12-13). But he has also warned them not to "exalt" themselves (8:14), for their prosperity will be solely a matter of divine provision—just as God guided them and cared for them in their dangerous wilderness journey (8:14-16). In those days God's constant provision was obvious. In the days of comfort, however, the Israelites will be tempted to lose sight of it and thus take credit for what they never earned themselves. Their life in the land is solely the result of God's own faithfulness: "so that he may confirm his covenant that he swore to your ancestors, as he is doing today" (v. 18). Remembering God's fidelity fosters thanksgiving, which in turn fosters a reciprocating fidelity to God (see my discussion on "the logic of obedience" with regard to the LFM first reading for Trinity Sunday, above). The LFM Gospel reading from Mark follows this pattern insofar as Jesus summons the healed demoniac to credit "the Lord" for his personal restoration.

Psalmody
Psalm 126 (RCL)

Just like the first reading, this psalm anticipates the restoration of Judah's fortunes, when God will turn tears into laughter. Verse 6 offers an additional parallel in its promise of material provision. This promise accords well with the Gospel reading from Matthew, in which Jesus assures his hearers of God's material provision, an assurance intended to elicit thanksgiving and trust in the Creator.

Psalm 113:1-2, 3-4, 5-6, 7-8 (LFM)

The psalmist calls on the assembly to praise God, defending his summons with the claim that this God is not like any other god. This God is seated on the heavens (vv. 4-6) and yet raises up the poor and needy (vv. 7-8). The God of Israel is both uniquely exalted and uniquely merciful. Were the healed demoniac not a Gentile, one could imagine him singing this very psalm (see the LFM Gospel reading, below). Jesus raises him from the "ash heap" (v. 7) of death—literally from among the tombs—so that he can praise the Lord among his fellow Gentiles.

Second Reading
1 Timothy 2:1-7 (RCL)

In exhorting Timothy to pray for "everyone," the writer specifies "kings and all who are in high positions" (2:1-2). It is a bold reminder that Christianity's absolute allegiance to the one Creator God—an allegiance inherited from Judaism—does not preclude the supporting of "civil" authorities who, in the first century, would have been almost entirely pagan.

Note, however, that such prayer has a specific purpose: in order that we might "lead a quiet and peaceable life in all godliness and dignity" (v. 2). Timothy need not agree with specific policies and laws. Nor must he back individual rulers, as if the writer naïvely assumes a nonthreatening coexistence between "church and state." In fact, based on the scholarly consensus on the date of this letter, the writer very likely knows about Emperor Nero's ghastly persecution of Roman Christians in the year 64. The charge to pray for civil authorities is more radical than it initially seems.

Verses 3-6 explain why this is "right and acceptable" (v. 3), namely because there is only one God, with one mediator between God and humankind (v. 5). More to the point, this one God "desires *everyone* to be saved and to come to the knowledge of the truth" (v. 4). Christ's ransom was not for a select few—those who currently find themselves joined to him—but "for all" (v. 6). In this way Christianity's radical monotheism leads to an equally radical catholicism (universality): *one* God for *all* people. This is why the church does not remove itself from unbelieving (even hostile) humanity but rather immerses itself in it, praying for all people as it proclaims the God of all people, whether Jew or Gentile, weak or powerful, neighbor or enemy.

Colossians 3:12-17 (LFM)

These verses encapsulate what Dietrich Bonhoeffer famously called our Christian "life together." The importance of community is already implied in the opening verse, since one cannot be kind, humble, meek, or patient on one's own (v. 12). To cultivate such virtues necessarily requires having beneficiaries for those virtues, recipients of divine gifts. While the call to "endure" (*anechō*; NRSV: "bear with") one another can sound like a matter of mere coexistence or conflict avoidance, the ensuing call to forgive makes the church considerably more than that (v. 13). The church is a community in which God's own gracious forgiveness of sins has been realized, that is, where it has taken concrete form in the reconciliation of members to one another. It is a community sustained by love, the "bond of perfection" (*sundesmos tés teleiotétos*, v. 14). Verses 15-16 offer variations on this theme while clarifying that it is *Christ* who sustains his own body. What distinguishes the "one body" (v. 15) of Christ from a collection of competing human personalities? It is nothing less than Christ's own peace controlling (*brabeuó*; NRSV: "ruling"), and Christ's own word "indwelling," his various members. The community opens itself up to Christ's presence, not only through the practice of forgiveness and reconciliation, but also through teaching, mutual admonishment grounded in wisdom, and singing in thanksgiving (vv. 16-17).

Christians can never reduce faith to an individual journey isolated from other members of Christ's body. It is never strictly "our" faith but rather "our" faith, a collective discipleship devoted to what Paul elsewhere calls "building up" Christ's body to the glory of God (1 Corinthians 14). In this way the church is a light to the world, bearing witness to God's plan for all of creation.

Gospel
Matthew 6:25-33 (RCL)

The gist of this passage is summed up in the very first line: "Do not worry about your life, what you will eat or what you will drink, or about your body, what you will wear" (v. 25). Concern for bare subsistence preoccupied the vast majority of people in the first century. Without clothing and nourishment one cannot survive physically, much less thrive spiritually. Jesus did not draw false distinctions between physical and spiritual well-being. He treated the person holistically because the entire person—and not some special part of the person—is a creature of God.

It is no coincidence, therefore, that Jesus assuages human worry by reminding his hearers that they are in fact . . . creatures. He does not deny the fact that humans hold a privileged place within the hierarchy of creation. Yet this hardly makes them less creaturely, as if they did not have to depend on the Creator as much as the birds of the air or the lilies of the field. It would not be an oversimplification to say that the entire history of human sin is our striving to become something "more" than creatures (as if that were in any way possible), to achieve a state of self-sufficiency and autonomy. Jesus does not preclude the benefits of various human advancements. He simply wants us to understand our creaturely dependence on God—and to find comfort in that.

Of course, Jesus knows we will find comfort in our creaturely dependence only if we find the Creator *trustworthy*. So he calls on us to observe how God provides for the birds and the lilies. And if that is the case, then God will surely provide for humans. "Are you not of more value than they?" (v. 26). In not trusting God, humans show themselves to be "of little faith" (v. 30; cf. 8:26; 14:31; 16:8). They then attempt to secure for themselves their own survival by their own means. There is thus a vicious cycle at work: when we aspire to be something more than creatures, we misuse our

God-freedom in the pursuit of autonomy vis-à-vis God. But when that does not work (and it never does), we mistakenly accuse God of being untrustworthy. Our accusation need not be explicit. It is more often subconscious, implied by the way we live.

Note that this entire passage elaborates upon a commandment that the RCL has omitted: "No one can serve two masters; for a slave will either hate the one and love the other, or be devoted to the one and despise the other. You cannot serve God and wealth" (v. 24). Jesus underscores our creaturely dependency upon a trustworthy God because he knows the power of wealth to occupy our minds and shape our souls, luring us into the fantasy of autonomy that, when pursued, results only in misery. By contrast, true joy and fulfillment come only from a life of completely trusting the benevolent Creator: "Strive first for the kingdom of God and his righteousness, and all these things [i.e., for survival] will be given to you as well" (v. 33). Wealth can be used lovingly in this striving for God, or it can be accumulated out of anxious distrust of God.

In contrast to Jesus' original hearers, affluent Western culture pushes on us a litany of *unnecessary* worries based precisely on the accumulation of wealth (e.g., investment portfolios, mortgage payments, body image, inheritance). Many of us worry about the *kinds* of clothes we wear rather than the basic provision of clothing. Meanwhile, we are never far removed from those plagued by life-threatening (or near-life-threatening) poverty. Later on Jesus says, "You will always have the poor with you" (26:11), meaning there is always opportunity (or lost opportunity!) to strive for the kingdom of God. To strive for God is largely a matter of striving for the well-being of others (Matt. 22:34-40; 25:31-46), chipping away the layers of anxiety and realizing (not just cognitively but bodily) our creaturely dependence upon a trustworthy Creator. For it is in this dependence that we find ultimate fulfillment.

Mark 5:18-20 (LFM)

Throughout his Gospel, Mark emphasizes the importance of following Jesus and remaining in fellowship with him (e.g., 1:16-20; 2:13-17; 6:30-32; 8:34-38; 10:21; 10:52; 14:34). Yet in this passage Jesus seems to *deny* the possibility of fellowship with a man he has just healed! Formerly demon possessed, the man has been restored to wholeness and, understandably, wants to be with Jesus. But Jesus has different plans: the man must return home and proclaim Jesus' merciful healing, while Jesus departs for further ministry.

Has Mark contradicted himself? Only if we expect him to be a systematic theologian—which he is not. Mark is a storyteller who emphasizes various aspects of the Christian faith as he moves from scene to scene. In other passages, Mark wishes to emphasize the importance of following and fellowship. In this passage he wants to depict the extent to which Jesus' fame spreads to surrounding regions, particularly to *Gentile* regions. The famous "Gerasene demoniac" is a non-Jew who inhabits territory on "the other side" of the Sea of Galilee (5:1). In depicting the man's restoration, Mark goes out of his way to stress the ritual uncleanness of this territory (pigs, tombs, demons). There is no evidence of the disciples even getting out of the boat! Yet Jesus steps ashore undeterred, and instead of becoming ritually unclean because of the demoniac, the demoniac becomes whole because of Jesus. By the end of the story Jesus has become known throughout the Decapolis, the "ten cities" spread throughout the predominantly Gentile region east of the Jordan River. The small mustard seed grows into the greatest of shrubs (4:30-32).

Whenever a student expresses displeasure with Jesus' refusal of the man's request (after all, he was "begging"!), I like to ask, "Does the man seem sad to you?" Mark simply reports his immediate obedience. Interestingly, the man does not seem to follow Jesus' instructions *exactly*. He either bypasses his hometown—perhaps to avoid the people who shackled him among the tombs (5:4)—or he does not think the message should be restricted to such a small area. Either way, there is no indication that he was fighting back tears or pouting. In fact, if he proclaimed Jesus "in the Decapolis," then he covered a vast amount of territory, and it must have taken him quite some time. Even granting some hyperbole (cf. 1:6), the man exhibits impressive enthusiasm. So I imagine him responding to Jesus' refusal quite positively: "What a great idea!" Off he went, thankful for the wellness and freedom Jesus had restored to him. And of course, in this way, the healed demoniac proves to be a real follower of Jesus after all.

In a sense, the healed demoniac is the first evangelist, or at least the first Gentile evangelist (the Greek *euangelion* meaning "good news"). For much of mainstream Christianity, the word *evangelical* has acquired negative connotations—and understandably so, given the way certain fundamentalists reduce the church's mission to a strictly oral communication of heaven or hell. If that is evangelism, then we should certainly stay away. But as Christian fundamentalism gradually comes to embrace the material side of the mission—caring for the poor and outcast—mainstream Christians should learn to embrace the mission of sharing the story of Jesus. Ideally, neither form of evangelism should be practiced in complete isolation from the other. But if we really believe that Jesus heals us, restoring us to a communion with the Creator and with each other, then our silence about him is little different from Peter's outright denial. Christians must not wait for the explicit question "Are you one of his disciples?" They should instead heed the words of Jesus himself: "Tell them how much the Lord has done for you, and what mercy he has shown you" (5:19).